[TRANSLATIONS]

ARCHITECTURE / ART

WORKS OF SIGRID MILLER POLLIN
TEXT BY DR. MARGARET BIRNEY VICKERY

TABLE OF CONTENTS

[PREFACES]

ACKNOWLEDGMENTS

SIGRID MILLER POLLIN

I have many people to thank for having contributed in various ways to producing this body of work and this book.

I begin with Vassar College Professor Emeritus and architect Jeh Johnson. Jeh was the encouraging force that brought me into the field decades ago as an undergraduate art history major. He offered me my first studio experience. This was pure magic to me. Rem Koolhaas, James Polshek, and Kenneth Frampton inspired me as a grad student at Columbia University. Romaldo Giurgola was both a wonderful teacher at Columbia and, even more important, my mentor in New York City in the beginning of my career. I admired his drawing and design skills as well as his gentle manner with students, staff, and clients. After our first daughter was born and I had apprenticed in large offices in New York, Aldo encouraged me to start my own practice.

Eric Sautter and his team at Sautter Architecture have collaborated with me both in California and Massachusetts. Eric has done outstanding work taking my conceptual and schematic designs through construction documents while maintaining the integrity of my original design concepts. Eric, a talented architect in his own right, has generously helped me in the production of nearly all of my projects. I greatly value his professional work ethic and his long-term friendship.

Numerous people, largely aspiring architectural interns, have worked with my firm to draw, model, and digitize my designs over the years. Some who have stood out as collaborators include Ray Q. Galano, Rene Glynn, Serena Chow, and Ana Escalante Lentz in California; and Gustavo Pardo, Cecelia Valinotto, Hernan Barufaldi, Shinyoung Park, Neetu Singh, Andrew Bagge, and Sherry Ng in Massachusetts. Chris Mansfield and Cortland Knopp of Embrace Design have been invaluable in organizing images and graphics for this book. Cortland has inspired me with his level of care and precision in processing images of drawings, photos, and texts. This volume would not have come to fruition without his efforts.

Over the years I have taught in two major institutions—California State Polytechnic University Pomona and University of Massachusetts Amherst. I am grateful for the support from both of these universities and the faculty, staff and students that have been my friends, colleagues, and my immediate architectural community—in particular Marvin Malecha, Patricia Oliver, Barry Wasserman, Christine Theodoropoulos, Bill Adams, and Michael Folonis at Cal Poly Pomona; as well as long-term colleagues at UMass Amherst Kathleen Lugosch, Ray Mann, Max Page, and Joseph Krupczynski. I offer special thanks to three colleagues that have shared my passion to bridge art and architecture—Sandy Litchfield, Jane Thurber, and Steve Schreiber. And, of course, I owe much to Dr. Margaret (Meg) Vickery for the insightful text she has written for this book and for her kind friendship.

I am indebted to the many clients I have had over the years—the clients whose projects are contained in this volume. I especially want to recognize my very first client, in Riverside, California—Rufus Barkley, developer and surfer. Sadly, Rufus's life ended much too soon.

My work in Massachusetts has greatly benefited from the skill and craft of builder Larry Rideout, who can build a building or a table with equal grace and care.

My daughters, Emma Grock and Hannah Pollin-Galay, have given me so much love, support and encouragement though these past decades of work and family life. Two girls born in Manhattan and raised in Southern California are now strong independent women committed and passionate about the lives they have chosen. My granddaughters, Leah and Ruthie Pollin-Galay, have been a blessing whether they are donning helmets on a construction site, making drawings in my studio, or suggesting family trips to the Parthenon. My new grandaughter Laila Grock is lucky to begin seeing the world with fresh eyes.

Finally, I am deeply grateful to my husband of forty-two years, Bob Pollin, who has always, always encouraged next steps—supporting me to this day to push boundaries in both my architectural projects, artwork, and life in general. We have deeply shared a long and continuing journey with all the amazing fullness that life brings over the long haul.

DR. MARGARET BIRNEY VICKERY

I have been impressed with Sigrid's work since I first encountered it in 2007. Since working with her on this book and other projects, I have learned a great deal about the process of architecture. But Sigrid's work has also opened my eyes to wider issues surrounding women and design, from career choices to feminist concerns around the built environment. It has been a privilege to delve deeply into her career and reflect on its personal and professional significance. Warm thanks to Sigrid for her inspiration, design sensibilities, and generous friendship.

FOREWORD

BY CHRISTINE THEODOROPOULOS
Dean of the College of Architecture and Environmental Design California Polytechnic State University, San Luis Obispo

As an educator-architect, Sigrid Miller Pollin espouses the academic tradition of reflective practice informed by theoretical discourse and enriched by collaborations with colleagues in allied disciplines. She is also an extraordinary role model, particularly for women who continue to be underrepresented leaders in the field of architecture. As a sole practitioner, Sigrid leverages her intersecting identities (designer, artist, teacher, family member, administrator, business owner) to create a distinctive body of work.

Her career in the academy has been equally influential. She set new directions for design education for the established program at California State Polytechnic University Pomona, where she was the first woman promoted to the rank of full professor, and the first to chair the department. Under her leadership experimentation flourished as the department transformed its design curriculum to integrate technology with aesthetics. As one of the founding faculty of the successful new architecture program at the University of Massachusetts Amherst, she continues to inspire students and colleagues through her commitment to design excellence and interdisciplinary collaboration.

Sigrid's creative process uncovers the unique essences of places to shape sustainable architecture that participates in nuances of climate, orientation, and topography. In arid Riverside, California the Jumping Rocks Houses are elegant variations on topographic theme and an early example of Sigrid's particular interest in architecture's fit to site. Likewise, on the historic University of Massachusetts campus, Gordon Hall and Crotty Hall derive spatial richness as they step through a gently sloping landscape. And in the speculative realm, Sigrid's drawing and painting treats line as the trace of topography. Simultaneously exuberant and economical, her projects reveal a unified approach to sustainable design that combines social and ecological imperatives.

Throughout her work, Sigrid interweaves playful, unexpected elements that humanize into bold concepts. Surprise spaces, flashes of vibrant color, sculptural details and strategic views impart distinctive identity to building interiors. The houses she designed for her family, Jumping Rocks III in Riverside and the 1290 Studio and Residence in Amherst, Massachusetts, are especially interesting as spatial-social experiments. Although they differ in their fit to particular landscapes, they share a feminist approach to shaping space that sustains the simultaneous dualities that define contemporary life. Be it work-play, personal-professional, individual-family, parents-children, or partner-partner, Sigrid embraces the value of those intersections by making places for each that acknowledge the other.

Sigrid Miller Pollin draws deeply from her personal experience to further the relevance of architectural practice and education. In doing so she enables us to transcend the status quo with grace and power.

BIOGRAPHY

Sigrid Miller Pollin, FAIA was born in Trenton, New Jersey and spent most of her youth in Rhode Island. She received a Bachelor of Arts degree in Art History from Vassar College in 1971 and a Master of Architecture degree from Columbia University in 1975. Before moving to Amherst, Massachusetts with her family in 1998, she was Chair and Professor of Architecture in the College of Environmental Design at the California Polytechnic University Pomona. Sigrid is Professor of Architecture Emerita at the University of Massachusetts, Amherst Department of Architecture and principal of Miller Pollin Architecture.

Sigrid has practiced architecture and been registered through the National Council of Architectural Registration Board (NCARB) in New York, California, Nevada, and Massachusetts. Her work has been published in numerous publications over the years including *Global Architecture, Progressive Architecture, Hauser Magazine* in Germany, *Ville Giardini* in Italy, *Boston Home*, and *Design New England*. It has been featured in various books including *World Cities Los Angeles and 21st Century Houses: 150 of the World's Best*. She has received architectural awards from AIA New England, Inland California AIA, Western Massachusetts AIA, and the Boston Society of Architects.

In 2009 Sigrid was elected to the American Institute of Architects College of Fellows. In 2010 she was awarded a UMass Amherst Chancellor's Award for Creative Activity. She was also selected to give the campus-wide Distinguished Faculty Lecture in 2010. In 2017 she received the Women in Design Award of Excellence from the Boston Society of Architects.

Miller Pollin's design studios at UMass Amherst have been grounded by her experience in practice, and inspired by the interpretive possibilities of site and the integration of environmental concerns with inventive design. Sigrid has produced LEED Gold and Platinum projects and recently completed Crotty Hall, a net-zero energy academic building at UMass Amherst.

Throughout her long career in architecture she has explored connections between art and architecture. In 2011 Sigrid began collaborating with architect Stephen Schreiber and landscape architect Jane Thurber in exhibits of drawings, bas reliefs and paintings related to interpretations of patterns found in the landscape, called *Field Notes*. The overlaps they have explored between art and architecture, the natural environment and the built environment have led to a total of eight collaborative exhibits thus far. In 2018 an exhibit of architectural models produced in California and Massachusetts by Miller Pollin Architecture was held at the John Olver Design Building Gallery at UMass Amherst. In fall of 2018 Miller Pollin's mixed media drawings exploring the cellular structure of selected plants were featured in a three-person show at UMass's Hampden Gallery along with works by New York artists Joan Weber and Paula Elliot. She describes this recent body of work as "looking inward beyond the surface and into the space that nature creates every day."

Sigrid has been involved with strengthening the identity and the opportunities for women in architecture since her professional career began in New York City and California. In her role as a teacher she has mentored hundreds of young aspiring architects. Among other related activities, she participated in the Women, Design, Theory series in Los Angeles, the CD entitled "You Can be A Woman Architect" produced by Margot Siegal, and in 2011 organized and participated in the Smith College lecture series entitled "Daughters of Invention." She, along with three other female AIA Fellows, founded the Western Massachusetts Women in Architecture organization in 2017.

Sigrid and her husband, economist Robert Pollin, have two daughters — Hannah Pollin-Galay of Tel Aviv and Emma Grock of Carlton, Oregon. They are the very proud grandparents of Leah and Ruthie Pollin-Galay and Laila Grock.

INTRODUCTION

BY SIGRID MILLER POLLIN

Before we began collaborating on this book, Meg Vickery and I had been engaged in a number of discussions about the relationship of work life to home life. From my perspective, even as a college student, I wanted to think that there could be a way to have a family and a satisfying work life and that these could complement each other. Practically speaking, I chose architecture, thinking I could ultimately work at a home studio and be near my family. This wasn't as simple as I had imagined but ultimately it did come to fruition. Meg and I decided that, in compiling the work in this volume, we could show how it has been possible to build a small but highly engaging architectural practice tailored as much as possible to allow time and space for raising kids with my husband, Bob Pollin.

The nature of my approach to an architectural practice has been very personal. It is a practice built on direct relationships with my clients. As is true with many small practices, I often found commissions from whomever came through the door. I was able to jump-start my practice in California by specifically targeting local developers. I thought of my work as creative production that emerged out of investigating questions in conjunction with a wide variety of client aspirations and circumstances. I think that Meg has seen this in part as a feminist approach to nurturing a professional practice. So we decided to take a personal approach to grouping projects in categories according to a project's potential offered either by the client, site, budget, or program. This seemed like a more focused way to organize the work rather than in a chronological sequence or by the dry categories of residential, commercial, and institutional.

We conceived this book as something that would both record my work while also providing reflections on the fluidity of approaches to projects. In my experience, every client calls for translations at every turn. The thorny job of the architect is to take large amounts of information and transform this information into physical form. This is always the case, regardless of a project's scale. In this sense we architects are simplifiers. The imperatives of site, program, and client goals interweave with larger aspirations of providing human comfort and hopefully, when everything comes together, an aesthetic contribution.

I was engaged as both the developer and the architect in some of these projects. Having myself as my client was different than the client-commissioned projects. These personal projects brought different rewards. For example, with the Jumping Rocks project that included my own family's home as one of the three houses on a dramatic 10-acre site in Riverside, California, I was able to investigate challenges and tenets that have interested me throughout my career. These include, among other things, searching for the genetic imprint of any given site and the essential relationships between built form and the natural environment.

Eight categories emerged as we looked at structuring this book: **Researching, Interpretations, Home, Transformations, Community Housing, Questions, Learning and Performing, and Drawing and Painting.**

The goal of projects in the **Researching** category was to create environments conducive to in-depth study as well as collegiality. The two university building projects in this category, Gordon Hall and Crotty Hall, house largely faculty and graduate student research offices. They also include group spaces such as conference rooms and common areas for meeting and socializing. **Interpretations** are projects that evolved through introducing metaphor as a guide in the design process. Such metaphors include built form as rock formations, the eye as a space opening up to a large view, the structure of a leaf as a shelter, a protective masque as a southern sun-sheltering element, and a cocoon-like transparent form as a chamber. **Home** is simply home—the base from which we operate in the larger arena. **Transformations** are essentially renovations—in a couple of cases aiming to make "silk purses from sow's ears." They are generally modestly budgeted projects. **Community Housing** is a glimpse into multi-unit dwelling as a building type for providing affordable housing. **Questions** includes my submissions into various architectural competitions. Competitions allow architects the opportunity to pose theoretical problems and investigate answers that stretch beyond the daily practice. **The Learning and Performing** projects shown here include educational facilities outside of mainstream schools.

In all phases of my architecture practice, I have maintained a strong interest in both linkages between art and architecture and in creating artwork as a counterpoint to architectural projects. Architectural projects are inevitably team-based whereas art pieces allow for immediate, individual expression and decision-making. The last section of the book, **Drawing and Painting**, includes examples of artwork completed for exhibits outside of the architectural profession.

My work in art and architecture continues. In 2019, I retired from the academic studio after 35 years of teaching. This step will allow me more time for exploring the critical issues that we face as architects in our current era. I look forward to opportunities for creating more translations with time, building from the ideas and projects presented in this book.

[RESEARCHING]

GORDON HALL

CROTTY HALL

GORDON HALL

University of Massachusetts
Amherst, Massachusetts
| 2003 |

The University of Massachusetts has recently experienced a building boom. Over the last fifteen years, the red brick and brutalist concrete campus has made way for a series of new contextual buildings with an emphasis on energy efficiency. One of the first to herald this new trend was Gordon Hall, designed by Miller Pollin in 2003. This was Miller Pollin's first larger scale work since leaving California. The site is located between a 1950s brick church and a narrow future building site. The program for the Political Economy Research Institute (PERI) and the Department of Economics at the University required a series of offices for faculty and graduate students, conference rooms and flexible spaces for special events such as lectures and receptions.

After Miller Pollin's move to Amherst she was particularly struck by the tobacco barns of the Pioneer Valley, and their practical yet elegant form. Inspired by this functional aesthetic, Miller Pollin's design scheme houses the repetitive office spaces in two shed-like forms. They recall the long simple forms of the tobacco barns. These two wings angle into the site and unite at a vertex forming the triangulated atrium and small kitchen. The V-shaped atrium space is lit by a translucent skylight supported by exposed sloping steel beams. On the exterior, gray ground face concrete block forms a plinth for the structure. Vertical cedar siding stained in a deep red clads the wings. The siding is rhythmically divided by narrow battens above and below the windows. These add texture to the wall surface and echo a board and batten building tradition in New England. A key objective in the design scheme was to follow the contours of the existing topography. This resulted in a ground floor located below the main entry level, allowing the building to step down the site.

The cladding technique of the exterior continues inside on the angled wings that form the triangular atrium filled with natural light from large skylights. The warm reds of the interior cladding contrast with a white elliptical form near the entrance that houses two private conference rooms. These receive natural light through scattered apertures that puncture the curved white walls. The crown of the oval form slopes downwards to the south, creating an energetic tension with the plane of the roof as it angles upward in the opposite direction. The atrium is a dynamic space with implied movement coursing through the angular geometry integrated throughout the building design.

These angled forms continue on the southern elevation where a larger conference space on the third floor projects out from the southern wing to accommodate lectures. The resulting overhang creates a shaded, protected patio/entry to the lower level. It also adds a sculptural quality to the uniform rhythm of the office block. Seen from the east, Gordon Hall, like so many of Miller Pollin's projects, is an assemblage of volumes, each often identified by color but, in this case, by the texture and material of the siding choices. Anodized aluminum sandwich panels sheath the western wing libraries while the warm, red board and batten siding identifies office space. The projecting conference room, a triangular volume, shares the red, ochre color but here horizontal clapboards sheath the form. In keeping

SITE PLAN

1. Main Entrance
2. Side Entrance
3. Entry Court
4. Balcony
5. Parking
6. Skylight

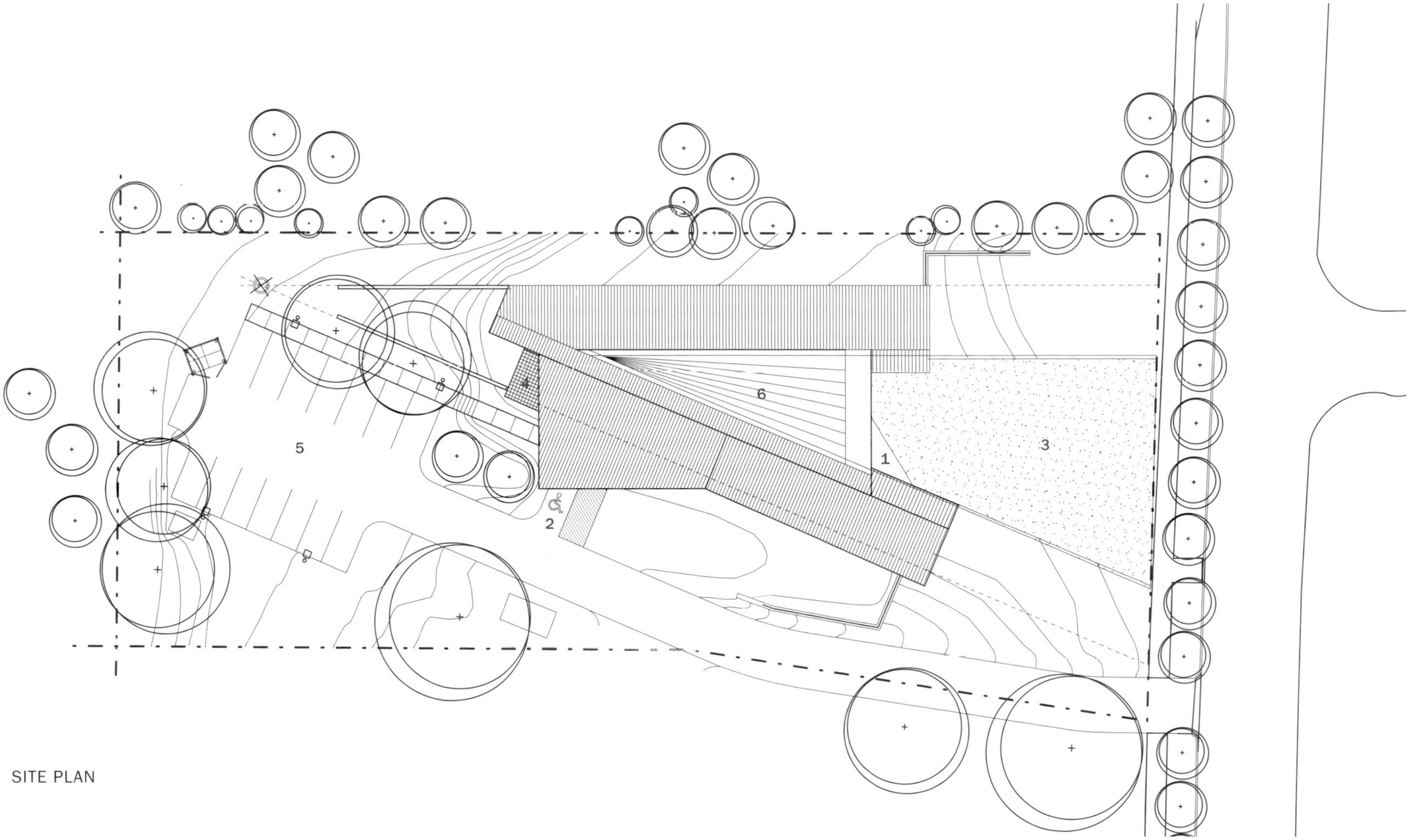

SITE PLAN

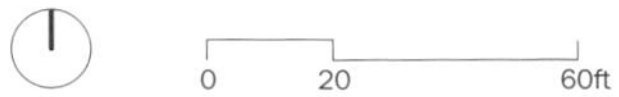

The angled roof and oval conference rooms frame the glazing of the northern façade. Below, radiant floor heating in the concrete warms the space with comfort and efficiency.

with her expressive bent, Miller Pollin creates variety, warmth, and interest in this structure, tying it to an architectural tradition while integrating forms, colors, textures, and materials to identify interior spaces with a vibrant modernity.

On the interior, the elliptical volume of the conference rooms in the foyer punctuates the street side of the atrium. The placement of this space within a space also achieves a level of privacy from the street. The office-lined corridors have views into the atrium through operable windows that can be opened for cross ventilation or closed for acoustical purposes. High clerestory windows on the south side of the atrium can be opened automatically on summer days. In winter the atrium is warmed with radiant floor heating. At the vertex of the V where the two wings meet, Miller Pollin carved out playful rectangular voids of bright teal and red. These are top lit and provide display spaces for small artwork pieces by UMass faculty artists and graduate fine arts students. These small, affordable details animate this circulation space.

As in her earlier California projects, Miller Pollin paid close attention to siting, natural lighting, materiality, and details. Each office has access to natural light and cross-ventilation. This reduces the electrical load and gives occupants fresh air options, particularly during the warmer season. Other details in the building include the wall sconces that line the atrium. Miller Pollin designed these tall narrow copper units mounted on redwood strips with notched side openings that filter light onto the redwood finish of the walls. These units provide patterned light and ambient warmth with forms harmonious with the verticals of the interior and exterior cladding.

The nuances of site and context acted as a springboard for the building design. Non-institutional materials and colors create a building that is synchronized with its surroundings, adding character to its context with angular drama.

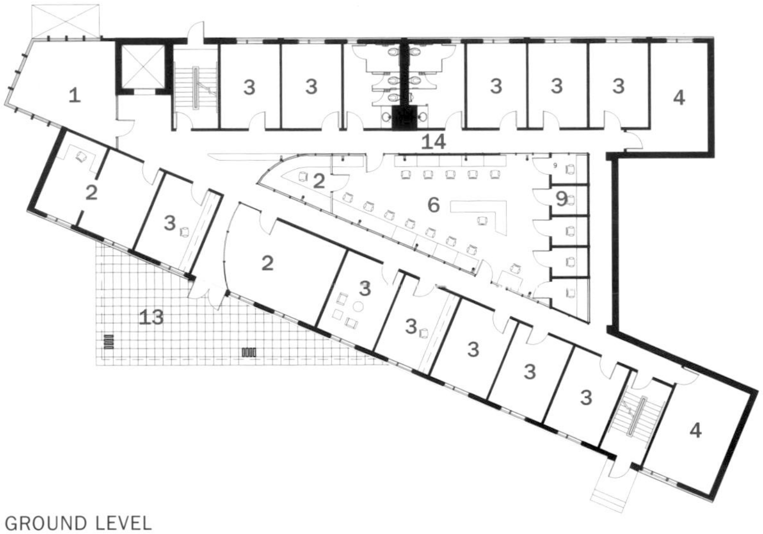

GROUND LEVEL

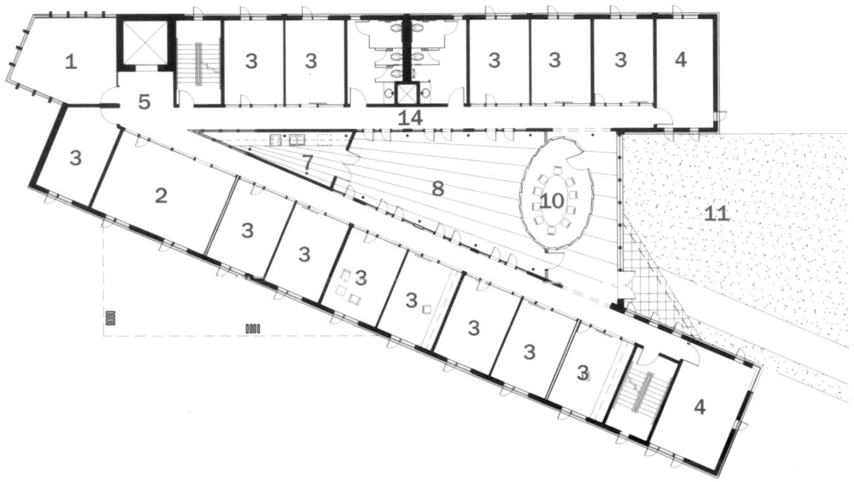

MAIN LEVEL

FLOOR PLANS

1. Library
2. Double Faculty Office
3. Single Faculty Office
4. Graduate Student Office
5. Lobby
6. Computer Laboratory
7. Kitchen
8. Atrium
9. Telephone Research Rooms
10. Conference Room
11. Entry Court
12. Lounge
13. Terrace
14. Restrooms

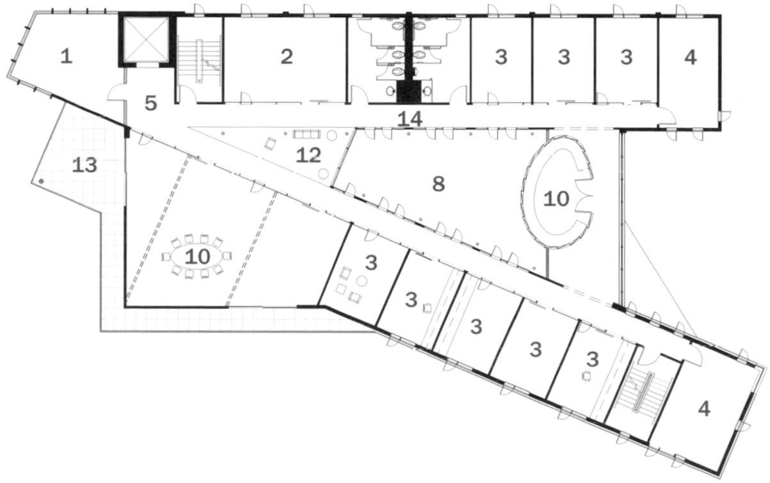

THIRD LEVEL

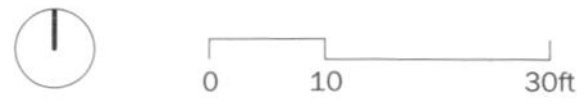

CROTTY HALL

CROTTY HALL

University of Massachusetts
Amherst, Massachusetts
| 2017 |

Crotty Hall, on the southeastern edge of the University of Massachusetts Amherst campus, is a remarkable building designed to operate under stringent net zero energy and emissions standards. It is located just south of Miller Pollin's Gordon Hall of 2003 and houses the UMass Department of Economics. Its name honors Economics Professor Emeritus James Crotty and his wife Pamela. The site is extremely narrow and the challenges of designing a building for this site were daunting. The overarching goal was to allow an architectural solution to emerge out of this virtual sliver of land and, at the same time, accommodate the requirements of a robust program of 35 offices, four conference rooms, a small kitchen/café and a sprinkling of student lounge spaces. As in her previous work, Miller Pollin began with the site and its contours; a gentle slope downwards toward the west, a tight boundary line and restricted street access. To accommodate setback requirements and a driveway between Gordon and the new construction, the street façade was limited to a 27' width.

The building stretches westward away from the road. Miller Pollin angled the building approximately two thirds of the way down the length of the site just as the slope begins to level out as a way of folding the north and south elevations. The fold softens the length of these façades. By breaking the orthogonal geometry at various points, she simultaneously created interest in the interior spaces and signaled the two entrances on the north side. Crotty Hall's angled form embraces the northern exterior space between the two buildings. The exterior is clad in two tones of zinc siding—warm gray siding that refers to the western aluminum cladding and gray ground face plinth of Gordon Hall, and a charcoal gray similar to the metal roof of Gordon Hall. While the approach via North Pleasant Street is modest and narrow, as visitors approach from the north, the building provides a concluding sight-line and a powerful presence as it spreads across the hillside.

Interior corridors break into "nodes"—small entry spaces for groupings of four offices. Punctuating the progression through the building in this way opens up the long expanse: spaces narrow and billow out as one walks through its length. These office nodes are further articulated by dropped, translucent ceilings of warm, indirect, LED lighting that complements the white opaque glazing of the offices and clerestory windows of the corridors. As seen elsewhere in Miller Pollin's work, she compresses and opens spaces to express different functions. Lighting emphasize these shifts. Through a combination of lighting techniques, changes in materials, and gentle spatial manipulations, Miller Pollin creates subtle variations that break up the regularity of the office block.

Construction began with the drilling of eight geothermal wells 450 feet deep as the primary ground water source for heating and cooling the building. The building has a tight, super-insulated envelope, triple glazing and a sophisticated system of sensors that can adjust air flow to an office if the window is opened. A computerized system notifies occupants when the weather conditions are right for natural ventilation with operable windows. A high efficiency solar array on the roof produces a significant portion of the electricity for the

building, and a dashboard on the first floor is intended to allow occupants access to real-time data on energy use, heating and cooling loads, and renewable energy production.

This building is beautiful with its rich blending of materials, colors, and lighting. It is also the first building on campus designed to operate under net zero standards. The design places a high level of value on spatial variety even within a constrained building envelope. Color and light bring warmth and comfort to public and private spaces. The site design reflects an integrated approach to sustainability by knitting together the architecture and the landscape architecture. The terraced rain gardens that line the northern bank of the building are fed by run-off from the roof, which is directed into vertical channels rendered in a dark gray zinc on the north elevation. The run-off irrigates the native plantings on the site. The plantings, in turn, filter the storm water as it flows down to a local wetland area. As these plantings mature, they will provide a soft, transparent layer composed of colorful perennials, woody plants and small deciduous trees between the driveway and the gray zinc of Crotty Hall.

CONTEXT PLAN

1. Crotty Hall
2. Existing Gordon Hall
3. Haigis Mall
4. Campus Visitors Center
5. Visitor Parking

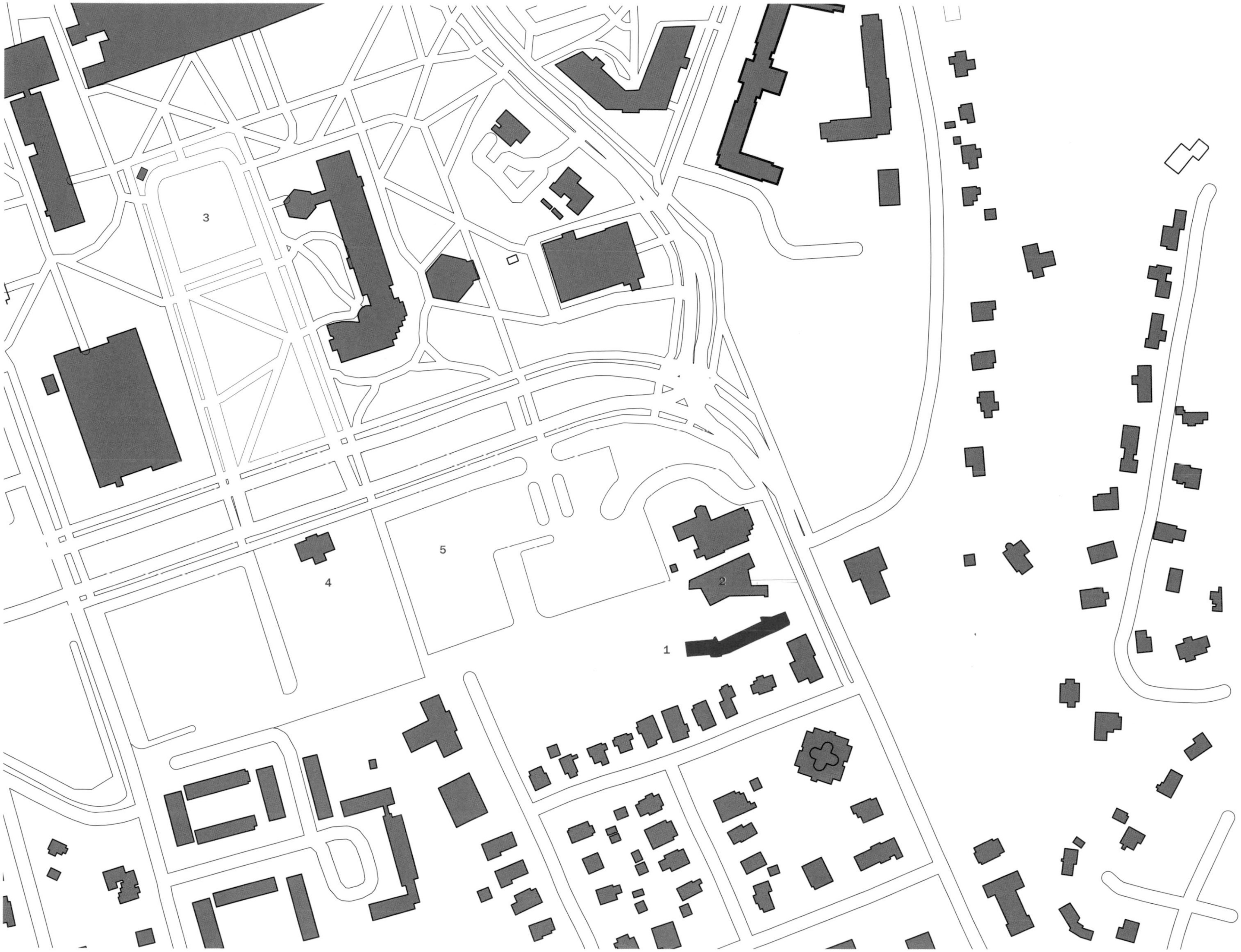

3
5
4
2
1

SITE PLAN

1. Crotty Hall
2. Existing Gordon Hall
3. Rain Gardens
4. Solar Panels
5. Parking Area
6. Wetland

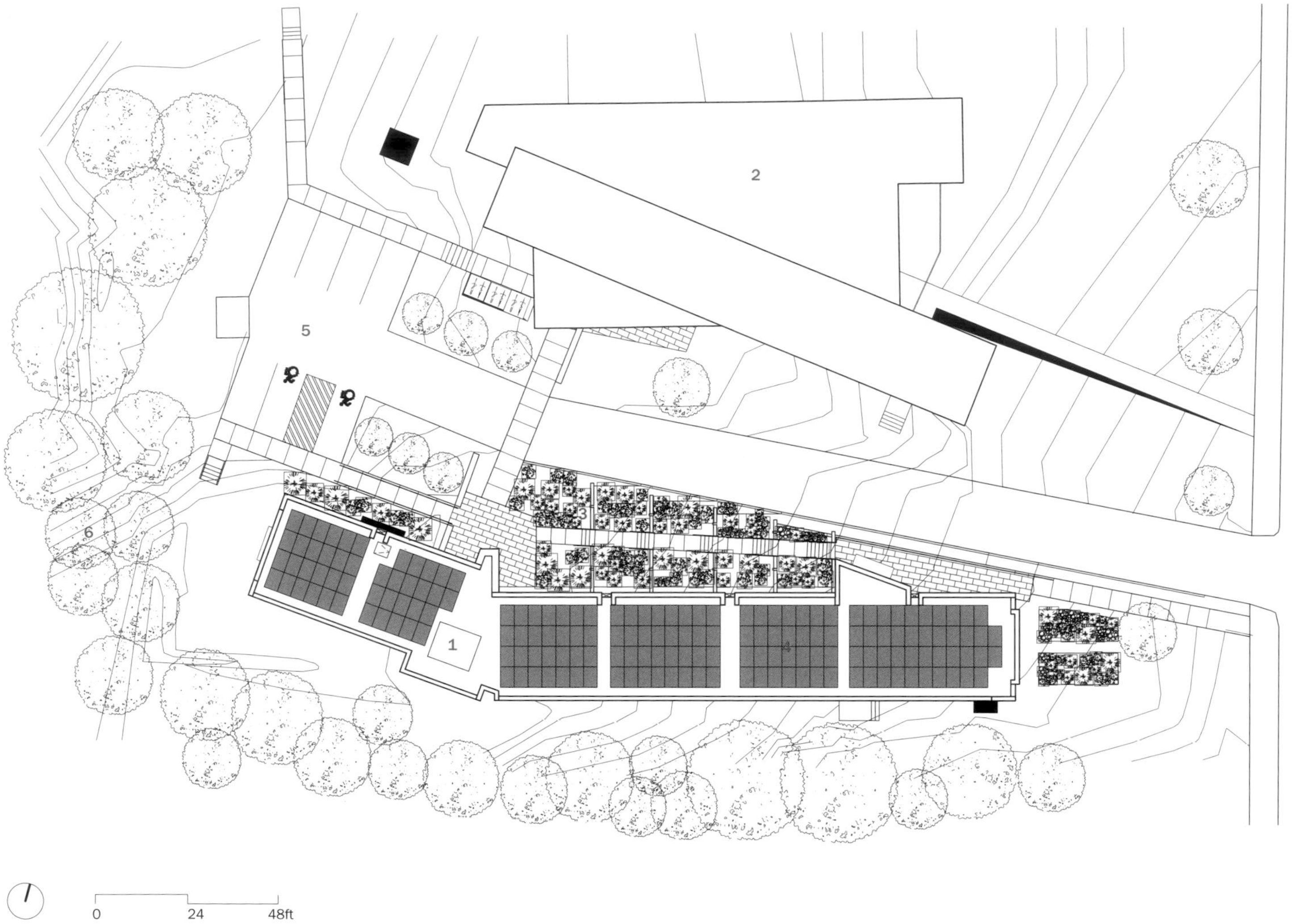

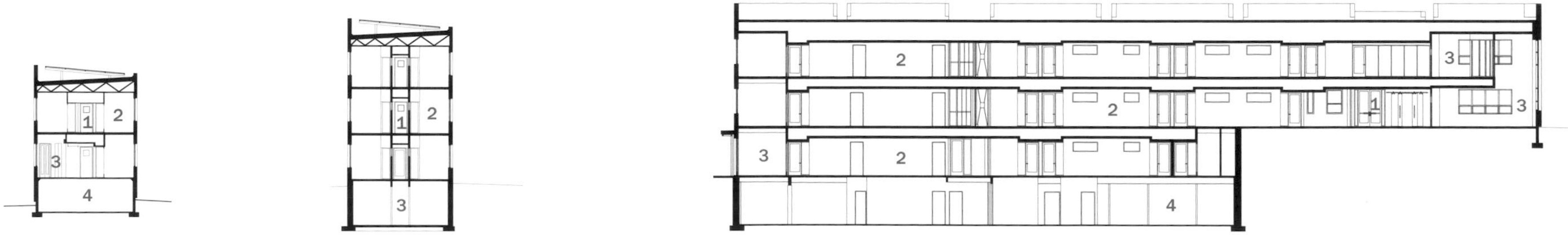

A-A

B-B

C-C

BASEMENT PLAN

1. Mechanical Storage
2. Shower Room
3. Restrooms

FIRST FLOOR PLAN

1. Central Circulation Stair
2. Office Corridor
3. Office Space
4. Restrooms
5. Conference Room
6. Lower Level Entry

SECOND FLOOR PLAN

1. Main Entry Lobby
2. Conference Room
3. Office Corridor
4. Office Space
5. Central Circulation Stair
6. Restrooms
7. Kitchen

THIRD FLOOR PLAN

1. Conference Room
2. Office Corridor
3. Lounge Area
4. Restrooms
5. Office Space

SECTION A-A

1. Main Entry Lobby
2. Office Corridor
3. Conference Room
4. Mechanical Storage

SECTION B-B

1. Office Corridor
2. Office Space
3. Mechanical / Storage

SECTION C-C

1. Main Entry
2. Corridor
3. Conference Room
4. Mechanical / Storage

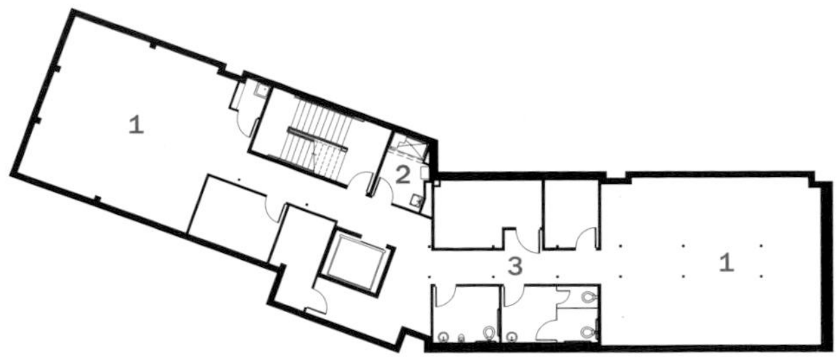

BASEMENT PLAN

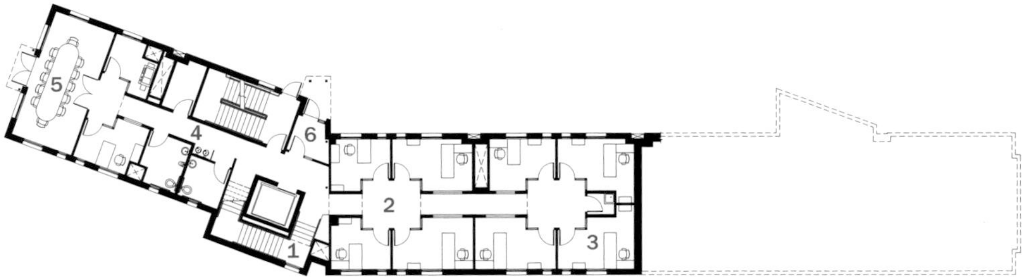

FIRST FLOOR PLAN

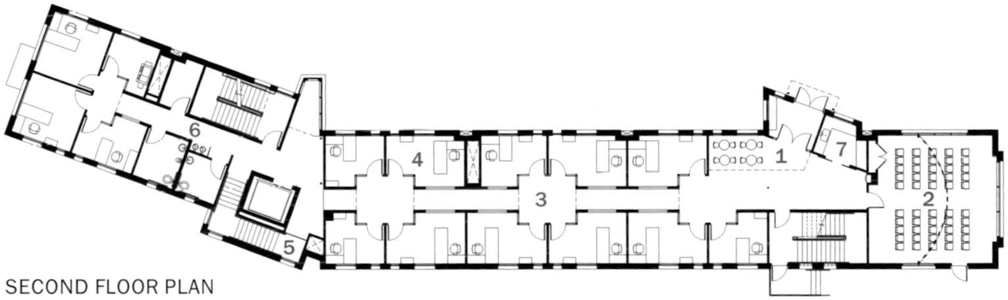

SECOND FLOOR PLAN

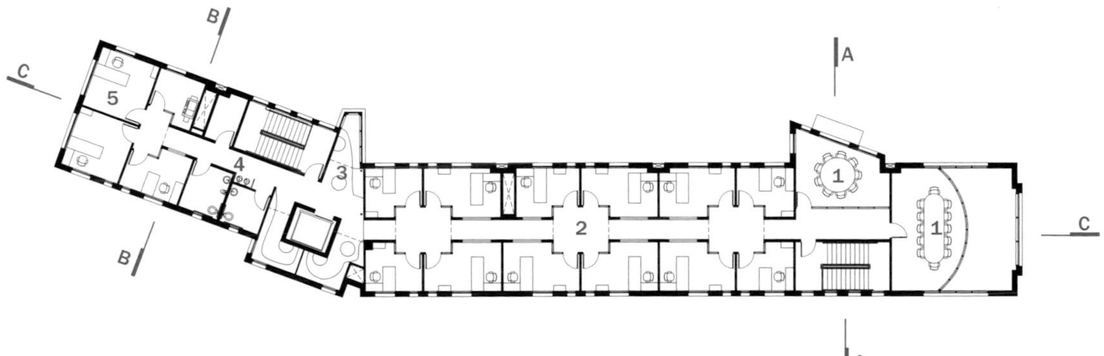

THIRD FLOOR PLAN

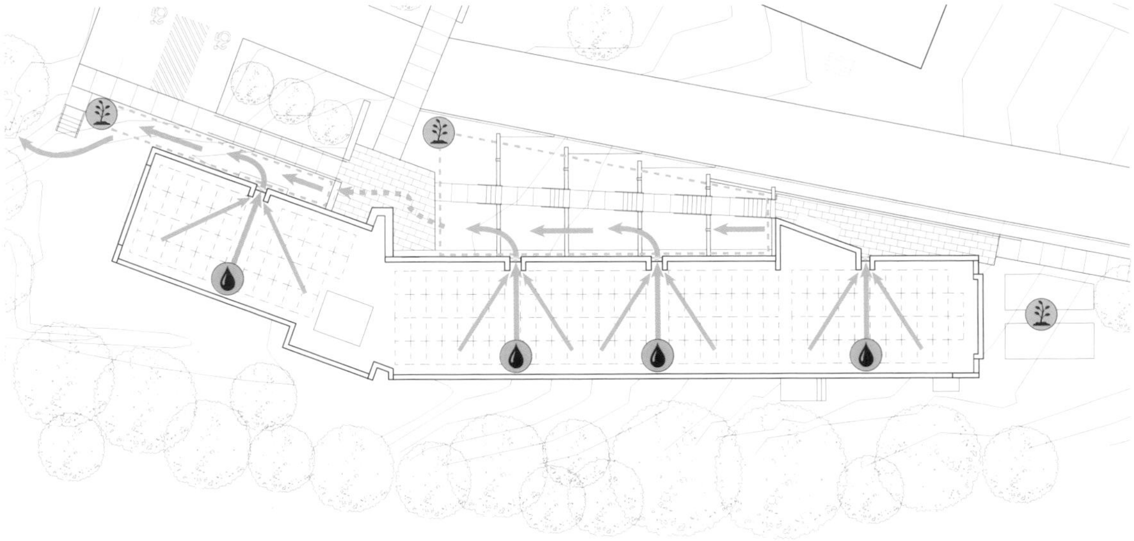

RAINWATER RUNOFF SITE PLAN

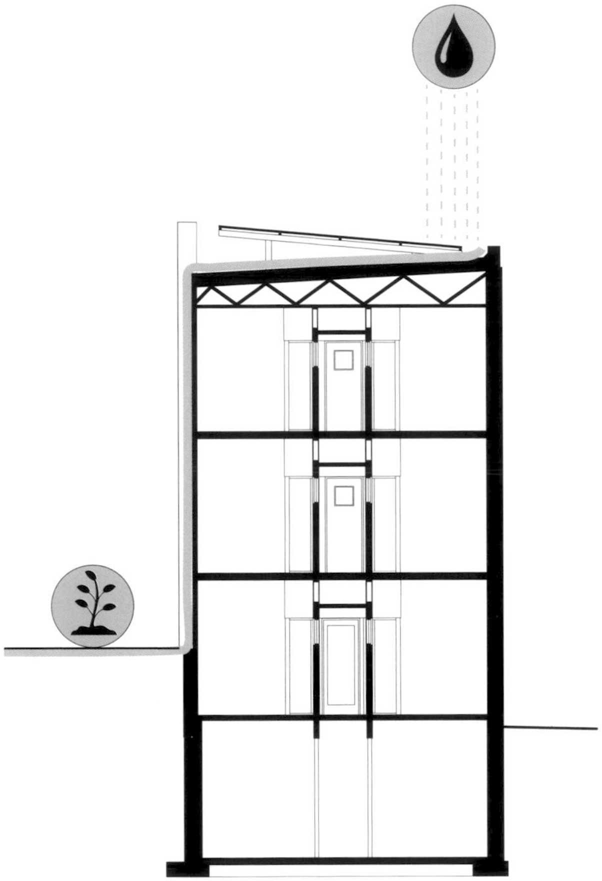

RAINWATER RUNOFF SECTION

0 12 24ft

RAINWATER RUNOFF ELEVATION

0 24 48ft

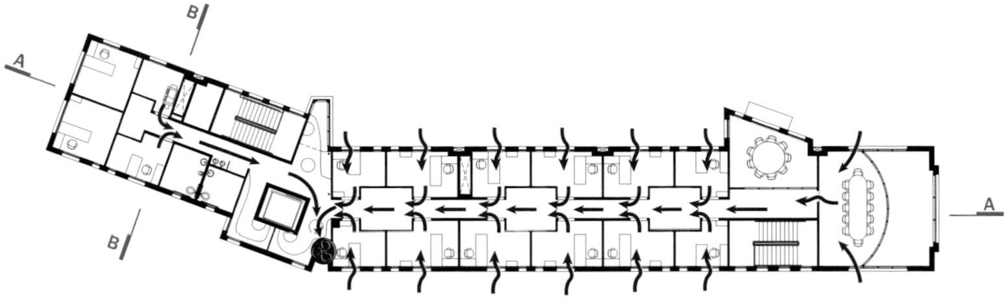

VENTILATION PLAN

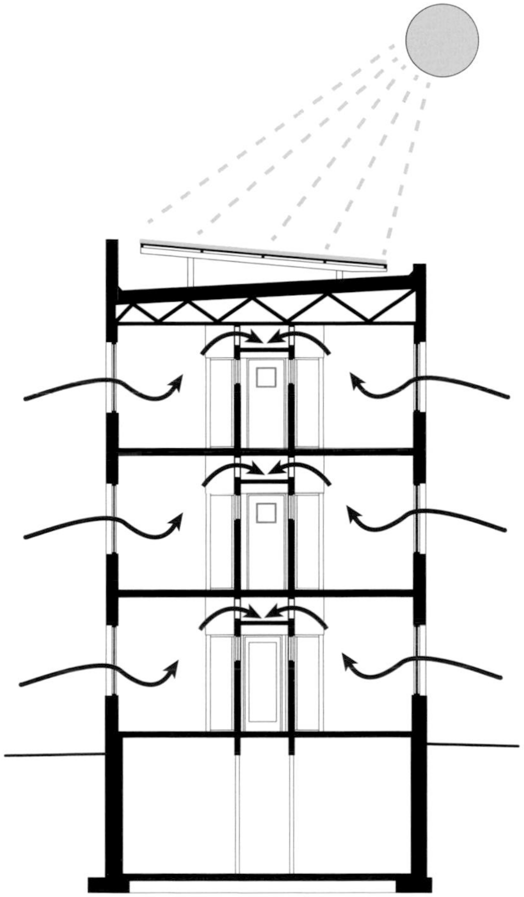

VENTILATION SECTION B-B

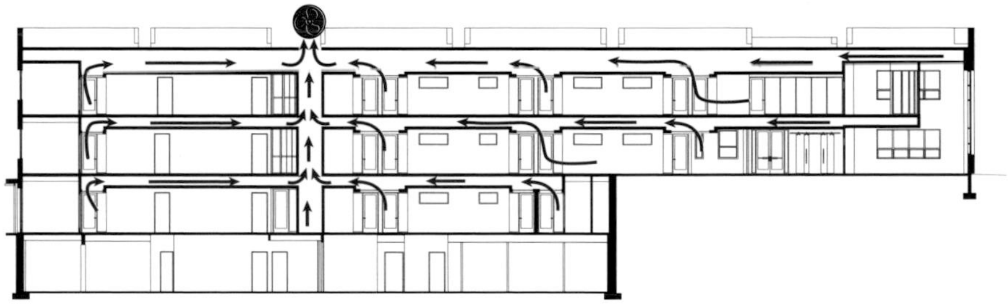

VENTILATION SECTION A-A

0 12 24ft

0 24 48ft

[INTERPRETATIONS]

JUMPING ROCKS: HOUSE I, II & III

1290 STUDIO & RESIDENCE

HOUSE FOR A MAGICIAN

WAVE HOUSE

LA SIERRA COMMUTER RAIL STATION

RIVERSIDE CHAMBER OF COMMERCE

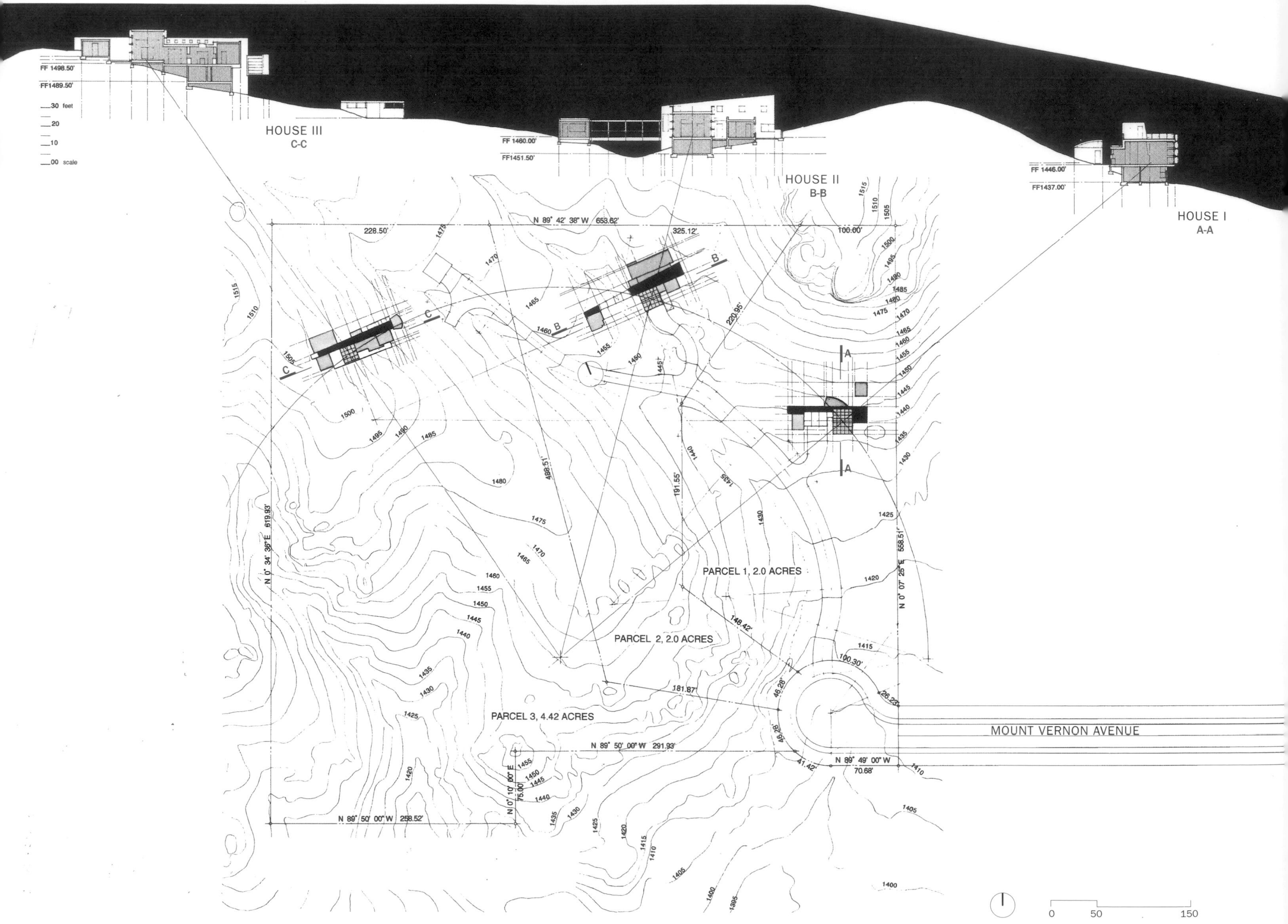
FF 1498.50'
FF1489.50'
30 feet
20
10
00 scale
HOUSE III
C-C
FF 1460.00'
FF1451.50'
HOUSE II
B-B
FF 1446.00'
FF1437.00'
HOUSE I
A-A
N 89° 42' 38" W 653.62'
228.50'
325.12'
100.00'
220.95'
488.51'
191.55'
N 0° 34' 36" E 619.93'
N 0° 07' 25" E 558.51'
PARCEL 1, 2.0 ACRES
PARCEL 2, 2.0 ACRES
PARCEL 3, 4.42 ACRES
148.42'
100.30'
181.87'
46.28'
26.23'
N 89° 50' 06" W 291.93'
N 89° 49' 00" W
70.68'
41.42'
N 0° 10' 00" E
75.00'
N 89° 50' 00" W 258.52'
MOUNT VERNON AVENUE
0
50
150

JUMPING ROCKS: HOUSE I, II & III

Box Springs
Mountain Park
Riverside, California
| 1993 |

This hilly, rocky ten-acre site is located at the boundary between the Box Springs Mountains and a suburban residential section of Riverside, California. Miller Pollin and her husband purchased this varied and dramatic site in 1989. They divided the property into three flag lots with the intention of building three houses, one for Miller Pollin and her family and the other two for friends. These houses show Miller Pollin exploring program, heightened sensitivity to site, and the natural world. Varied volumes in the context of home converged with an interest in material expression. The rugged landscape of the foothills around Riverside provided her with an opportunity to understand how an architectural vocabulary could root itself in and grow out of this terrain.

At the same time, exposure to the Los Angeles area work of California modernists such as Rudolph Schindler and Richard Neutra prompted a strong interest in their approach to architecture in Southern California. Having purchased the land and found clients for two of the houses, Miller Pollin began the design process by investigating the site's topography: the hills, shallow ravines, and jagged rocks. She observed and photographed the site extensively, experimenting with the impact of siting structures within this particular landscape. She found the various topographical conditions of the site could be distilled into distinct potential relationships to built form. For example, a valley or ravine cued concepts of infilling or bridging. A strong slope could be paired with cantilevering or precariously restraining built form. Inspired by the powerful rock outcroppings whose gritty gray roughness contrasts with the feathery desert undergrowth, Miller Pollin studied these spatial conditions in the topography and the rock formations. These were geological phenomena whose relationship to built form could establish a set of ground rules for these structures.

These striking rock formations represented an invulnerable permanence on the site which is subject to potentially severe brush fires fueled by the infamous Santa Ana winds. Furthermore, there was evidence on site of stone "bowls" created by Native Americans who used their surfaces for milling grain. Miller Pollin responded to these age-old rocks, interpreting their strength as protective walls. This idea was explored in her drawings in which colored shards representing brush fires and the winds buffet the stone surface but cannot reach the inner protected spaces. Such ruminations helped Miller Pollin formulate the idea of datum walls protecting against the elements and uniting different spaces in this case for three residential programs. In the final analysis, these were each sited with a distinct physical relationship to the varied topography. House I is parallel to the slope, House II bridges a ravine, and House III is perpendicular to the sloping hillside. Though each house is angled slightly differently, forming the broad arc seen in the site plan, their unifying datum walls essentially face north towards the undeveloped landscape and act as protective barriers. The deeply saturated Tuscan red color complements the hues of the semi-arid site. While it ties in with the flora of the landscape's underbrush and spring wild flowers, the deep red seems to emerge from the land itself. The concrete block walls create a dialogue with the tone and solidity of the rock formations.

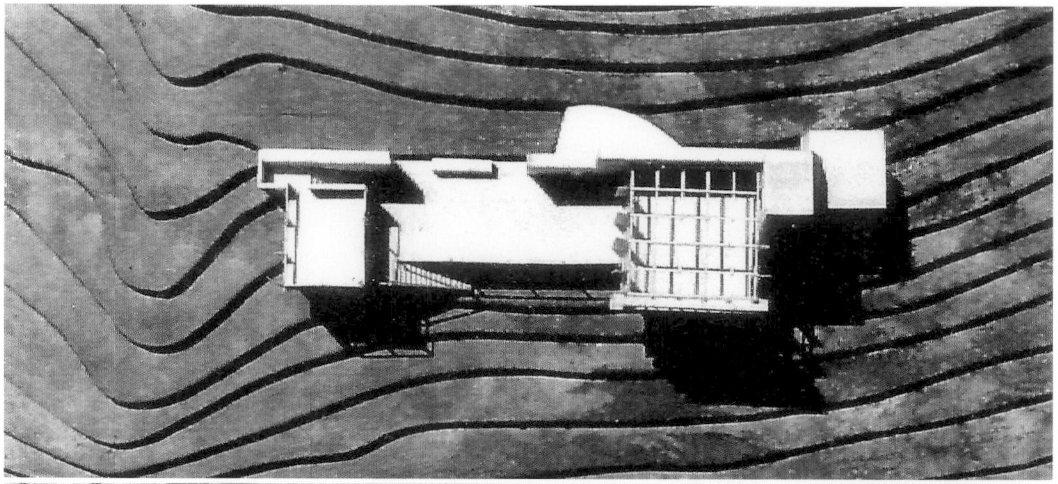

HOUSE I

HOUSE II

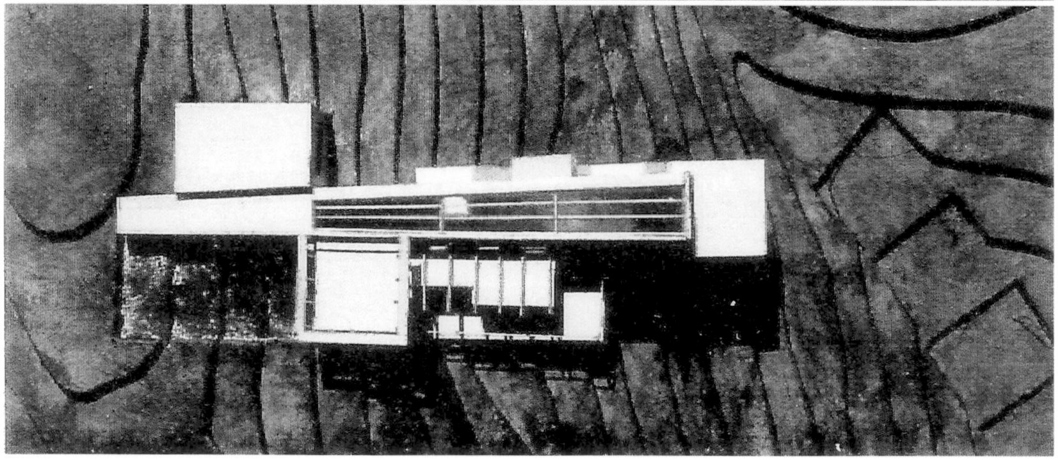

HOUSE III

HOUSE I

The Houses

The landscape provided an inspiration for the unifying datum of the red walls, at the same time the tenets of architects such as RM Schindler inspired Miller Pollin to think about spatial volumes in expressive ways. Miller Pollin credits Schindler and less directly Adolf Loos and the architects of the de Stijl movement with inspiring her to think about how space can be identified and defined. In contrast to Le Corbusier's "free plan" and the modernists of the International Style, architects like Loos and Schindler expanded thinking about what Loos called the Raumplan. This was realized in Loos' work, as rooms were separated by changing floor levels or ceiling heights to identify individual spaces. Schindler thought about spaces in the home in a similar way. Loos' view that interior space should be thought of as a series of vertically related horizontal platforms was a theme to which Schindler was to return again and again. Miller Pollin was particularly impressed with seeing Schindler's work in Los Angeles first hand. The "living cubes" of this project were directly inspired by the wood frame "sleeping baskets" of the Kings Road House.

Building on Loos and Schindler and with her own interest in identifying and organizing domestic spaces, Miller Pollin laid out these houses with clearly articulated forms defining various spaces. As these axonometric drawings indicate, spatial units such as bedrooms, "living cubes," and libraries are spliced onto the unifying spine datum wall. The "living cubes" are discrete living room units defined by double height walls of glazed Douglas Fir wood grids providing light and expansive views across the hillside. Miller Pollin explains, "What unified the project overall was the use of the red wall as a collective element as well as the 'living cube' in each house. The spaces and volumes varied depending on the program and specific site condition."

Miller Pollin explores space here with a rational clarity of parts. Her clients, for Houses I and II, had strong voices in these distinctive spaces. For example, the clients for House I both worked from home a good deal and needed work spaces that were clearly separate from living spaces. Miller Pollin's solution to this request shows her working on ideas that play out again in the 1290 Residence and Studio on the East Coast.

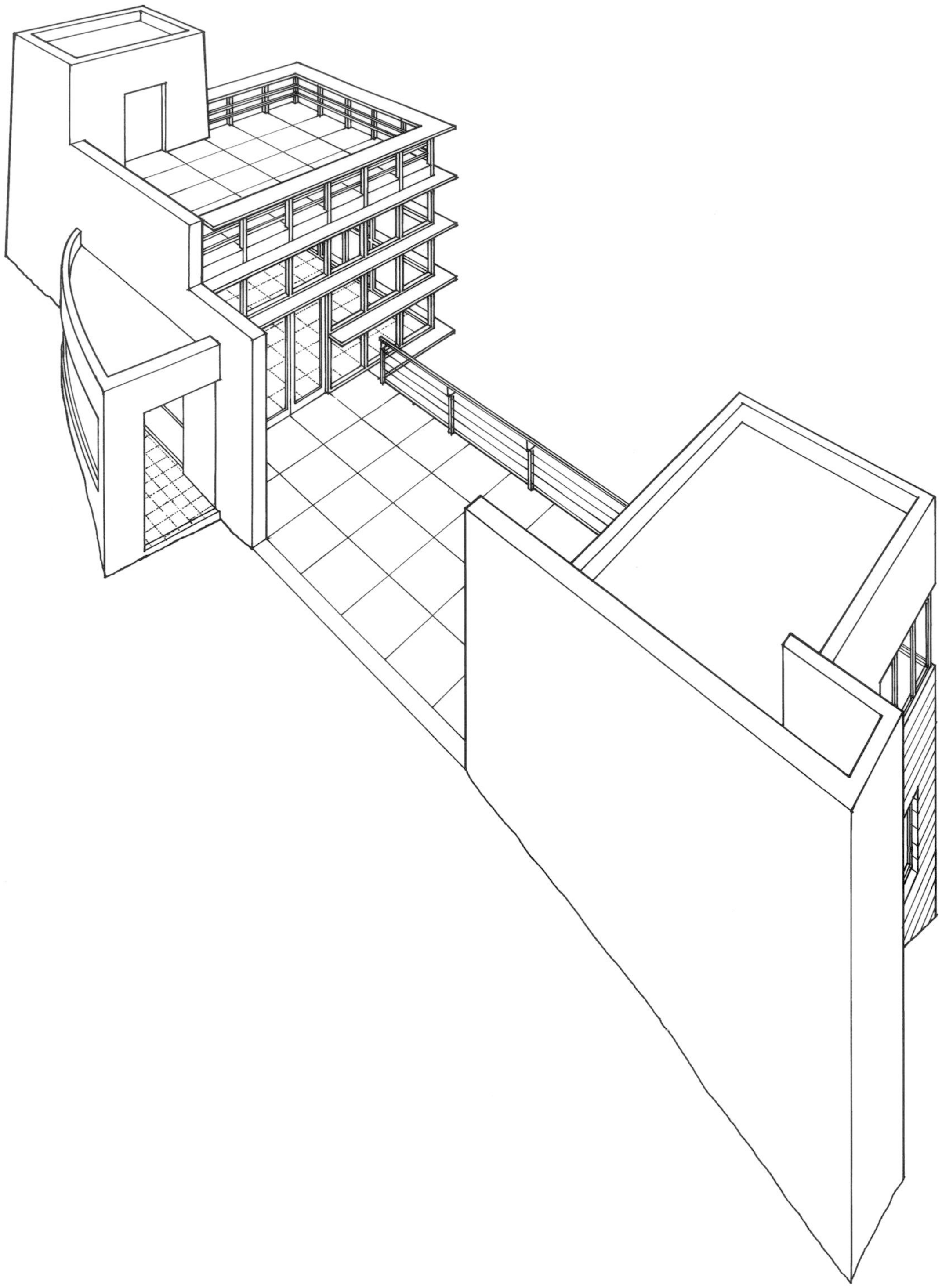

HOUSE I - 2,900 S.F.

1. Living Room / Dining Area
2. Kitchen
3. Stair Tower
4. Study / Bedroom
5. Floating Room
6. Deck
7. Master Bedroom
8. Bedroom
9. Carport

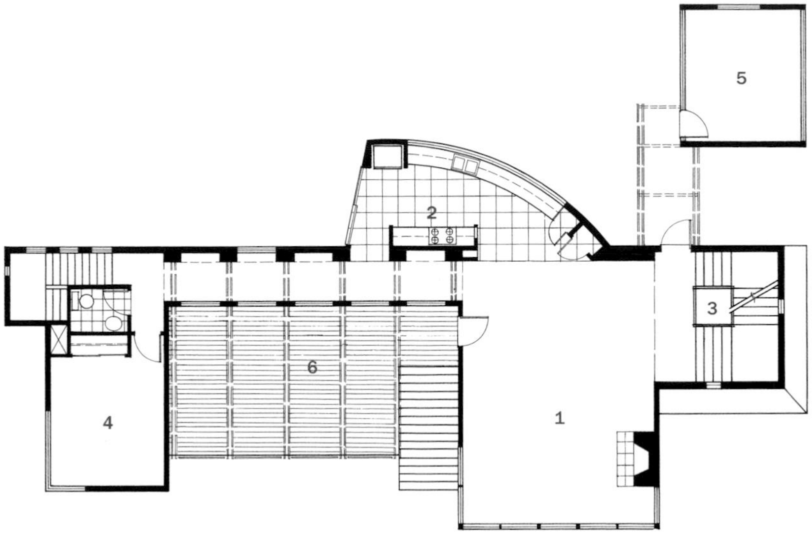

MAIN LEVEL

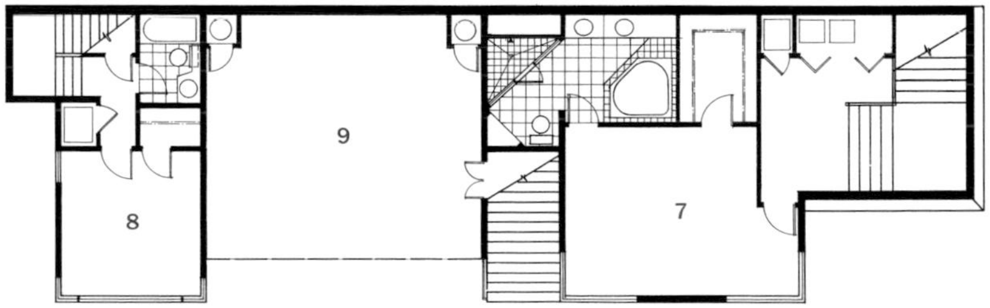

LOWER LEVEL

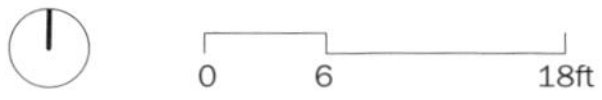

In House I, one of the two studies is separated from the living spaces via a wide deck on the main level and the second study becomes a separate structure on the slope just to the north. The "living cube" provides views to the south, but the study, clad in cedar, has views that look westward into the site. Both studies are purposefully positioned away from the public sphere to provide a space for work, free from domestic distractions. The bedrooms are on the ground level tucked into the hillside and sheltered from the sun. As we will see in her Amherst residence, Miller Pollin is concerned with the intersection of work and home life and how to craft spaces for both on one site. House I has a long red wall off of which living spaces project. This wall culminates in a stair tower. The tower rises up from the landscape, its substantial red walls reminiscent of traditional adobe architecture of the Southwest.

In House II, the red wall, the datum, connects the house parts and serves as a spine stretching across the landscape, uniting spaces and angling upwards out of the terrain, much like the rocky outcroppings do on the site itself. The library is accessed via a bridge that spans a seasonal ravine. In this instance, daily domestic activities occur on one side of the bridge and the quiet work space located on the library side. Corner windows frame views to the landscape and concrete block walls provide protection against the winds and sun. They are also the backdrop for bookshelves. Further to this clear separation of parts, the bedrooms are placed in a single volume sheathed in tan stucco grafted onto the north side of the red core along with the "living cube" and concrete block dining room to the south.

House I is parallel to its site slopes. House II bridges a ravine creating a spanning relationship to the slope. House III projects outward from the hillside, as if emerging from the ground and reaching out across the landscape. It too has a central spine off of which living spaces open. This was Miller Pollin's house for her family, and here the library lines the walls of the spine, spreading book shelves throughout the house, affording easy access for all of the family. All three houses address the needs of the clients via expressive assemblages of parts. Though distinct from each other, they share protective red walls that unite different spaces in the houses, protect against brush fires from the north and are deeply rooted in the landscape.

HOUSE II

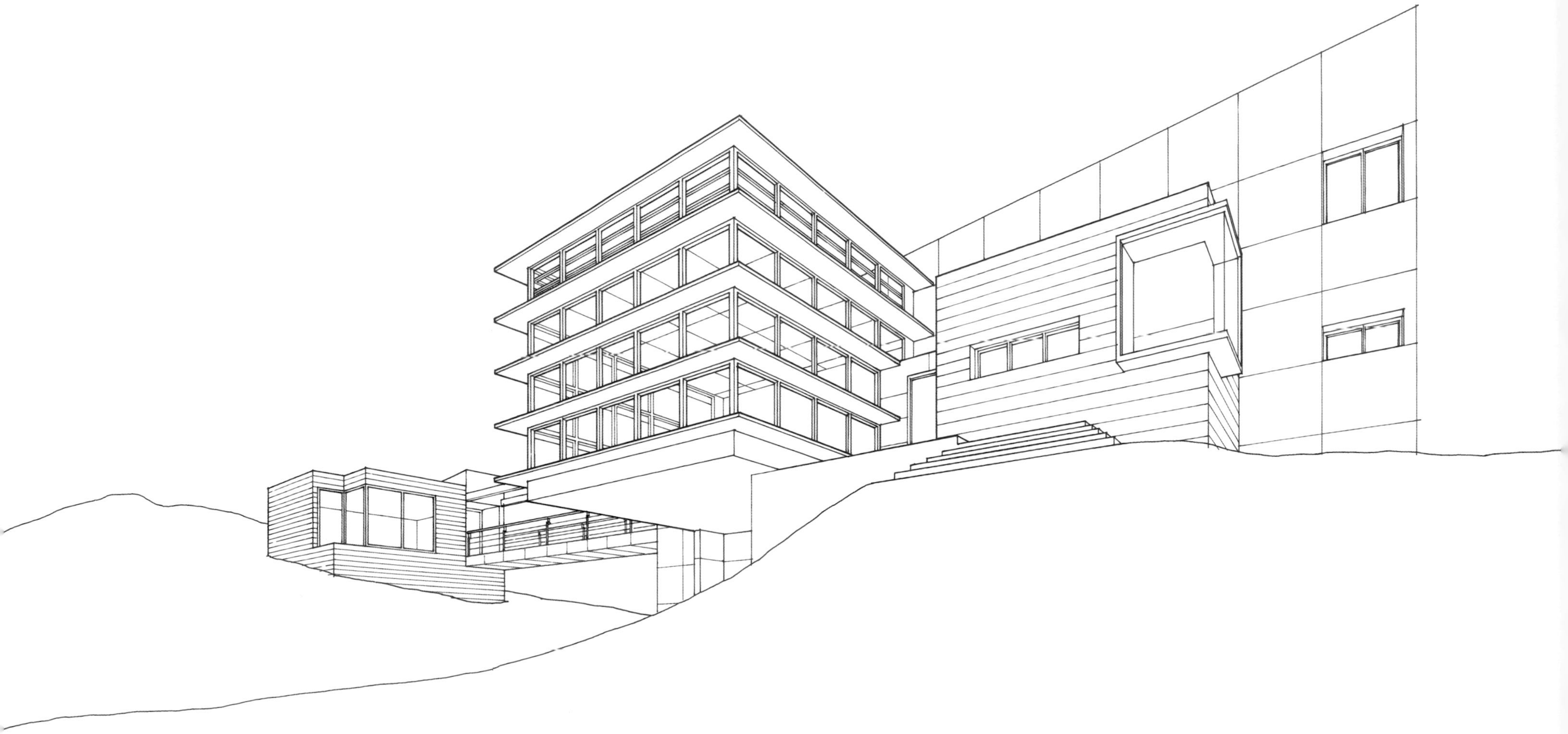

HOUSE II - 3,400 S.F.

1. Living Room
2. Dining Room
3. Kitchen
4. Media Room
5. Jacuzzi Room
6. Master Bedroom
7. Bridge
8. Library
9. Floating Room
10. Bedroom
11. Deck
12. Carport / Storage

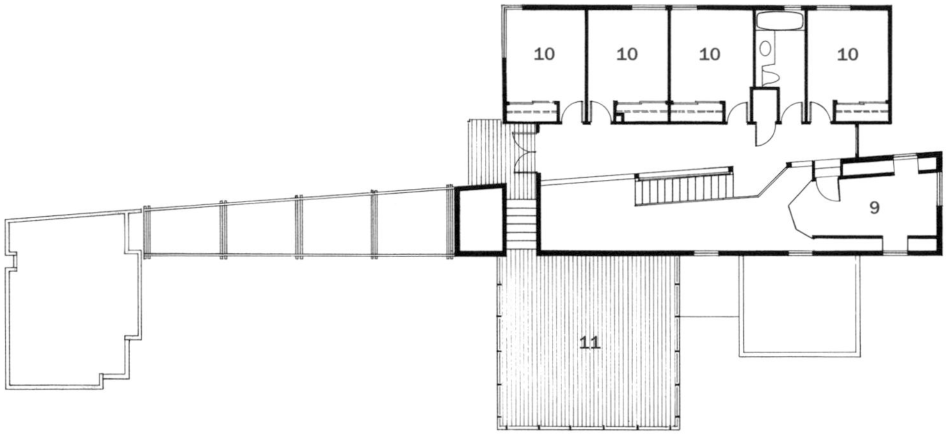

UPPER LEVEL

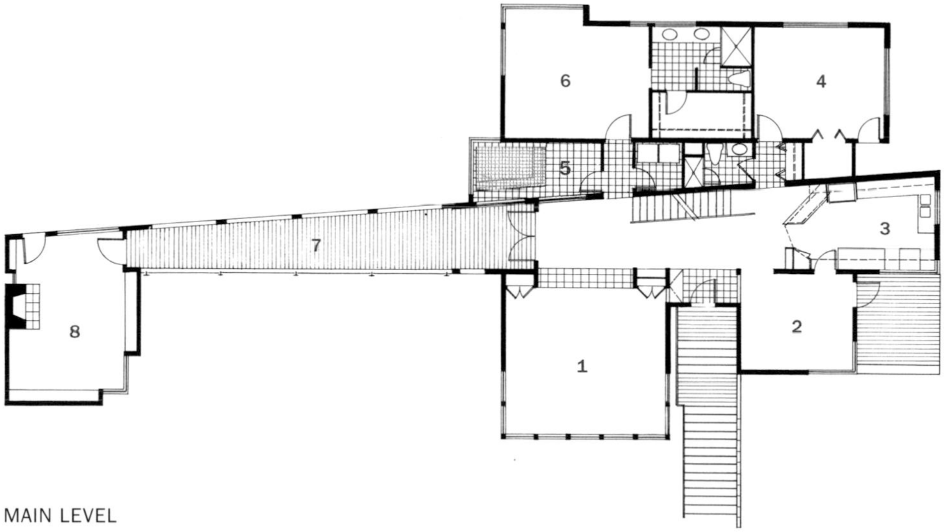

MAIN LEVEL

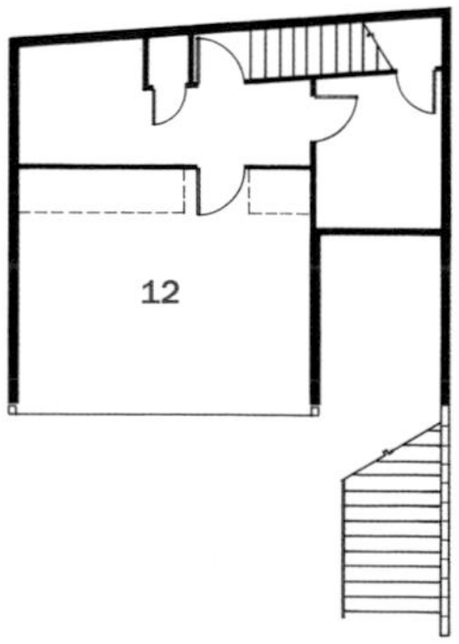

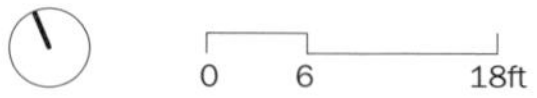

LOWER LEVEL

HOUSE III

Similarly, each house has what Miller Pollin calls an "anomaly space." In House I, the separate curving study is placed at the bottom of a slope north of the stair tower. It is a playful counterpoint to the main house. In House II, the "floating" room is tucked within the house, suspended within the central double-height circulation space. It is a space within a space, a segmented glass form that defines a reading room. In her own house, the "floating" room projects out from the house proper, a bold cantilevered volume with a curving wall. These counter-punctal spaces occur in many of Miller Pollin's projects.

The layered warmth of the wood is set off in part by concrete block walls whose light gray color, scale, and toughness tie in with the site's granite outcroppings. There is a staccato-like interplay between these materials which further articulates spaces. Just as the rocky outcroppings contrast with the feathery textures of the undergrowth across the hillsides, so do the redwood walls, thin mullions and wooden deck rails stand out against the solidity of the red and gray walls. This creates a tension between the delicate and the solid which adds interest and warmth. Schindler, Wright, and Aalto purposely collaged materials in numerous residential projects. In tandem with a varied material palette, Miller Pollin adds color to spaces following a personal interpretation. For her, color gives spaces definition and distinction, like punctuation in a sentence, adding clarity to her cubic clauses.

Consistent in her work is an attention to the detailed crafting of the house. The staircase of House II illustrates the point. The client for House II was interested in Japanese joinery. Miller Pollin translated this interest by making visible joints woven into the wood screen guard rail of Douglas fir struts. This screen reveals the stairs as both open and closed. The joints are made by a tectonic method used to connect the three rudimentary elements of a stair, namely: the tread, the riser, and the guard rail. At the joint the aluminum tread is kerfed into the thick wood tread and the horizontals of the guard rail slide onto and overlap the tread. This assembly then forms the expressed joints that create an ascending zig-zag pattern. Similarly, in the bookshelves that lined her family's library, small wooden blocks at the upper corners of each shelf give refined definition and ledger support to the shelving. Miller Pollin designed the drawer and cabinet pulls in House III kitchen, creating small collage compositions.

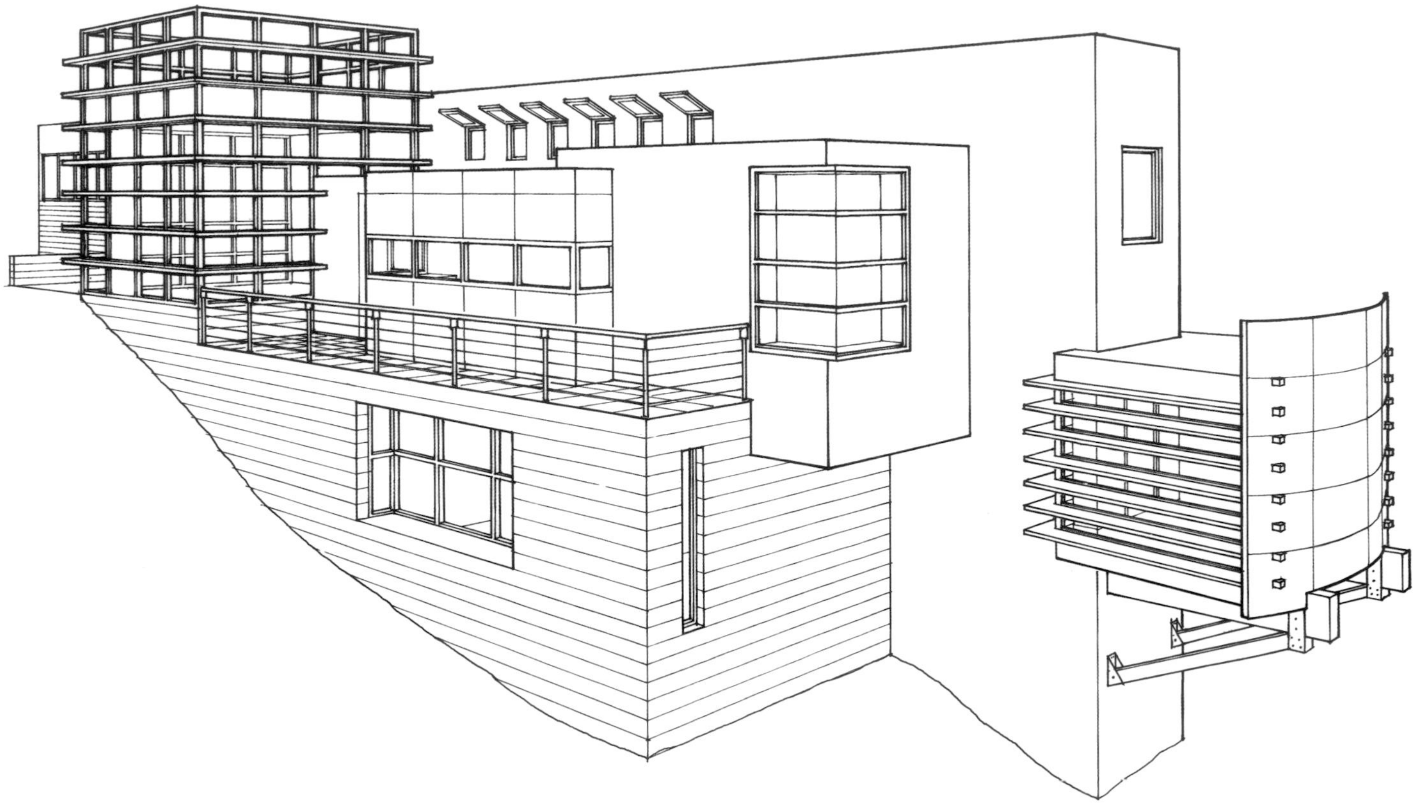

HOUSE III - 2,900 S.F.

1. Living Room
2. Dining Room
3. Kitchen
4. Floating Room
5. Library
6. Study
7. Guest Room / Study
8. Master Bedroom
9. Bedroom
10. Sitting Room
11. Storage

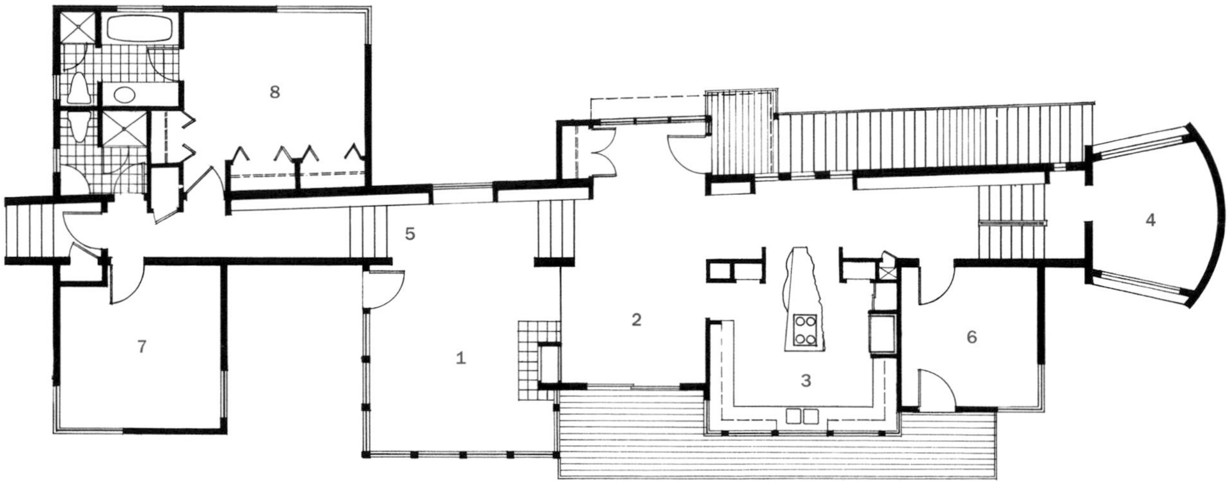

MAIN LEVEL

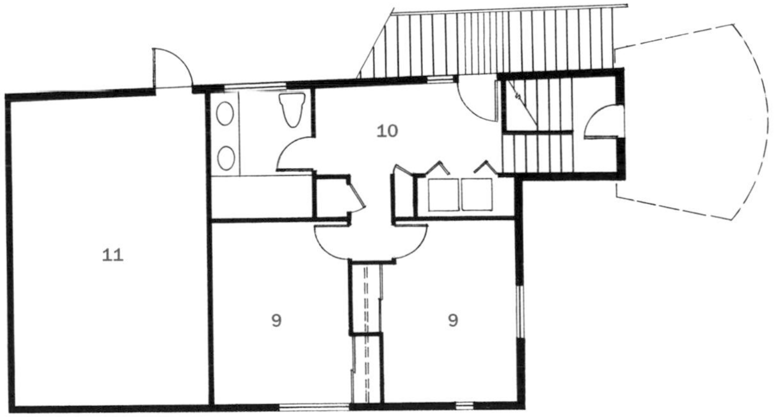

LOWER LEVEL

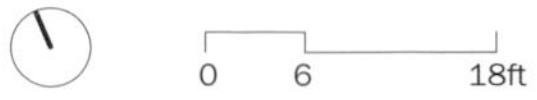

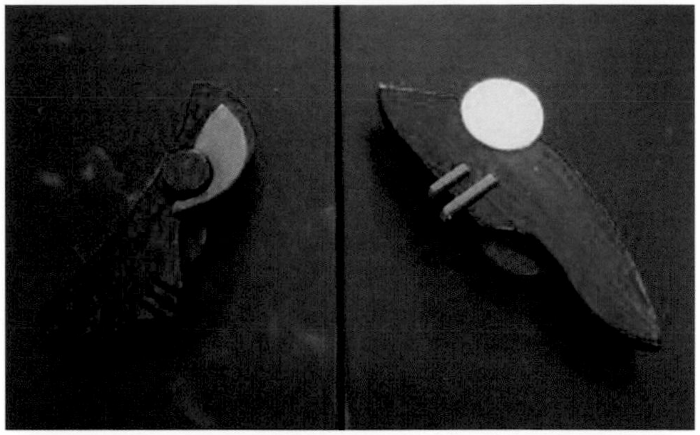

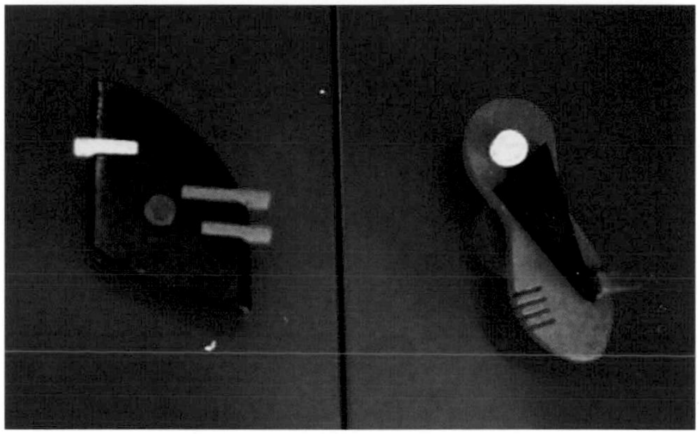

CABINET PULL DETAILS

Selected works of art inspired these California houses. In 1992 Miller Pollin wrote a piece for *Architecture California* titled, "Media Crossovers." In this article, she discussed how she was inspired by the black and white photographs of ruins taken by Mexican photographer Juan Rulfo as well as drawings by the German Expressionist painter Lionel Feininger. When the land was first purchased, Miller Pollin walked the site taking in the orientation, breezes, and the aesthetic vigor of the protruding rocks. Studying the topography, together with Rulfo photographs and Feininger's drawings of ruins emerging out of sloped terrain, was part of Miller Pollin's creative process.

Miller Pollin used photocopies of photographs of the landscape to investigate ways to site her houses. This process of drawing on the photographed landscape embedded the section diagram in the contours of the topography.

A background in art history, fine arts, and architecture undergirds this design process wherein landscape, art, and architecture work together. This congruence of nature, art, and craft has informed her architecture for decades. Consistently, the character of the site informs design ideas. This is a clear departure from most of our current building stock wherein style is imposed on the land, adjusting the topography to fit the design. Instead, Miller Pollin's designs are informed by the land, by the rocks and hills, lichen and brush. Art, as seen here in the case of Feininger's and Rulfo's related subjects, is a piece of that design process as well. It provides a means of seeing and understanding the landscape that prompts responsive structures with minimal site disturbance.

1290 STUDIO & RESIDENCE

Amherst,
Massachusetts
| 2007 |

Miller Pollin's house and studio reflect her long-term interest in the landscape, her concerns about women's home and work life, and her continuing commitment to contemporary architecture. Miller Pollin and her husband, Bob Pollin, found a stunning five-acre site for a new home and studio in South Amherst. Miller Pollin explored the surrounding meadows and woods for inspiration in the early design process. The site opens onto an expansive meadow skirted by a wooded conservation area with the Pelham hills as a backdrop. As in the design process of the Jumping Rocks project, she worked with photos, sketches, and watercolor studies of the land and the region's seasonal changes.

Early models and sketches show an intersection of two main forms for the house and studio—one running east-west and the other north-south. First sketches illustrate the east-west volume rising to the east where the meadow is located. Later sketches become more complex with both ends sloping upward—one toward the Pelham Hills and the other toward the public street where her studio would be housed. The north/south volume evolved as a rectangular bar parallel to the slope and perpendicular to the volume housing primarily work spaces—the studio, a study, and a tool workshop. A section through the rectangular living/dining space depicts space opening up like an eye to the view beyond. Most spaces in the house are focused to the east, toward the morning sun and the changing seasons. These two forms create an "L" shape that defines an open courtyard area oriented to the south. The courtyard would become home to colorful plantings, a granite cobblestone drive, and local Goshen stone walls. This is a crucial nexus, where a vehicle passes on its way to the garage, where visitors enter the house and is the transitional space for Miller Pollin between home and work. Inclusion of the designed garden within the courtyard fosters an opportunity to create dialogue between two very different kinds of landscape spaces—the garden and the meadow. In the garden perennials, woody plants and small trees provide planned color and texture. By contrast, the sprawling meadow beyond is largely the result of long-term natural evolution.

The sloping roofs of the east/west volume rise up to accommodate upper stories in both the house and studio. They also funnel rainwater into downspouts leading to a round stone cistern which captures rainwater for garden irrigation. Exterior walls are finished with ground face concrete block and painted shiplap cedar siding. As seen in Walter Gropius's house in Lincoln, Massachusetts, the white shiplap siding ties the house to a New England tradition without the traditional domestic forms. The concrete blocks were produced regionally and contain recycled granite chips. These not only provide texture and visual contrast to the siding, but also serve as a plinth against which snow accumulates, thus protecting the wood siding from the harshest effects of winter.

Inside radiant floor heating provides an even warmth throughout the house and studio in the colder seasons. The roofs and walls are heavily insulated.

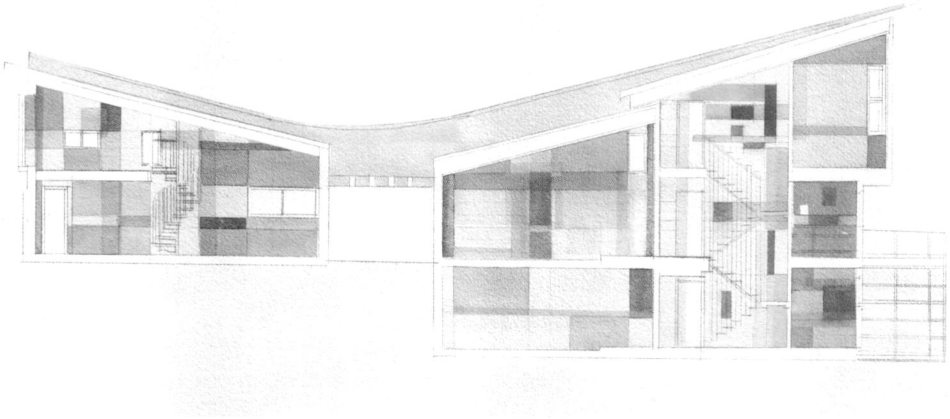

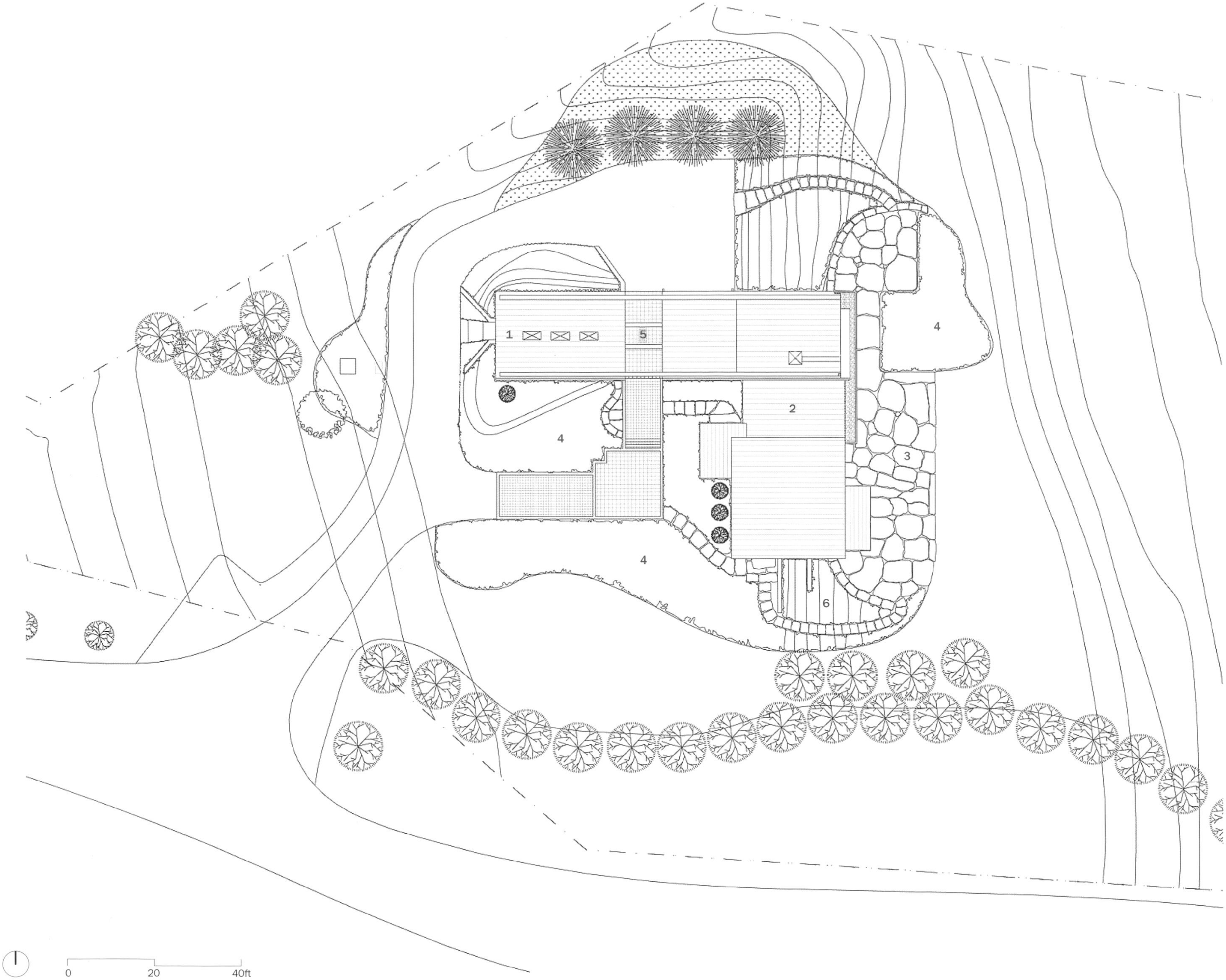
1
5
2
3
4
4
4
6
0
20
40ft

SITE PLAN

1. Studio
2. Residence
3. Patio
4. Garden
5. Driveway
6. Side Walkway

The clerestory windows on the western side of the living room capture westerly breezes, cooled by the row of hawthorn trees in front of them. Natural ventilation and careful planting help cool the house in summer. Other materials and features, such as bamboo flooring, the low-maintenance steel standing seam metal roof system, and an abundance of natural light make this a highly efficient and environmentally responsible structure.

The house itself illustrates Miller Pollin's understanding of the work of 20th-century architects such as Frank Lloyd Wright, Alvar Aalto, and Rudolph Schindler. The entry is a compressed space with a low ceiling that expands upward as one enters the living/dining room in the manner of Wright, directing the eye outward towards the meadows and woods beyond. Bundled wooden door handles and the stair with its carefully joined vertical slats compose a wood screen, coupled with the ergonomics of smooth, mahogany stair nosings, echo elements of Aalto's Villa Mairea. Spaces within the open floor plan of the ground floor are articulated by differing ceiling and floor heights in a manner traceable to Adolf Loos and Schindler's ideas of the Raumplan. While these historical references exist, they do so with personal interpretation with respect to material, form, and color.

The space created for the living-dining area has a distinct warmth that is largely due to the sloping cedar ceiling with its recessed azure blue light boxes. The kitchen and dining alcove have a saturated color array derived from the moss greens of the adjacent forest and a Scandinavian blue that Miller Pollin links to the Swedish part of her heritage.

In two rooms on the lower level, Miller Pollin designed built-in beds that serve as couches when not in use. She is acutely aware of the changing nature of a family. Children fill a space, leave for college and work, and return for visits with grandchildren. The flexibility of these rooms, as studies or bedrooms, distinguishes them from traditional bedrooms. A bathroom for these spaces includes a Japanese soaking tub with elegantly curving steps in a dark mahogany.

This bathroom combined with a cedar-lined sauna imbue the guest level with a sybaritic quality. At the end of the hall is a library. Here the stacks run perpendicular to the corridor axis. Miller Pollin cut a series of square "view portals" out of the bookshelves, allowing the eye to travel beyond the hallway. These lead the eye into the library with a perspectival view to the far wall and a chosen art object. This unique feature came from simple observation of what could be seen looking through library stacks. The library has an adjacent aluminum-framed screen porch for summer dining or a launch space for cross-country skiing onto the meadow in winter. Some spa-like features woven together with a library reflect ideas about rethinking domestic space for family and guests.

The studio itself is both separate from the main body of the house and linked with two substantial, continuous curved walls that produce a unified, dramatic visual backdrop for the garden and simultaneously create a shaded courtyard between garage and studio. The exterior courtyard affords Miller Pollin a transitional space between home and work. Walking through this area, past the stone walls and lush plantings, signals a shift from the domestic sphere to the place of work and creativity.

In the studio, the main level is connected to a loft with a prefabricated steel spiral stair. The studio houses models, renderings, paintings, and drawings—products of Miller Pollin's art and architecture to date.

Miller Pollin's house and studio provide insights into her design process, her concerns juggling work and family, and her interest in historical and contextual precedents. But as is clear from her early drawings to the finished product, her architecture is, above all, responsive to the site, to nature and its processes. She explores materials, colors, and complex programs in her architecture. But as 1290 House and Studio make clear, the site and landscape always provide the bases from which a project emerges.

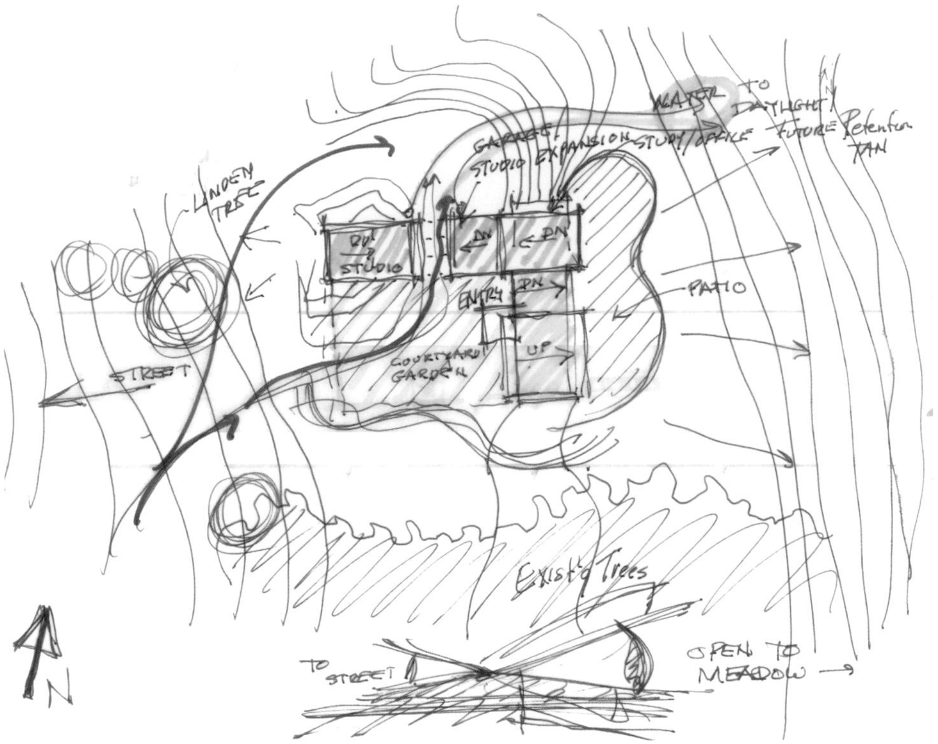

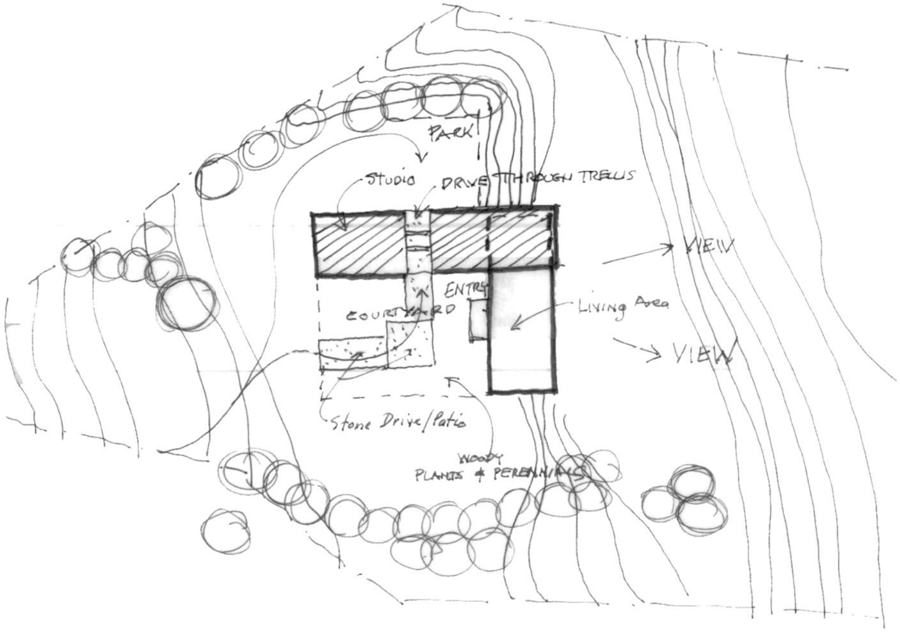

LOWER LEVEL

1. Bedroom
2. Library
3. Screened Porch
4. Sauna
5. Bathroom
6. Laundry Room
7. Stairway
8. Storage

MAIN LEVEL

1. Main Entry
2. Living Area
3. Dining Area
4. Kitchen
5. Study
6. Garage / Loft Workspace
7. Studio
8. Bath
9. Stairway
10. Deck

UPPER LEVEL

1. Master Bedroom
2. Master Bathroom
3. Closet
4. Stair

SECTION A-A

1. Studio
2. Pass Through
3. Garage / Loft Workspace
4. Master Bedroom
5. Bedroom
6. Storage
7. Stairway

SECTION B-B

1. Dining Area
2. Library

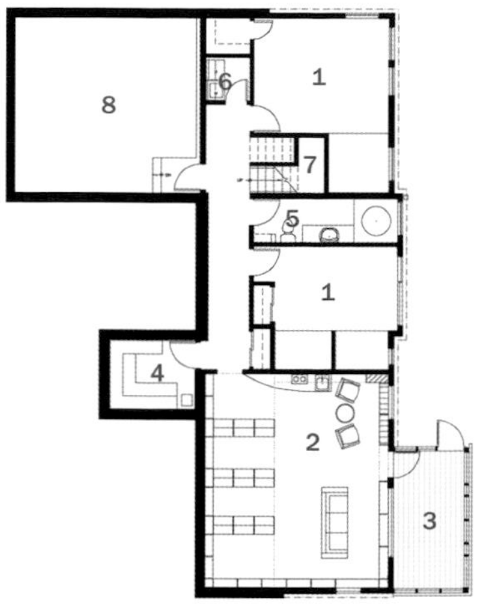

LOWER LEVEL

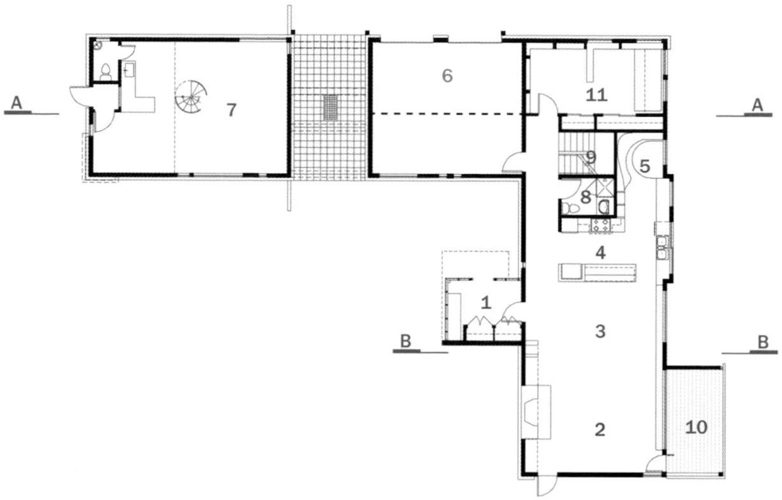

MAIN LEVEL

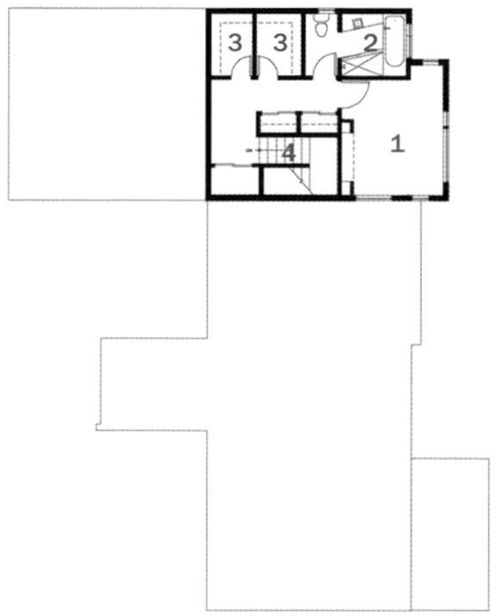

UPPER LEVEL

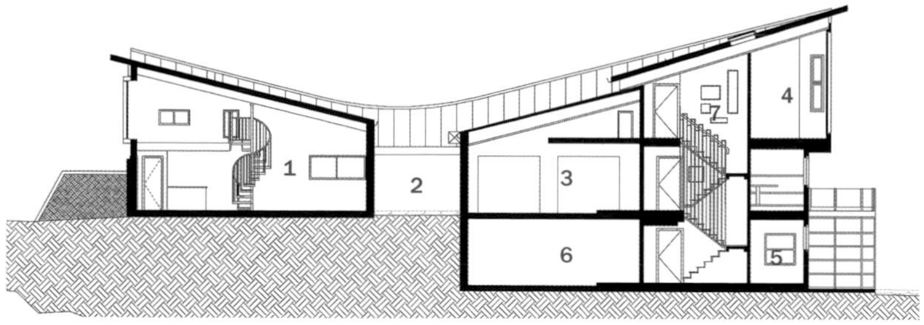

SECTION A-A

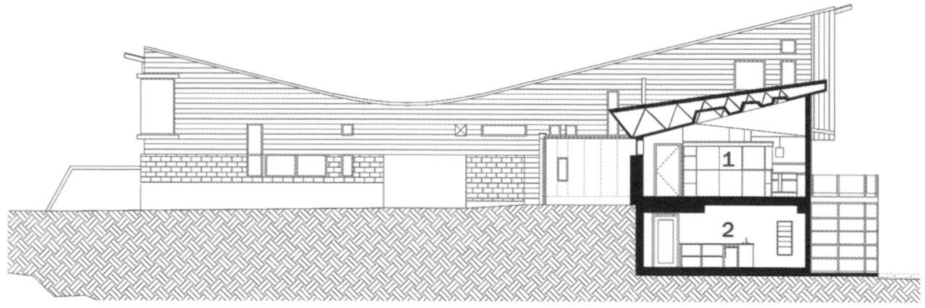

SECTION B-B

ON THE RISE
WESTERN ARCHITECTURE
ABC of Architecture
MANHATTAN
Ancient Arts of the Americas
BERNARD MAYBECK
JACQUES LIPCHITZ
Aalto
Henry Moore
MICHELANGELO
OSKAR KOKOSCHKA
DRAWINGS 1906-1965
alvar aalto
ABRAMS
Gordon Ernst Ludwig Kirchner
SAM MALOOF WOODWORKER
The Details of Modern Architecture
MALAPARTE
CONTEMPORARY AMERICAN ARCHITECTURE
HOME
INDIAN TALES
The Caravela
le corbusier
A HISTORY

JAMIE OLIVER
The Naked Chef Takes Off
STILL LIFE WITH MENU

HOUSE FOR A MAGICIAN

Las Vegas, Nevada
| 1997 |

In the desert hills above Las Vegas this house emerges like a boulder, sloping upward out of the sagebrush on the site. The client, Teller of the magic duo Penn and Teller, had seen Miller Pollin's Mount Vernon residences in a magazine and invited her and her partner at Siteworks Architecture, Kevin O'Brien, to come out to Las Vegas and see the site. Together they designed a house of strength and whimsy with touches of magic in response to Teller's vision. At the beginning of the design process, Teller and his partner named their two favorite pieces of "architecture" as the Hoover Dam and The Pirates of the Caribbean at Disneyland. This created the starting point for Miller Pollin and O'Brien's dramatic architectural interpretation.

Visitors approach the house from the south east intrigued by the bold southern wall "masque." This is a protective stucco-sheathed surface, broken into angled polygons which frame small, fortress-like windows. The small windows and dominant angular wall provide a protective shield against the powerful desert sun. On the narrow east end, the wall extends above the roof line to serve as a parapet for a "moon deck." Just below this, the wall breaks open with a corrugated metal balcony and views to the south east.

The southern side of the house is enveloped in a protective wall and the northern side of the house opens up with a large expanse of windows within corrugated metal siding. While Miller Pollin's bold datum walls of red protected against fire and the Santa Ana winds in the Mount Vernon houses, here this protective "masque" shelters against the Nevada heat. To the north, a filigree wall of glass and metal faces a protected garden space, and allows views of downtown Las Vegas.

Surprises abound in this 4500-square-foot house. The kitchen faces north east, with bands of aluminum windows and an industrial feel. Their metallic gray contrasts with the warmth of the wooden cabinets and the black counter tops. There is an openness to the space with an angular kitchen island that repeats the angled geometry of the southern exterior wall.

A central circulation spine runs through the south side of the house. A door at one end has an angled mirror that reflects the outdoors, a visual trick that obfuscates understanding of the interior spaces. Standing at one end, the corridor appears to conclude with views of the desert beyond. Yet what we see is actually a door, leading farther into the house: like a magician's visual tricks, things are not how they appear. Similarly, the library presents a wall of shelves. Yet, like the sleight of a magician's hand, one bookshelf pivots inward, providing ready escape to a room beyond.

Secret passageways and visual complexity are at play throughout the house. A catwalk hangs above the corridor spine. This was inspired by The Pirates of the Caribbean at Disneyland, a playful observation bridge looking down on the activities below. A spiral staircase in the studio adds an element of curvilinear drama and another means of visual escape to a balcony above. The house includes an "endless pool" enclosed in aluminum and glass with access from both the exterior and interior of the house.

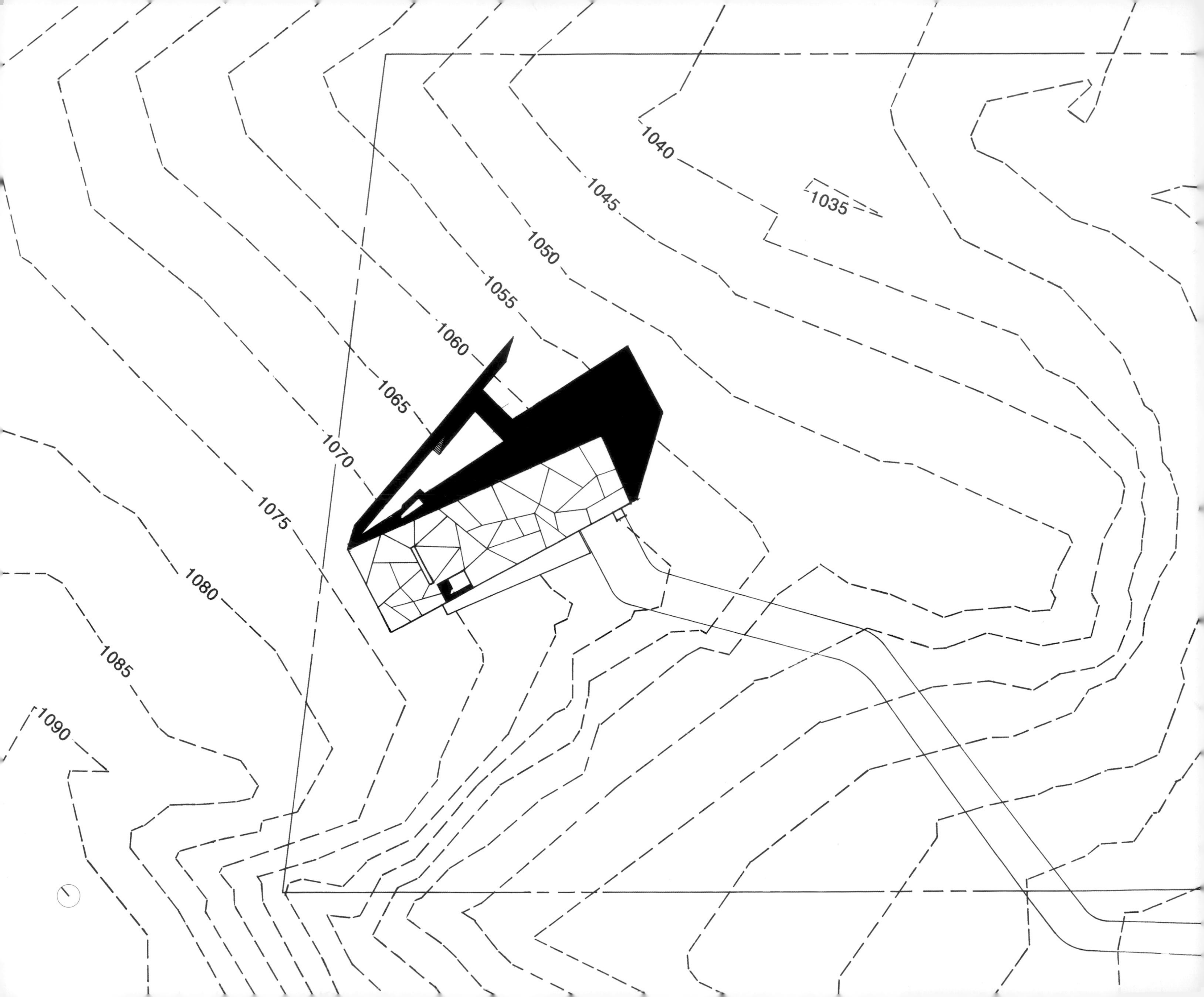
1035
1040
1045
1050
1055
1060
1065
1070
1075
1080
1085
1090

1020
1015
1010
1015
100

This house is a bold, cohesive volume rising out of the desert hills. Its angled "masque" wall shields a complex system of rooms and corridors housing the client's art work, memorabilia and tricks of the trade. Its singular appearance in the landscape belies a labyrinthine interior that wittily represents the client and his work. The house is sensitive to site, protecting the interior from the desert while embracing a shady oasis on the north. It is also responsive to the client's program, with a whimsical arrangment of rooms and spaces with both obvious and hidden connections.

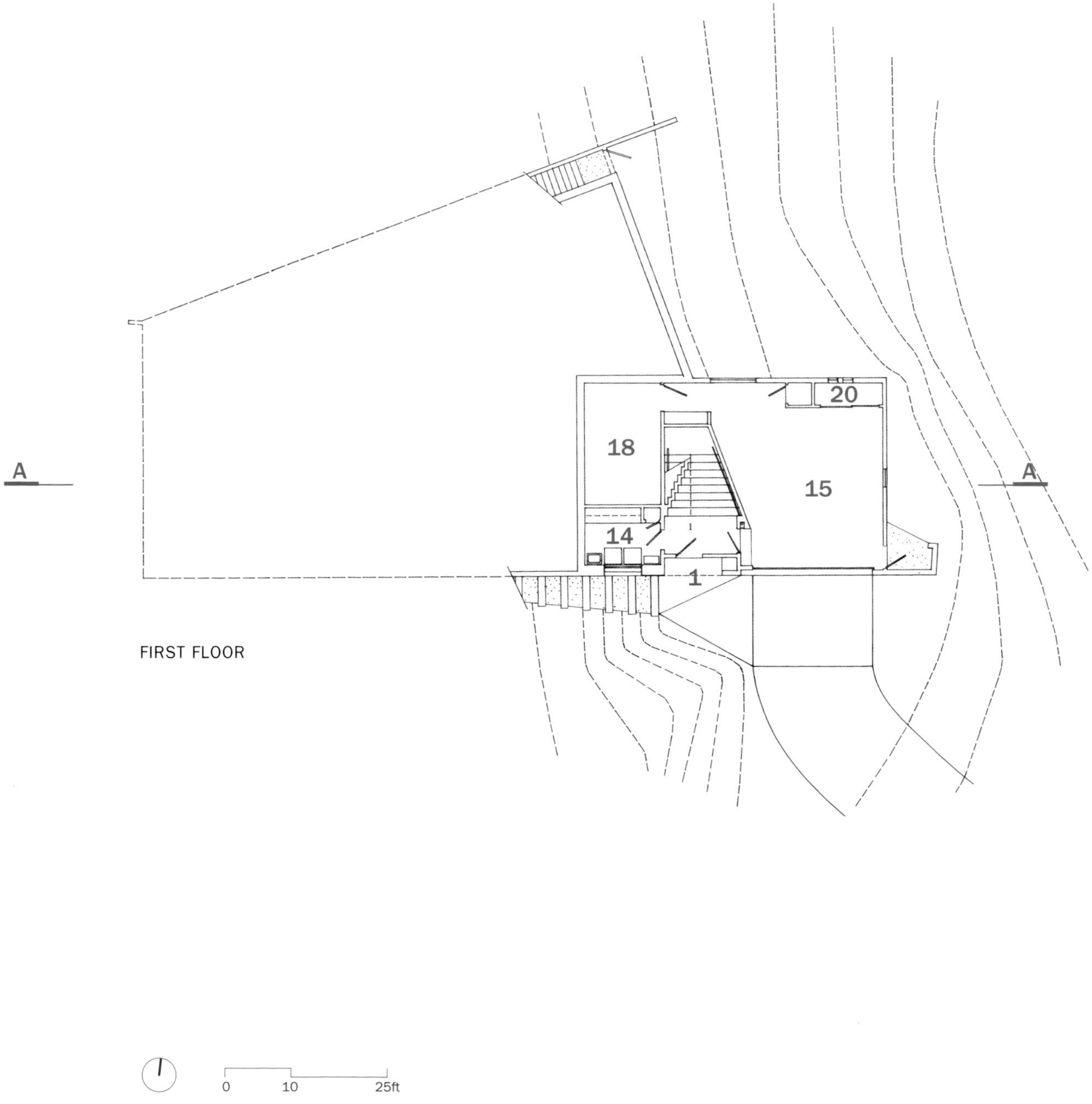

FIRST FLOOR

FLOOR PLANS

1. Entry
2. Gallery
3. Library
4. Bridge
5. Library Mezzanine
6. Magician Library
7. Bedroom
8. Dining
9. Exercise Room
10. Media Room
11. Kitchen
12. Endless Pool
13. Moon Deck
14. Laundry
15. Garage
16. Garden / Patio
17. Walk-in Closet
18. Storage
19. Loft
20. Closet

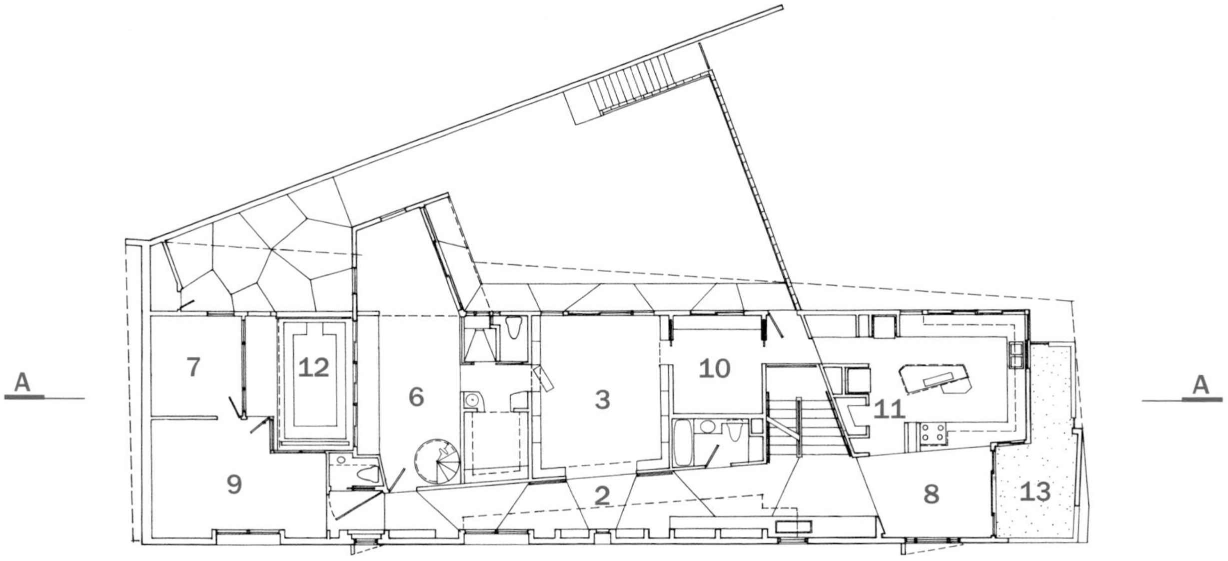

THIRD FLOOR

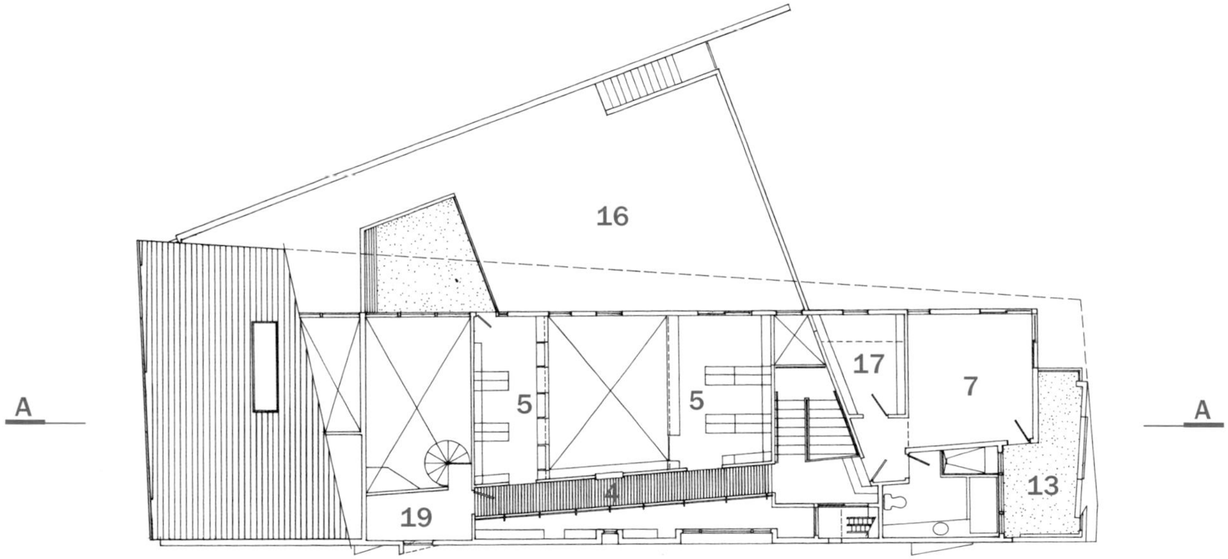

SECOND FLOOR

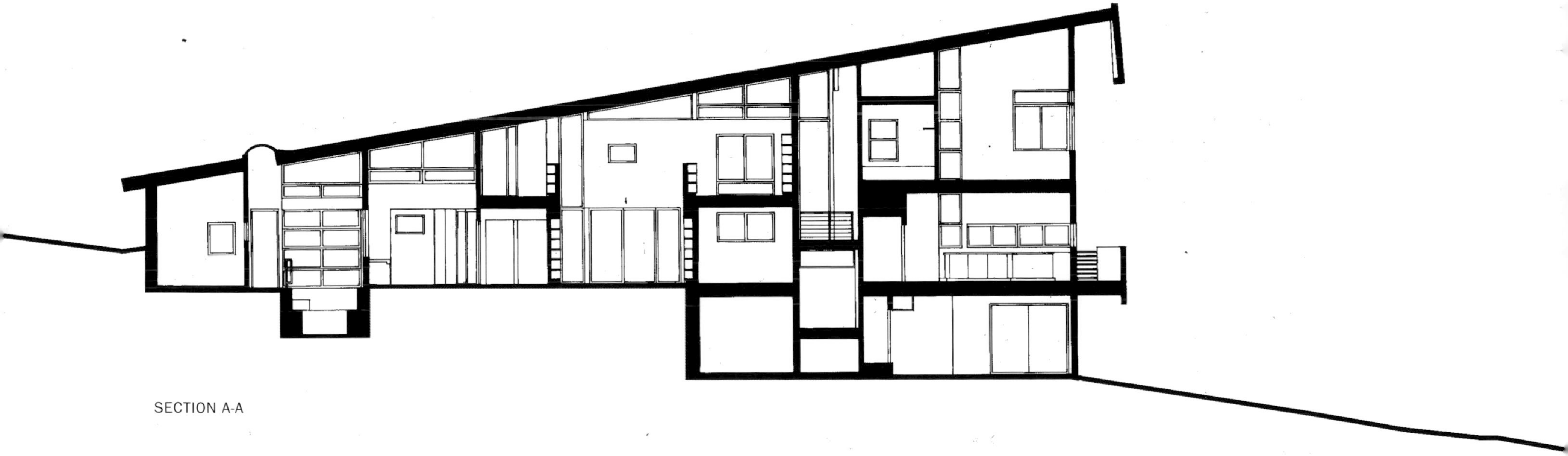

SECTION A-A

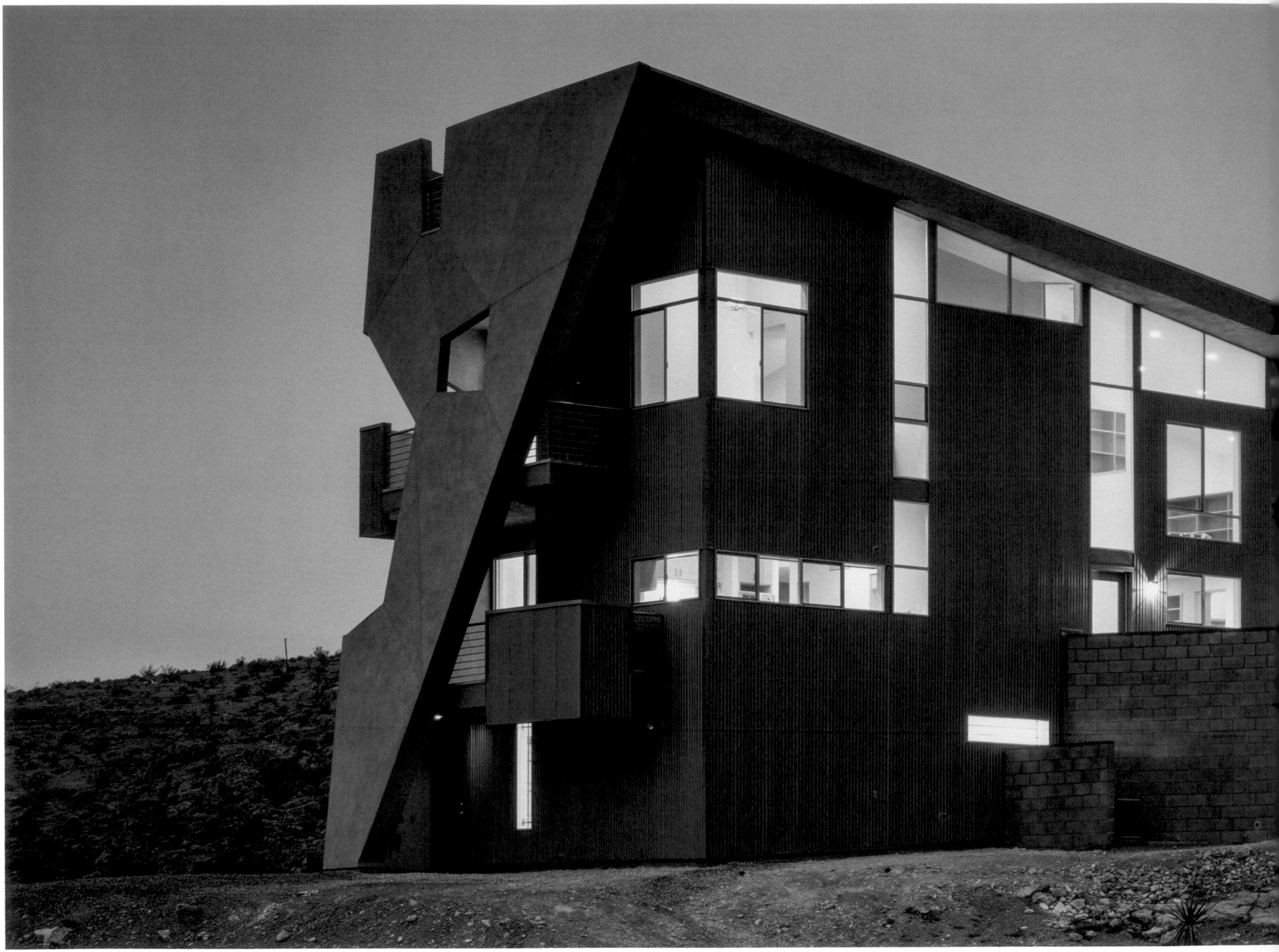

712

WAVE HOUSE

Laguna Beach,
California
| 2008 |

After leaving California to teach at the University of Massachusetts Amherst and establish an East Coast practice, Miller Pollin completed work on a house in Laguna Beach, California. Known as the Wave House, this project was informed by the steep slope with views of the Pacific Ocean, the requirements of an active family with three children, and the clients' love for the Spanish architect Antonio Gaudi. The organic forms of Gaudi's work and the challenging 40-foot grade change of the topography inspired Miller Pollin to design a house that spills down the site with three levels that follow the terrain and capture dramatic ocean views.

The house is organized along a cascading series of curved stucco walls. The children have private spaces on the upper level, while the living and kitchen areas are in the middle elevation. The parents' master suite at the lowest level has spectacular ocean views. The white stucco walls create a stunning backdrop for the brilliant colors of the landscaping.

The clients had traveled to Barcelona multiple times and were inspired by Antonio Gaudi's architecture. Miller Pollin honored their interest in his work by developing a curvilinear scheme in plan, elevation, and detail. Curving forms define spaces and movement throughout the house. In the central staircase, mahogany stairs wind down to the kitchen from the upper level. The sinuous forms of the banister follow the stairs. The stainless steel handrail at the bottom of the stairs curls up a steel column like a vigorous vine. Miller Pollin interlaced function with decorative form in several places throughout the house, from the escaping banister to the light fixtures enmeshed in the sensuous curves of the stainless steel above the fireplace.

Niches for art objects are carved into the walls of the living room. These rectangular niches play off of exterior windows that frame the ever-shifting views of ocean, sky, and land.

The levels of the house create layered decks which visually connect the upper and lower areas. On the pool level, the roof pulls away to provide shaded relief from the Laguna Beach sun. Walls retreat and expand according to programmatic needs within, while an organic rhythm synchronizes with the level changes of the terrain.

Such curving, sensuous forms pose particular challenges for architects in design and builders in the construction process. Here, Miller Pollin weaves art, history, and landscape into a unique expression of her clients' wishes and an exploration of organic forms. The Wave House courses down the slope, ebbing and flowing with the topography to create controlled forms inspired by the natural world.

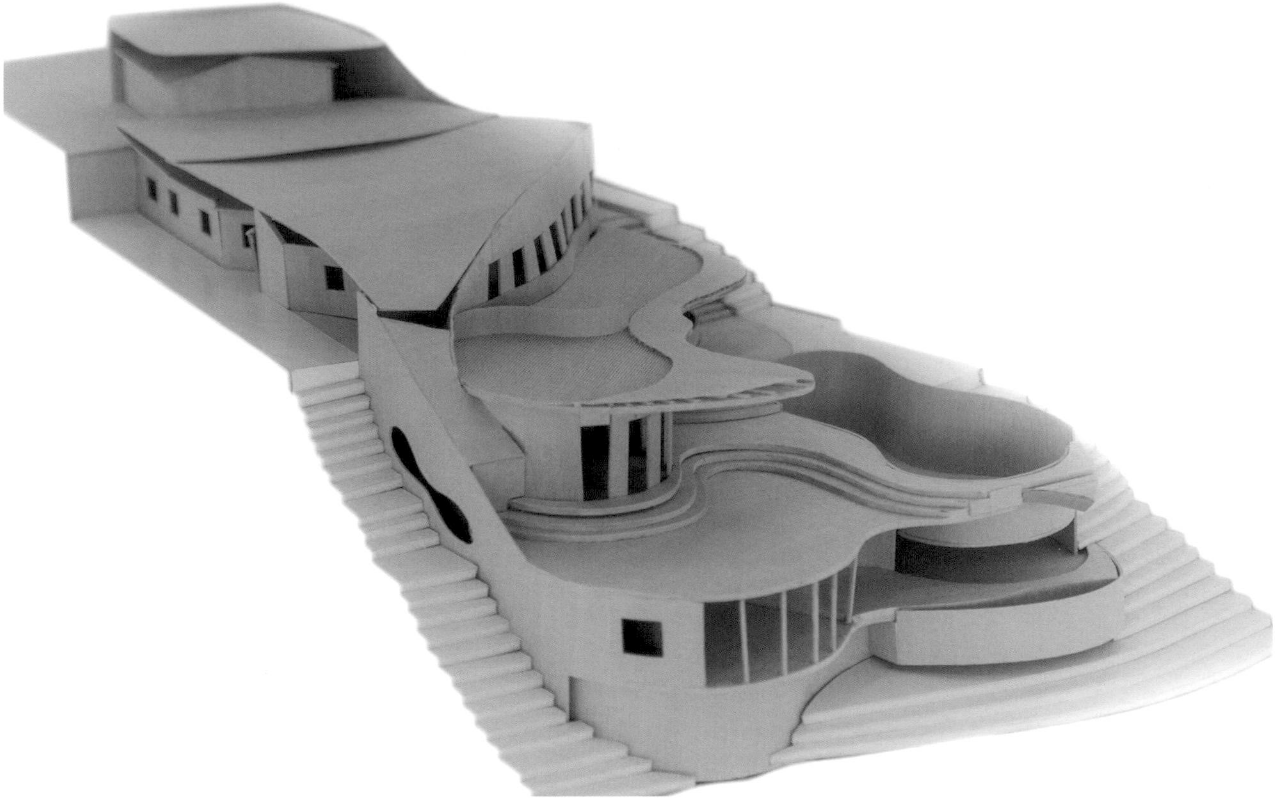

RIVERSIDE
LA SIERRA

LA SIERRA COMMUTER RAIL STATION

Riverside,
California
| 1996 |

In 1994 the Riverside County Transportation Commission invited women architects to submit designs for a series of Metrolink stations that would link Riverside County with downtown Los Angeles. Miller Pollin was one of the participants in the program. In 1996 the La Sierra station she designed opened to the public. The program required a number of small free-standing canopies for waiting passengers and an enclosed overpass across the tracks with stairs and an elevator.

The concept for the individual shelters emerged from the orange grove history of Riverside. Miller Pollin based her design for the canopies on the structure and shape of an orange tree leaf. Ridged green roofs shelter waiting passengers from the hot California sun and occasional rain. These leaf-like forms bow down more deeply in the center and curve upwards at each end. They are supported by concrete piers with steel ribs that arch upwards to meet the roof. Patina-coated copper up lights are set within the ribs like green buds in the center of four stems.

The station references the weathered copper of Hector Guimard's Art Nouveau metro stations in Paris, but here the structure and shapes are rooted in local California agricultural history. The sturdy, organic components are purposeful and create a modest but memorable stop on the transit line.

RIVERSIDE
LA SIERRA

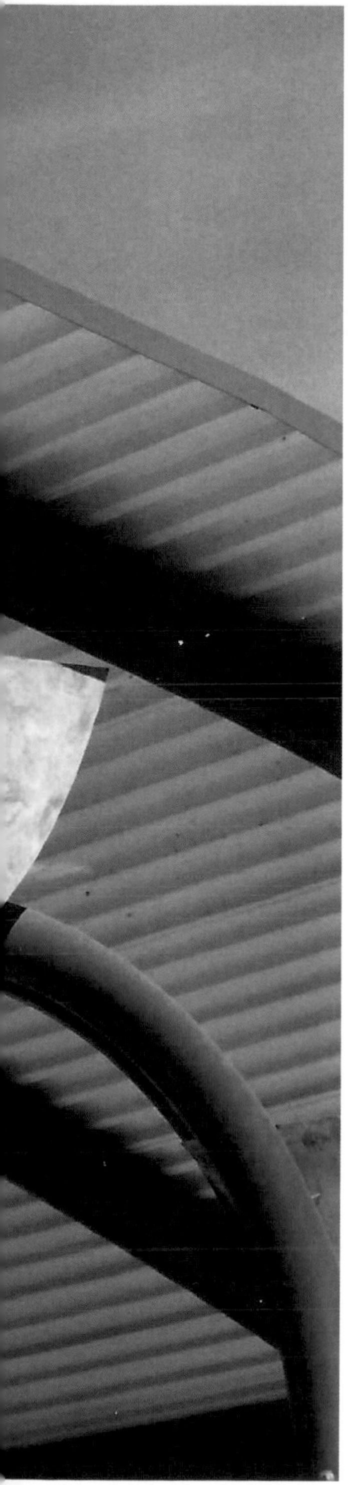

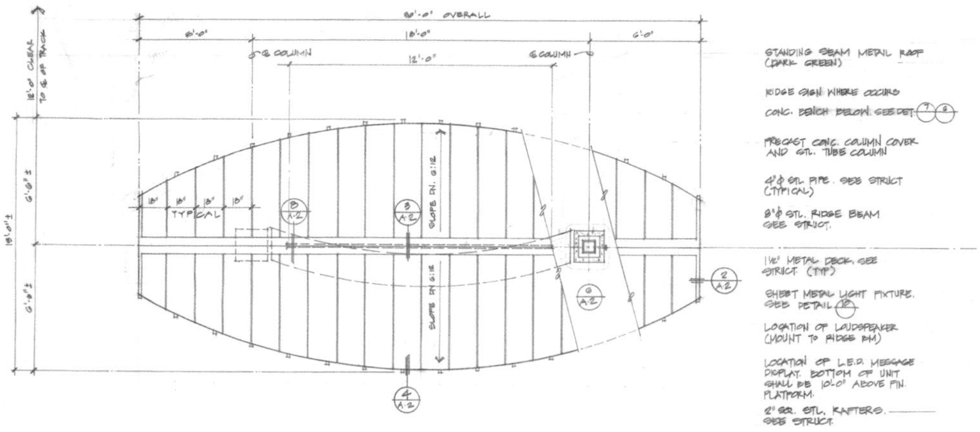

ROOF PLAN
3/8" = 1'-0"

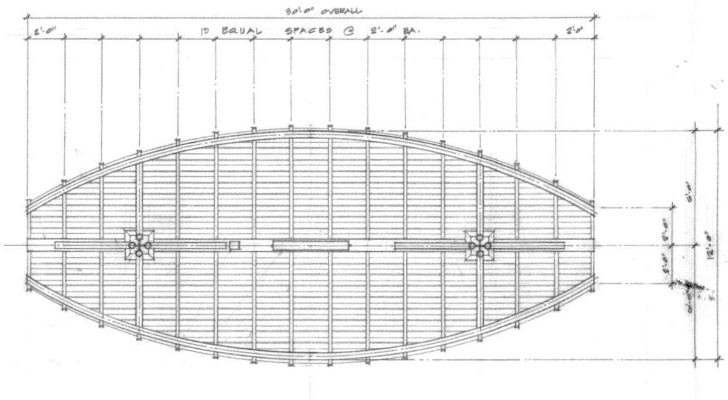

REFLECTED CEILING PLAN
3/8" = 1'-0"

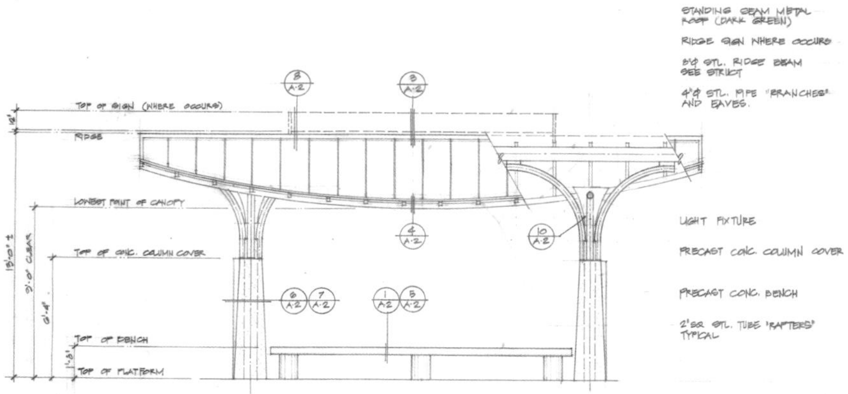

FRONT / REAR ELEVATION
3/8" = 1'-0"

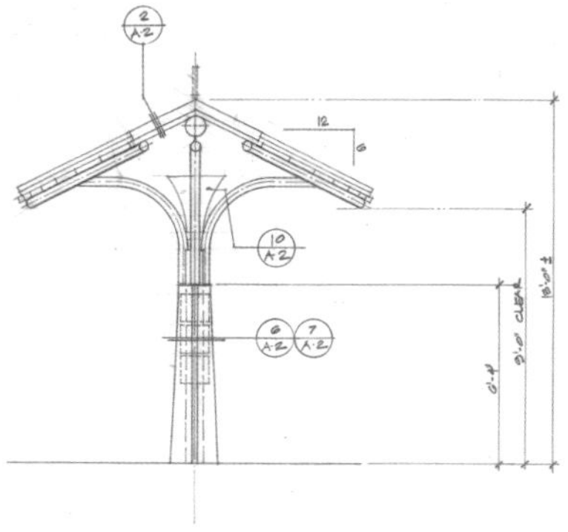

SIDE ELEVATION
3/8" = 1'-0"

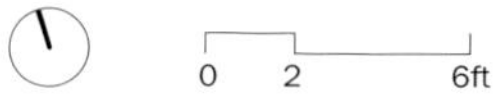

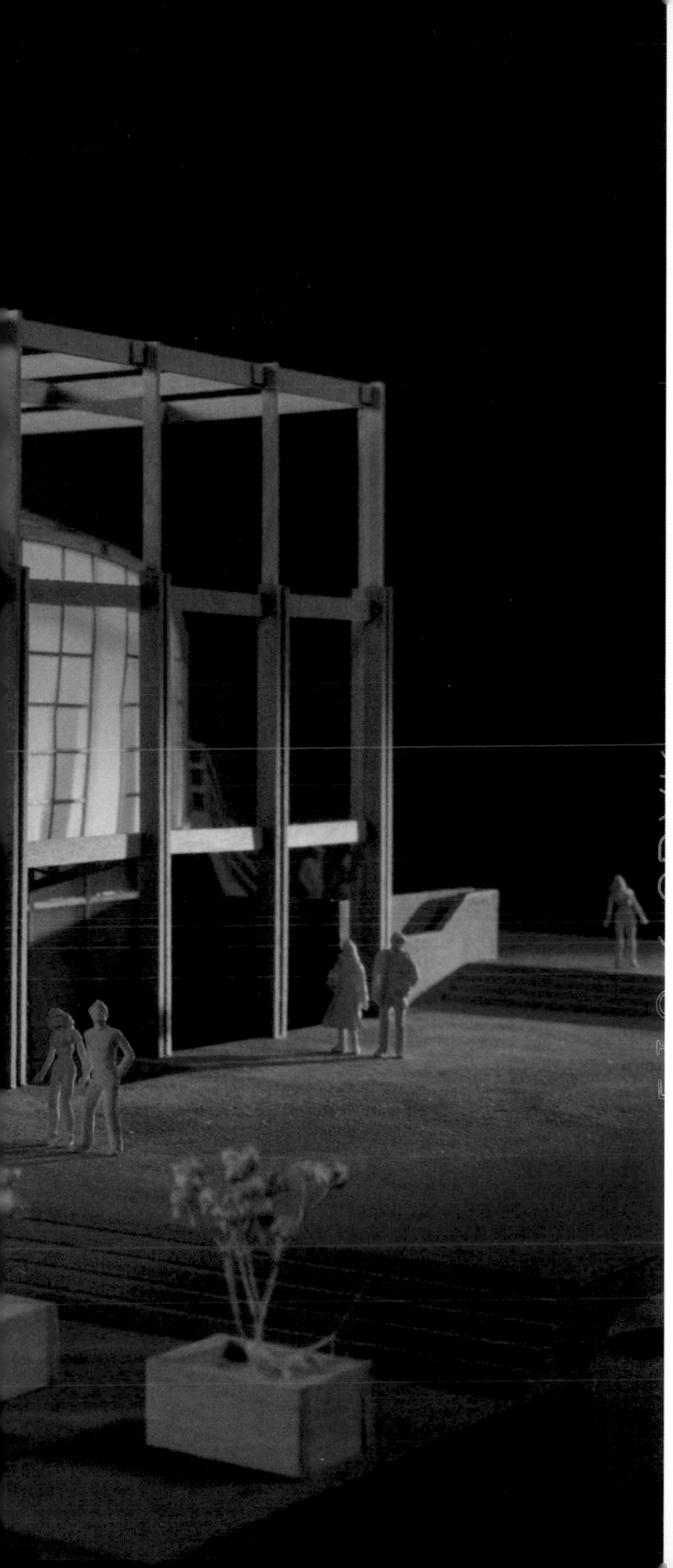

RIVERSIDE CHAMBER OF COMMERCE

Riverside,
California
| 1995 |

The client for this proposal was the Riverside Chamber of Commerce. This organization of business owners was considering a new facility on a block in downtown Riverside. The central program for the building was a large meeting space, conference rooms, and offices.

This proposal offered space for the given program with the large conference room interpreted as a visible, translucent, curvilinear chamber—a volume dramatically legible from the street scape. Miller Pollin suggested to the clients that they add a second half to the program that would be leasable commercial and office space which could support the Chamber expenses by bringing in rental income.

In this proposal both the curvilinear chamber and the orthogonal speculative space are contained within a collective form composed of an exposed steel grid frame. This frame also provided a structure for rooftop shade canopies in response to the strong summer sun of the region. The project was never realized, but it incorporated ideas that Miller Pollin developed in other commercial projects.

SECOND FLOOR

1. The Chamber
2. Kitchen
3. Storage
4. Small Conference Room
5. Office
6. Flexible Space

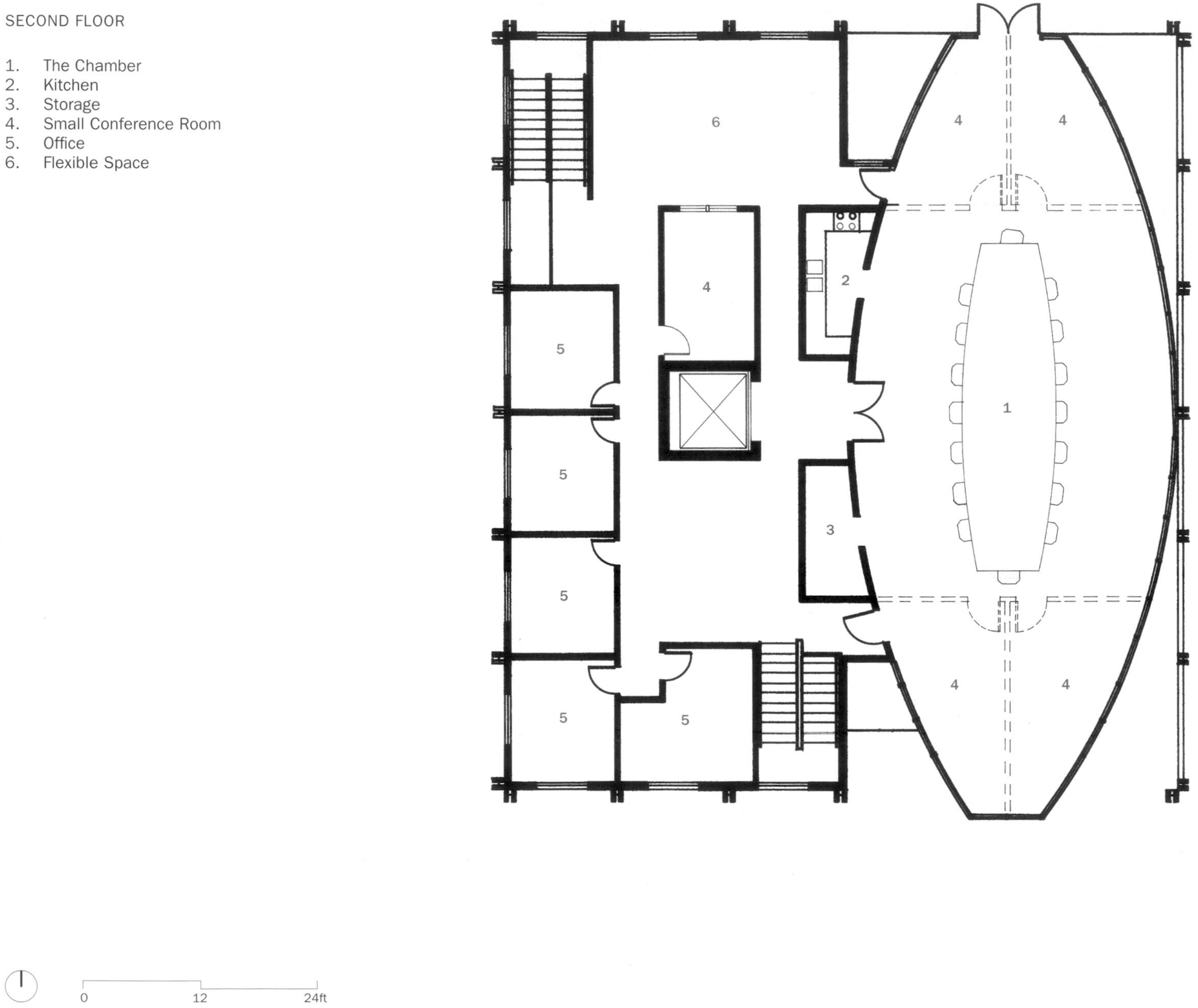

FIRST FLOOR

1. Lobby
2. Flexible Office Space
3. Tickets
4. Accounting
5. Mail Room
6. Break Room
7. Sales Office

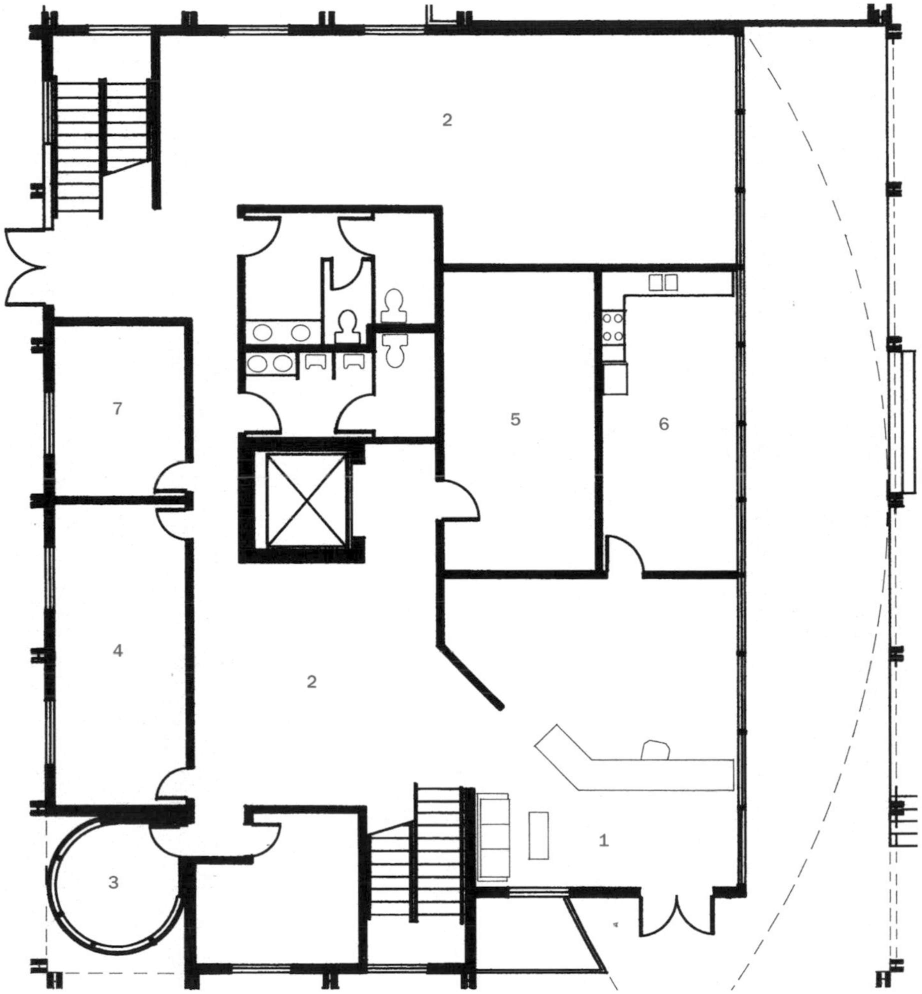

[HOME]

STRAW AVENUE

PAT'S HOUSE

MOORE HOUSE

HEMMER CORRALES HOUSE

RUTHIE LANE

111

STRAW AVENUE

Florence,
Massachusetts
| 2012 |

Often residential lots with challenging topography lie vacant for years while neighborhoods grow up around them. This was the case on Straw Avenue in Florence, Massachusetts. Straw Avenue is a modest street with easy access to local shops, schools, and offices. This small lot sheers down steeply to the east, away from the road. Looking to downsize, a couple bought the lot and hired Miller Pollin to design a house for them. Typical of her design process, this project is informed by the environment, by the steep slope and the scale of the residential neighborhood.

Miller Pollin designed a modern bungalow that breaks free of the context's traditional gabled and ranch houses while respecting the scale of the neighborhood. The street façade presents a friendly front porch beneath an overhanging roof angled to maximize solar gain for the photovoltaic and solar hot water panels. Typical of Miller Pollin's earlier houses, such as the Mount Vernon residences, she articulates different spaces with varied volumes. In this case, the roof-angle slopes to the north over the more private spaces of the house, creating a strong intersection of two volumes. Color also defines the volumes, shifting from the yellow of the garage to the blue of the larger volume to the east. This division of parts is clearly recognized from the back of the house where the blue, white, and yellow parts meet and define interior spaces.

There is a simple elegance to the house. The front porch shelters the living room from the western sun. Planters are finished with the same clapboard siding used on the house. The street level includes an entry foyer and open kitchen/dining/living area. The couple's bedroom extends away from the street, as does a master bath and study. Stairs off the central corridor lead to a suite of rooms which include a bedroom, bath, and laundry room, and an office. A separate entrance provides privacy and independent access to the lower floor. As the drawings illustrate, the house is carefully positioned on the inclined site in both plan and section. Miller Pollin's design is informed by the topography, with a respect for the existing slope. Varied ceiling heights and a rich interior color palette organize different regions in the home.

The site and house have many sustainable aspects and design features that contribute to its LEED Platinum Certification, the highest designation for sustainable building under the U.S. LEED system. The angled roofs are thickly insulated with dense pack cellulose and the windows are dual-glazed, low E with fiberglass frames for easy care and efficiency. The walls are two by six inches and densely packed with locally sourced cellulose insulation, then wrapped with a rigid insulation. Clerestory windows catch breezes for natural ventilation. Rain garden swales manage water down the steep slope and native plantings prevent soil erosion. While LEED certification at any level requires great attention to materials and site management, many of these approaches have been part of Miller Pollin's architectural approach for decades.

SITE PLAN

1. Main Living Quarters
2. Single Car Garage
3. Deck
4. Driveway
5. Recycling Bins / Bike Storage
6. Existing Single Family Residence
7. Existing Day-Care Center
8. Native Drought-Tolerant Ground Cover
9. Gravel Drainage Bed
10. Drought-Tolerant Turf
11. Local Stone Retaining Wall
12. Meadow
13. Existing Retaining Wall

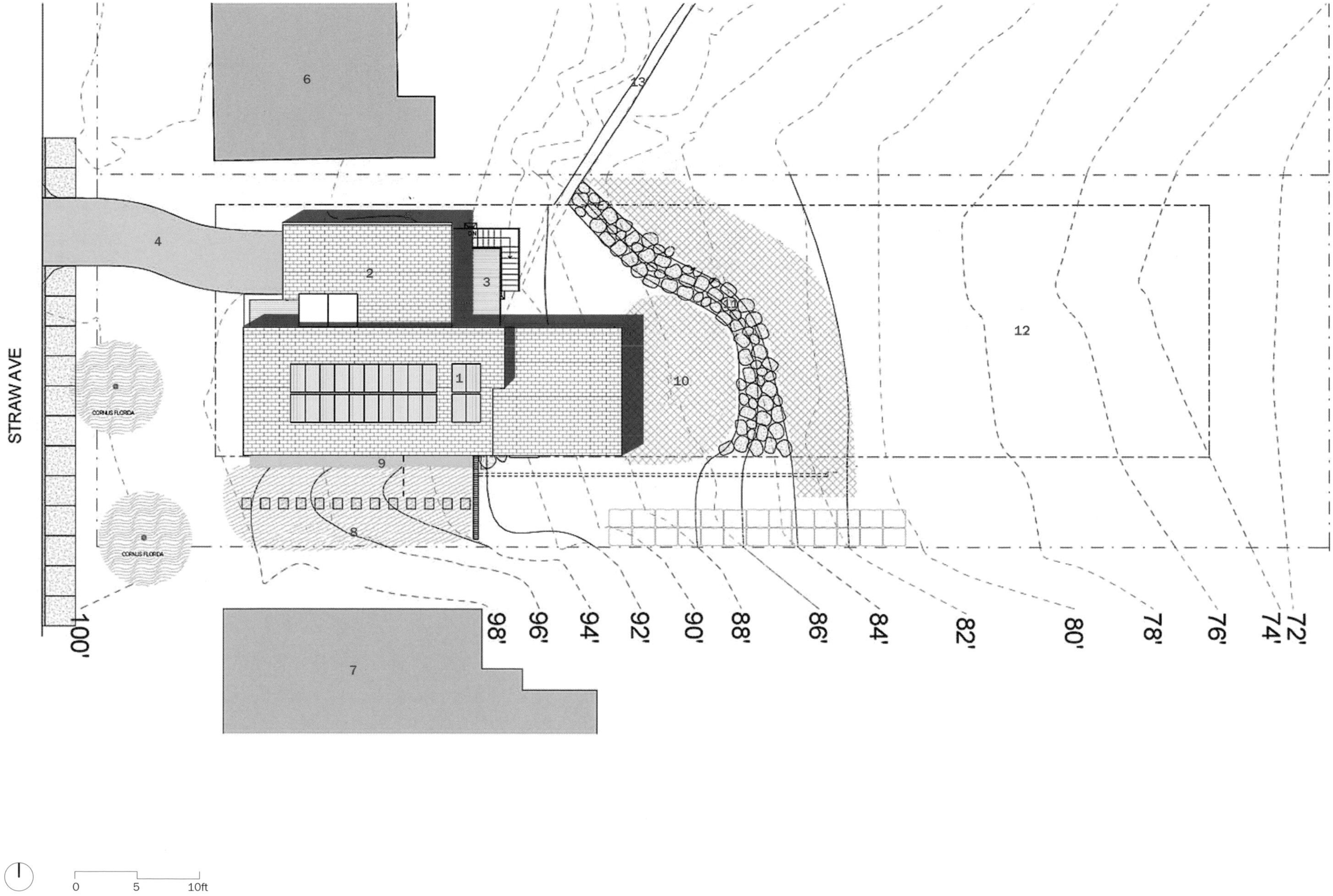
STRAW AVE
CORNUS FLORIDA
CORNUS FLORIDA
1
2
3
4
5
6
7
8
9
10
11
12
13
DN
100'
98'
96'
94'
92'
90'
88'
86'
84'
82'
80'
78'
76'
74'
72'
0
5
10ft

WALK-OUT BASEMENT

1. Storage
2. Mechanical
3. Office
4. Bathroom / Laundry
5. Bedroom

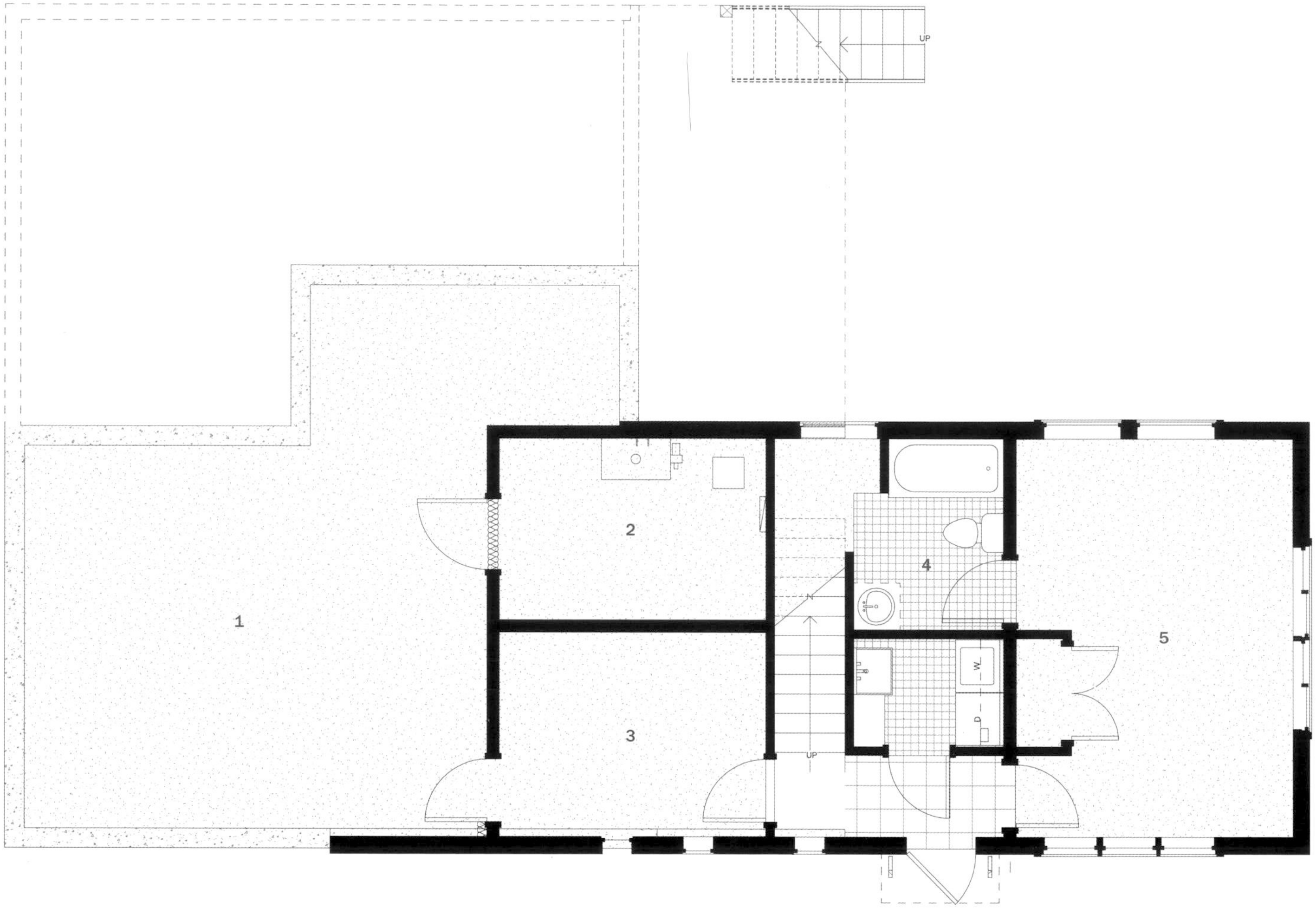

GROUND FLOOR

1. Garage
2. Foyer
3. Back Deck
4. Front Porch
5. Living Room
6. Kitchen
7. Study
8. Master Bath / Half Bath
9. Master Bedroom

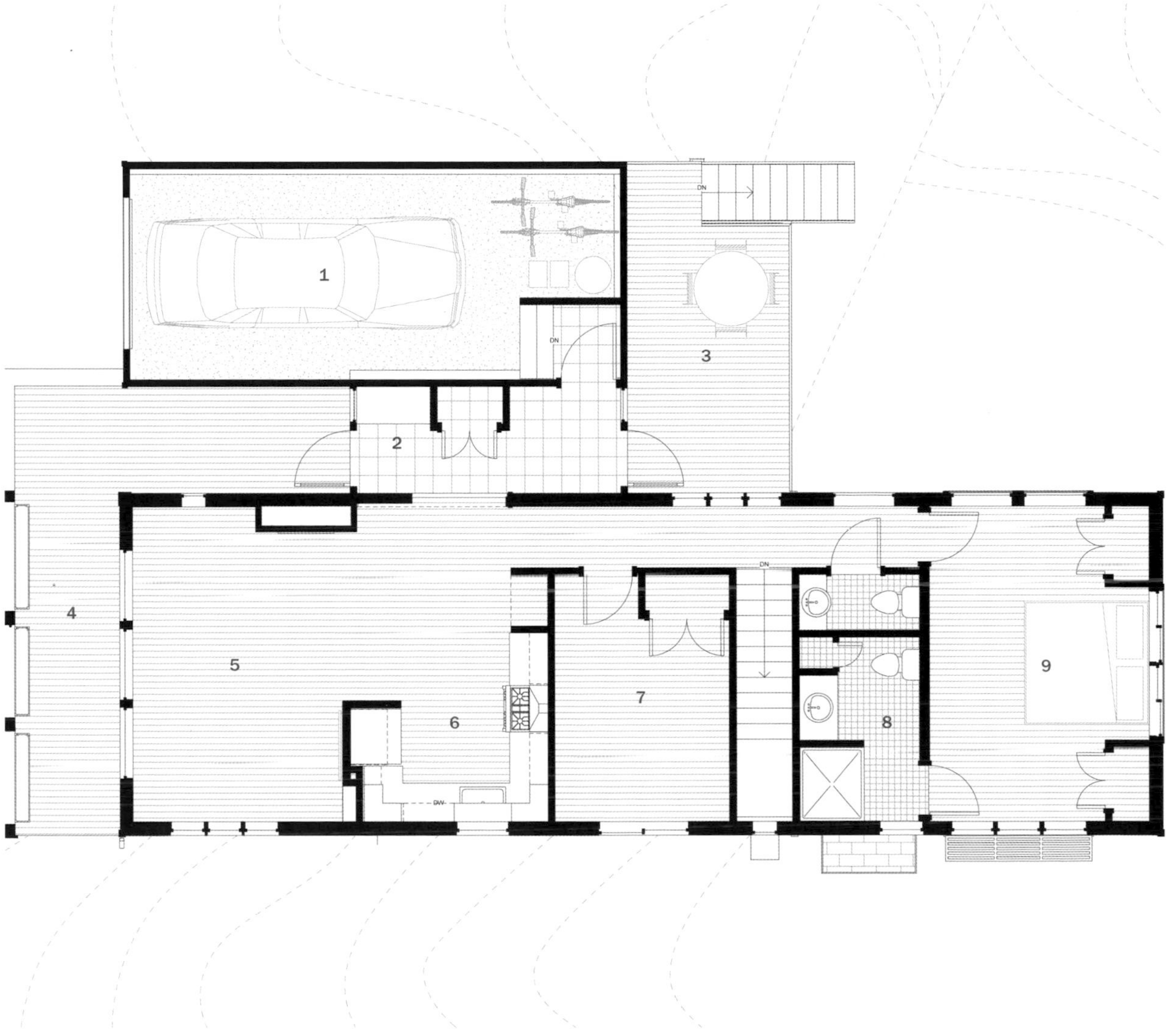

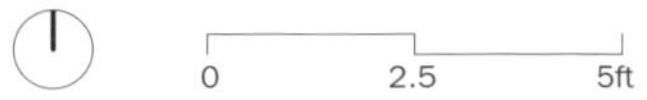

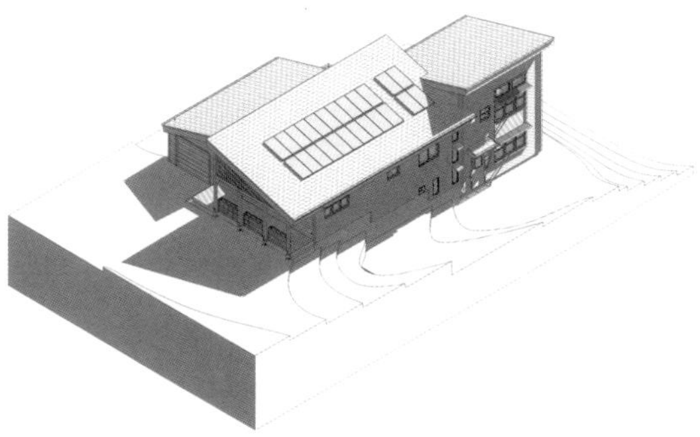

SUMMER SOLSTICE 8:00 AM

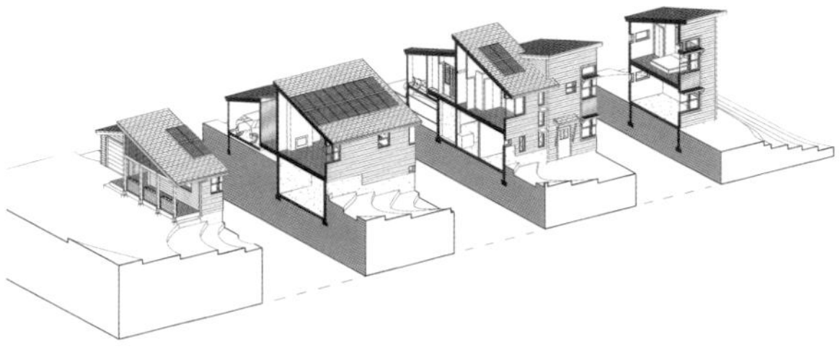

SUMMER SOLSTICE 12:00 PM

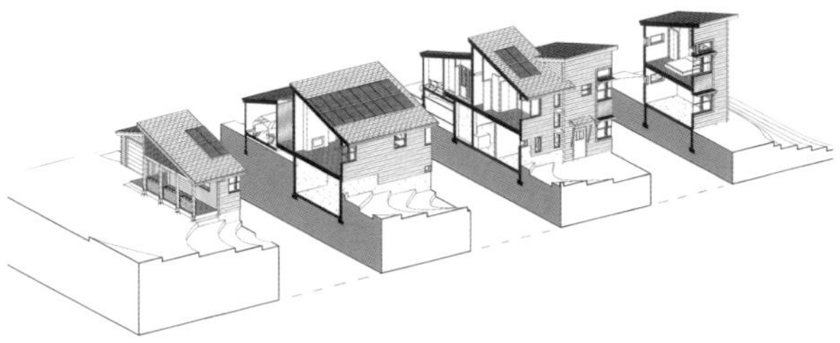

SUMMER SOLSTICE 4 PM

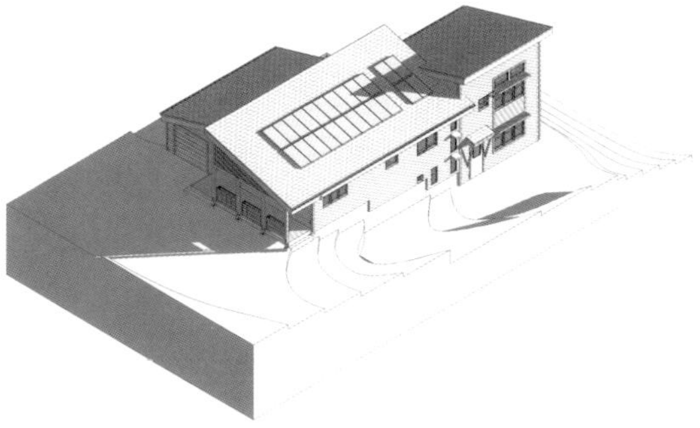

WINTER SOLSTICE 8:00 AM

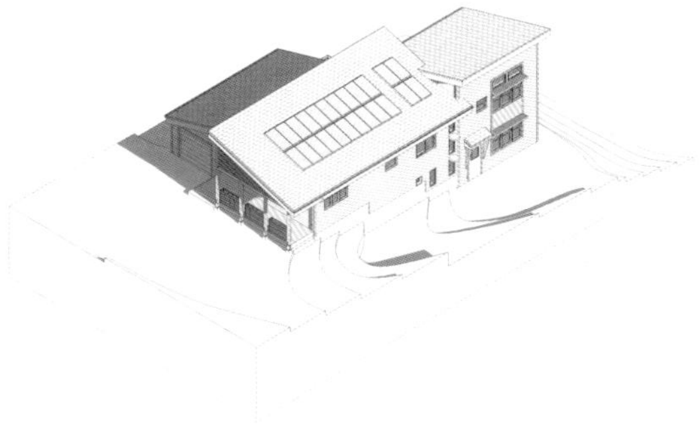

WINTER SOLSTICE 12:00 PM

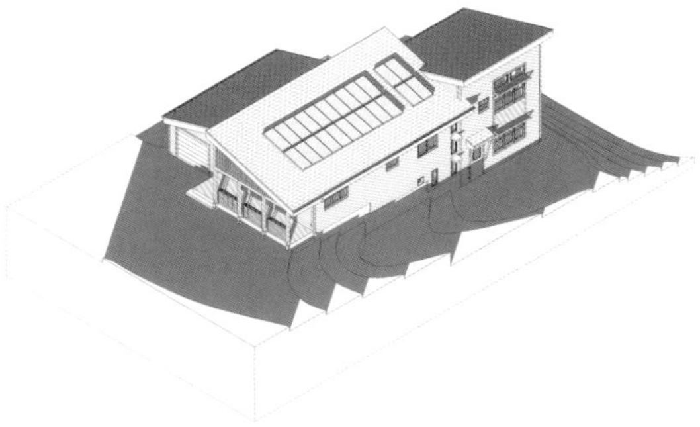

WINTER SOLSTICE 4 PM

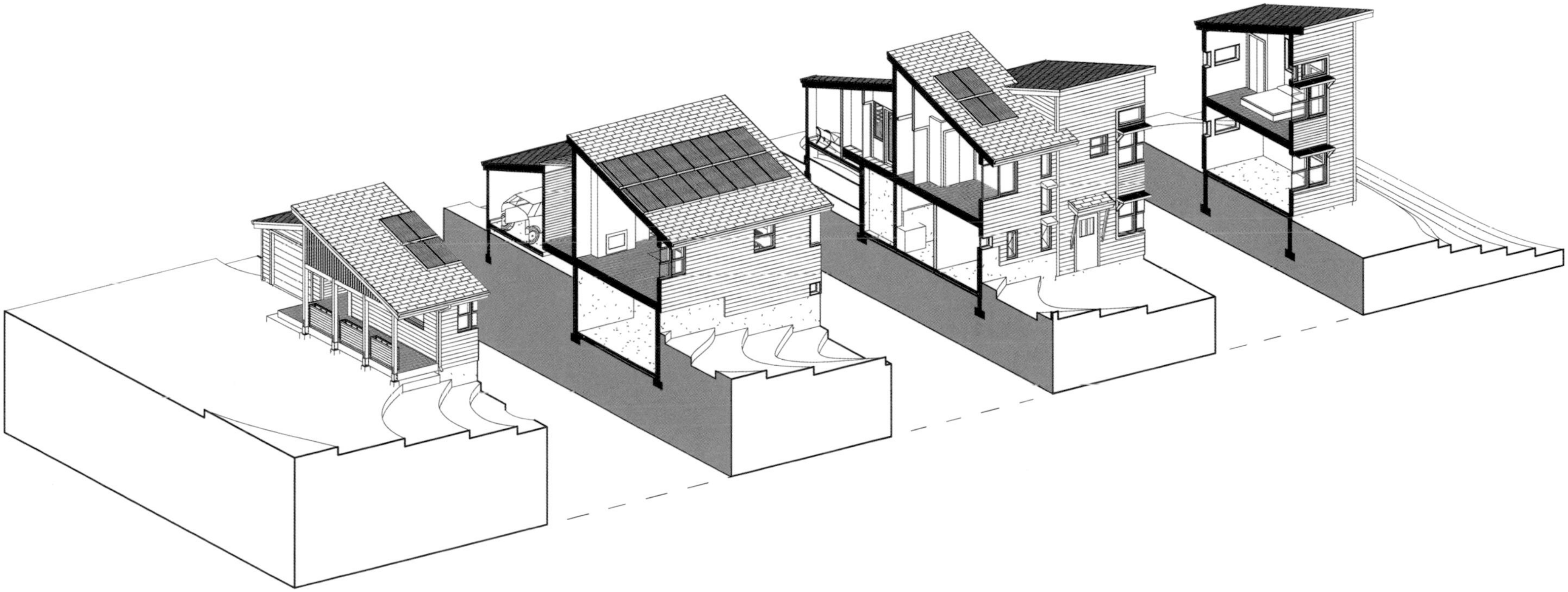

PAT'S HOUSE | A PREFABRICATED HOME

Pelham,
Massachusetts
| 2010 |

The town of Pelham, Massachusetts lies in the hills to the east of Amherst. It is a rural setting, with some historic churches, a small elementary school, and a police station. On the one major road that bifurcates the village, Miller Pollin designed a 2,500-square-foot house for her client, Pat. Pat's work requires frequent travel and she wanted a rural retreat as home. With a tight budget, Miller Pollin worked with the project contractors to create a highly efficient, pre-fabricated home whose shell was built over a seven-day period.

The house is tucked back from the street to minimize traffic noise. East of the house is a small pond and a mature stand of blueberry bushes. To the north is a dense forest. Miller Pollin sited the house to maximize the easterly view of the pond and the morning sun for the living area while the bedrooms face out towards the forest and quiet of the north and west. The underlying form is a simple square, forty-eight by forty-eight feet, with a two-car garage which creates a sheltered entrance to the south. This straightforward geometry accommodated the eight-foot prefabricated wall and roof panels that were shipped to the site from Southern New Hampshire. A heavy timber ridge line carries the roof loads and divides the basic square into halves, one for sleeping to the west and the second for the living space and open veranda to the east. Miller Pollin broke up the simple gable form with a small pop-up dormer that provides light and extra space to the in-home office in the upper loft space. This feature also adds interest and complexity to the otherwise straight-forward square footprint.

The color palette of lavenders, mossy greens and soft yellows further articulates interior spaces. Niches for decorative arts add depth to walls. On the exterior, cement board siding in a soft gray gives a nod to the historic buildings of Pelham, while the profile of the house with its dominant roof lines gives the home a simple contemporary appearance. Pre-fabricated panels provide high value insulation, with R-60 and R-40 for the roof and walls respectively. Radiant floor heating in a slab-on-grade provides an even warmth throughout the house. Respecting Pat's limited budget, Miller Pollin designed a home that is both intimate and expansive. The design provides ample space for work, living, and rocking on the veranda while the blueberries ripen.

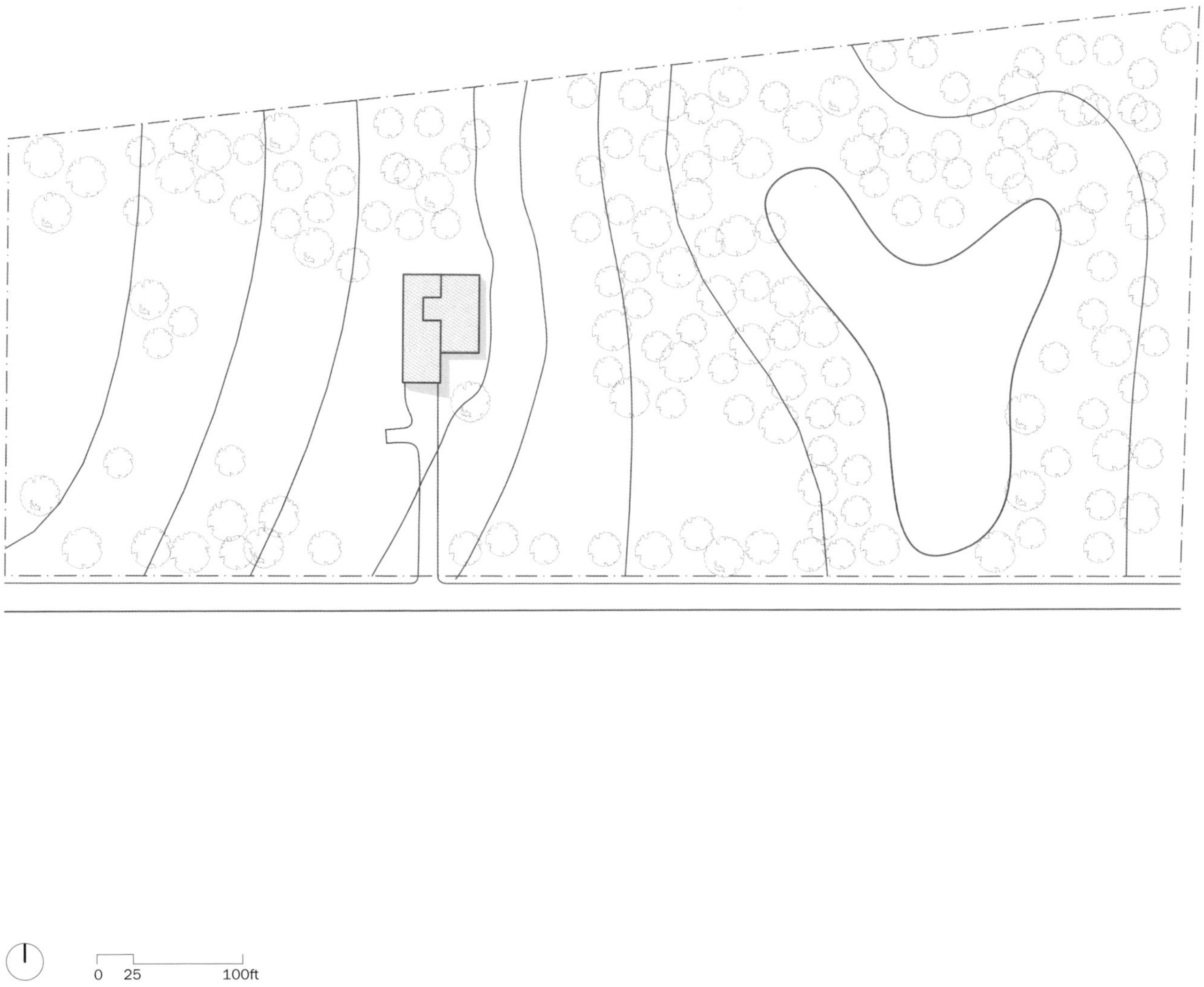
0 25 100ft

FLOOR PLAN

1. Entry
2. Living Space
3. Kitchen
4. Master Bedroom
5. Master Bathroom
6. Bedroom
7. Bathroom
8. Garage
9. Mechanical
10. Laundry

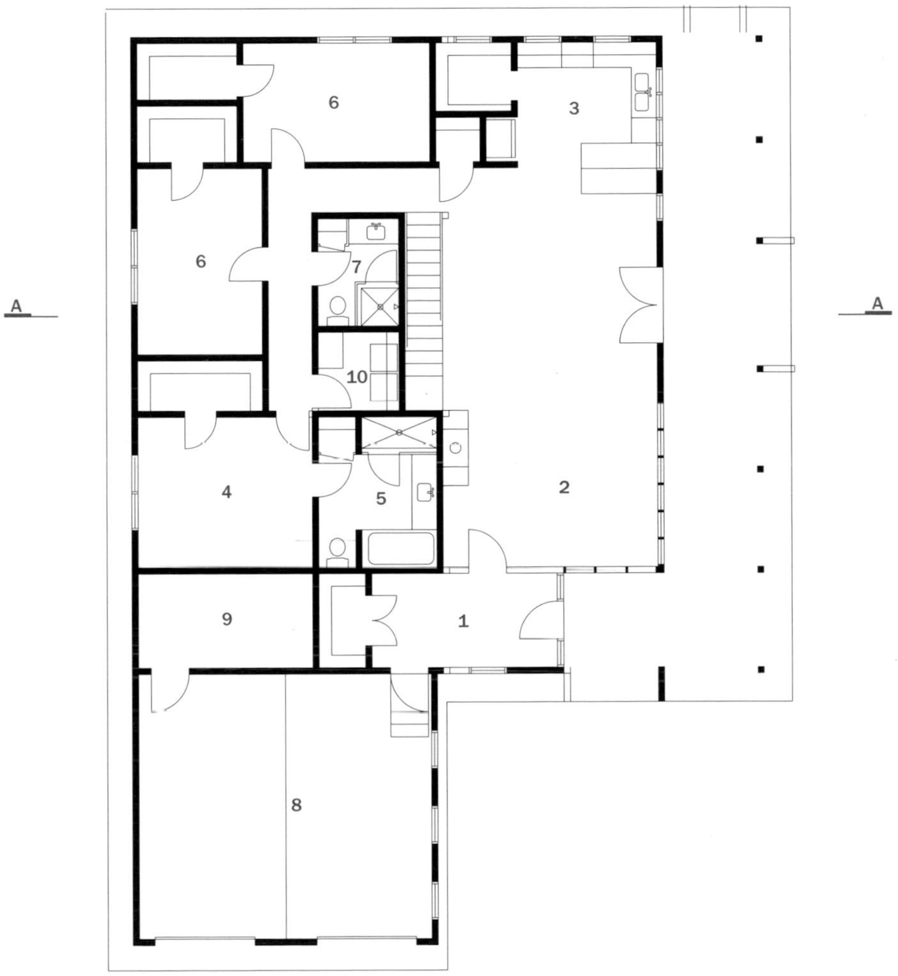

SECTION A-A

1. Living Space
2. Bedroom
3. Loft
4. Porch
5. Laundry

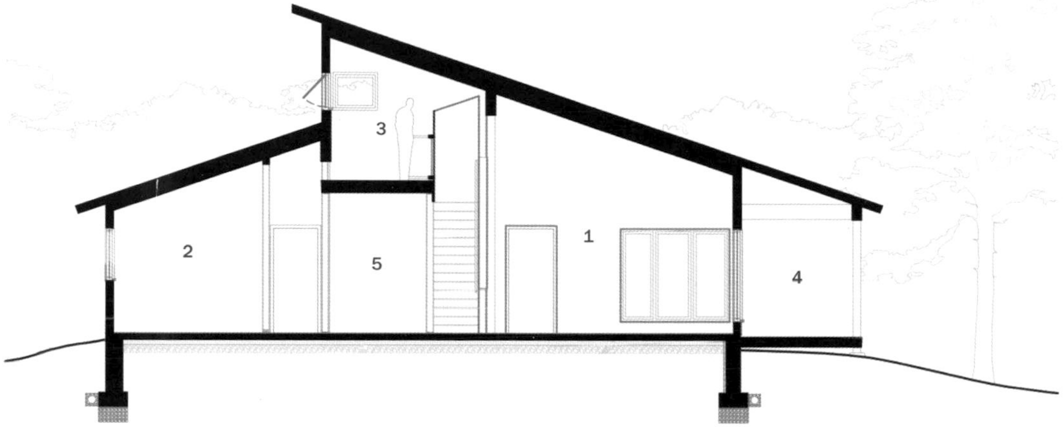

0 15 30ft

1

2

3

4

5

6

7

8

9

10

11

12

13

14

PRE-FABRICATION PROCESS

Panels Transported in from Bensonwood Homes
| Walpole, New Hampshire |

DAY 1

1. Step One
2. Step Two
3. Step Three
4. Step Four
5. Step Five
6. Step Six
7. Step Seven
8. Step Eight

DAY 2

9. Step Nine
10. Step Ten

DAY 3

11. Step Eleven
12. Step Twelve
13. Step Thirteen

DAY 4

14. Step Fourteen

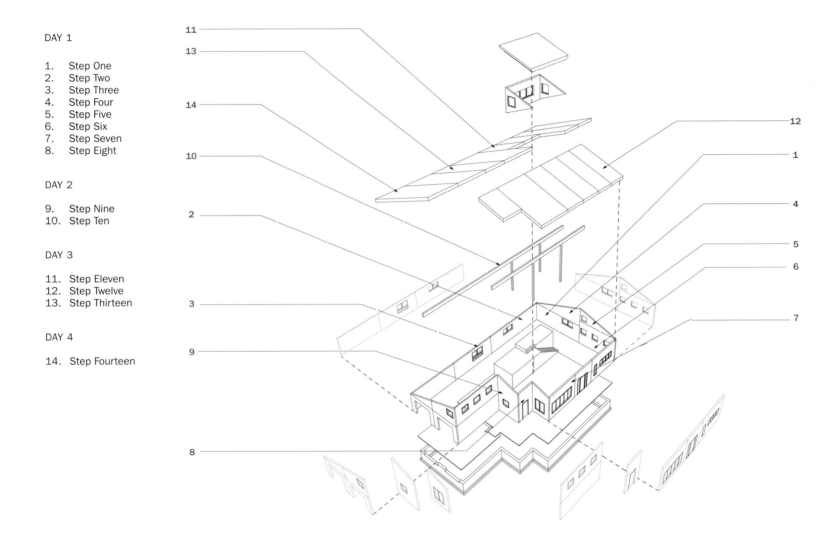

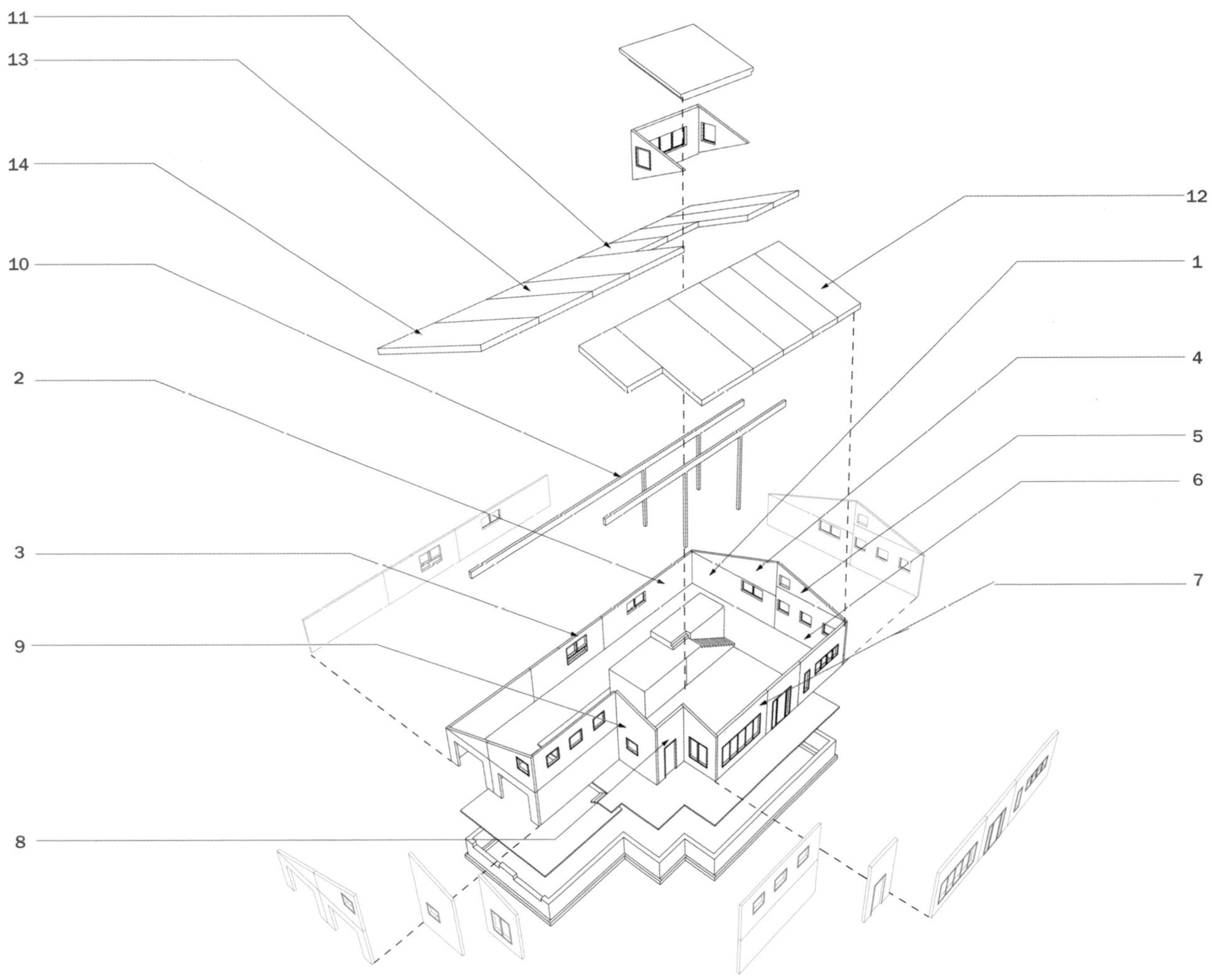

MOORE HOUSE

Sunderland,
Massachusetts
| 2004 |

For the Moore residence, Miller Pollin worked with an existing house—a large, barn-like two story volume that the owners, Lisa and Joe Moore, wanted to expand to accommodate their growing family. Here Miller Pollin inserted a stair tower which serves as a joint between the old and new. The addition with its sloping roof pivots off the tower and stretches out into the surrounding trees for privacy. The site is woody but with views that open out towards the western hills. There is a treehouse quality from the second-story porches, a sense that you can almost touch the forest. Glazing is limited on the entry side, but windows, both clerestory and casement, abound on the private western façade to better capture the views.

On the decks, a trio of narrow redwood balusters secure the stainless steel screen panels and create a rhythmic pattern around the perimeter. On the interior, guardrails on a bridge overlooking a double height space are detailed with balusters joined in pairs with a syncopated rhythm of redwood blocks. These details add a playful level of wood craft to this functional feature.

The existing house and the new portion were both clad in new cedar clapboards at the time of the renovation. This decision unified the new and the old forms of the house. Its original, simple form is now enlivened by two new volumes which stretch out across the hillside. Miller Pollin's addition connects with the spirit of the original house while simultaneously introducing a variety of new views and a more intimate connection with the landscape.

UPPER FLOOR

1. Living Room
2. Kitchen
3. Dinning Room
4. Master Bedroom
5. Master Bathroom
6. Walk-in Closet
7. Studio
8. Bridge
9. Deck
10. Bathroom

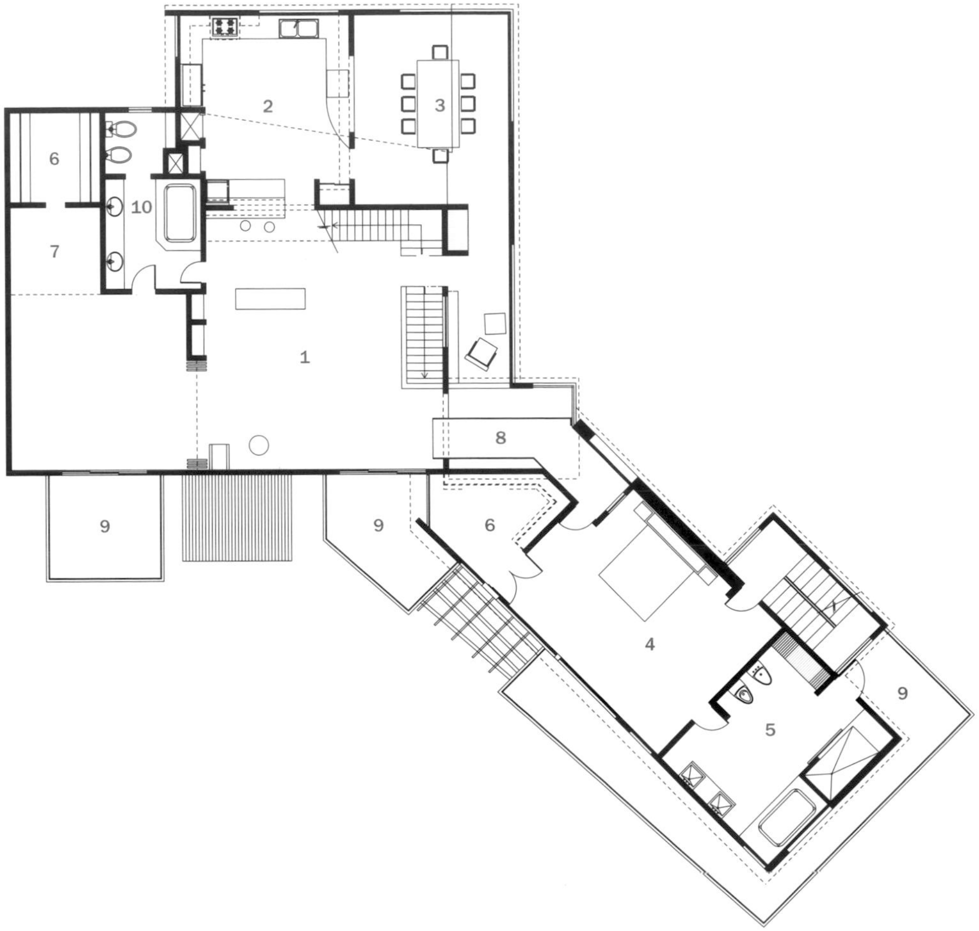

LOWER FLOOR

1. Entry
2. Playroom
3. Sun Room
4. Bedroom
5. Bathroom
6. Storage
7. Garden Storage
8. Garage
9. Pantry
10. Mechanical Room

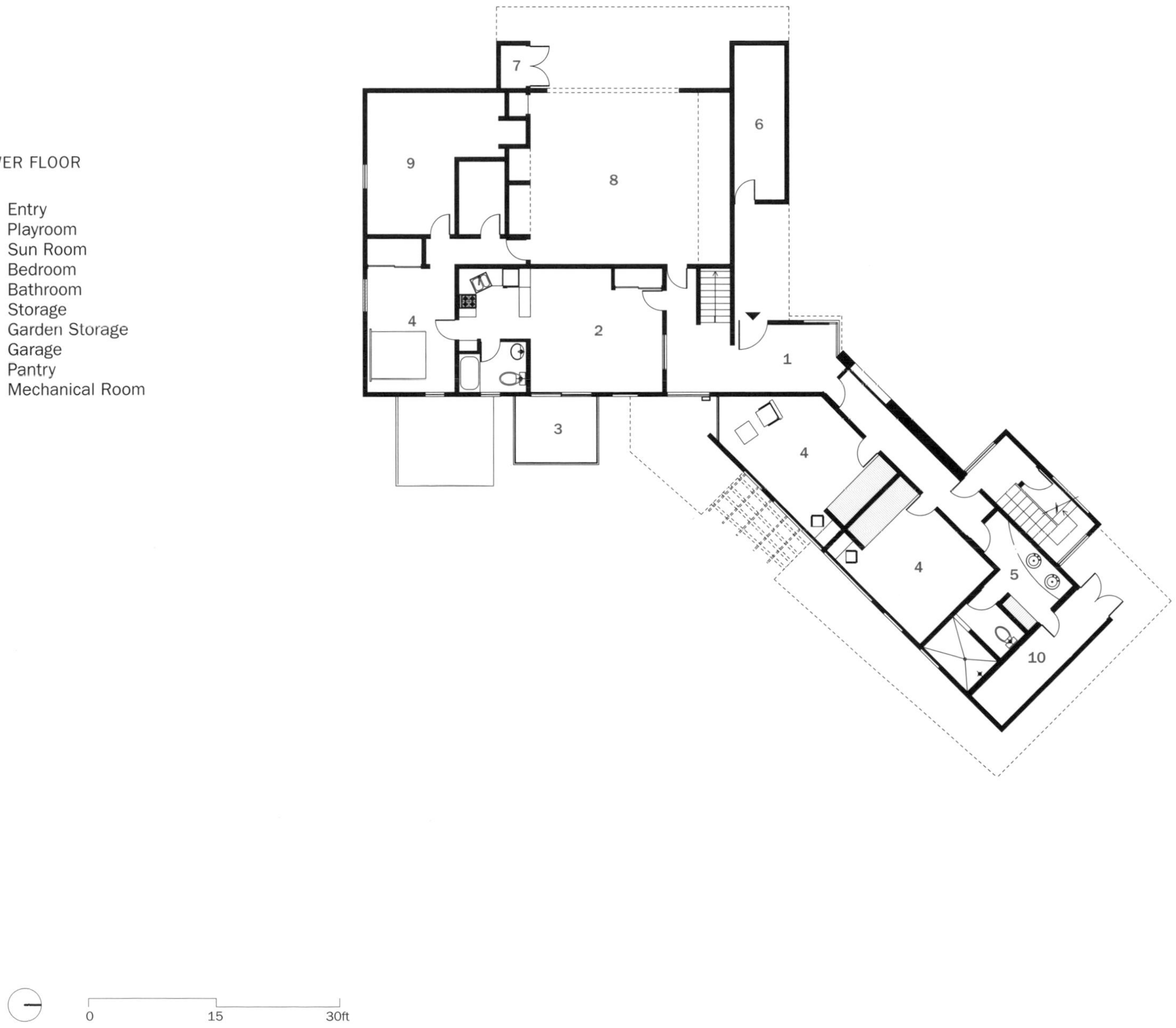

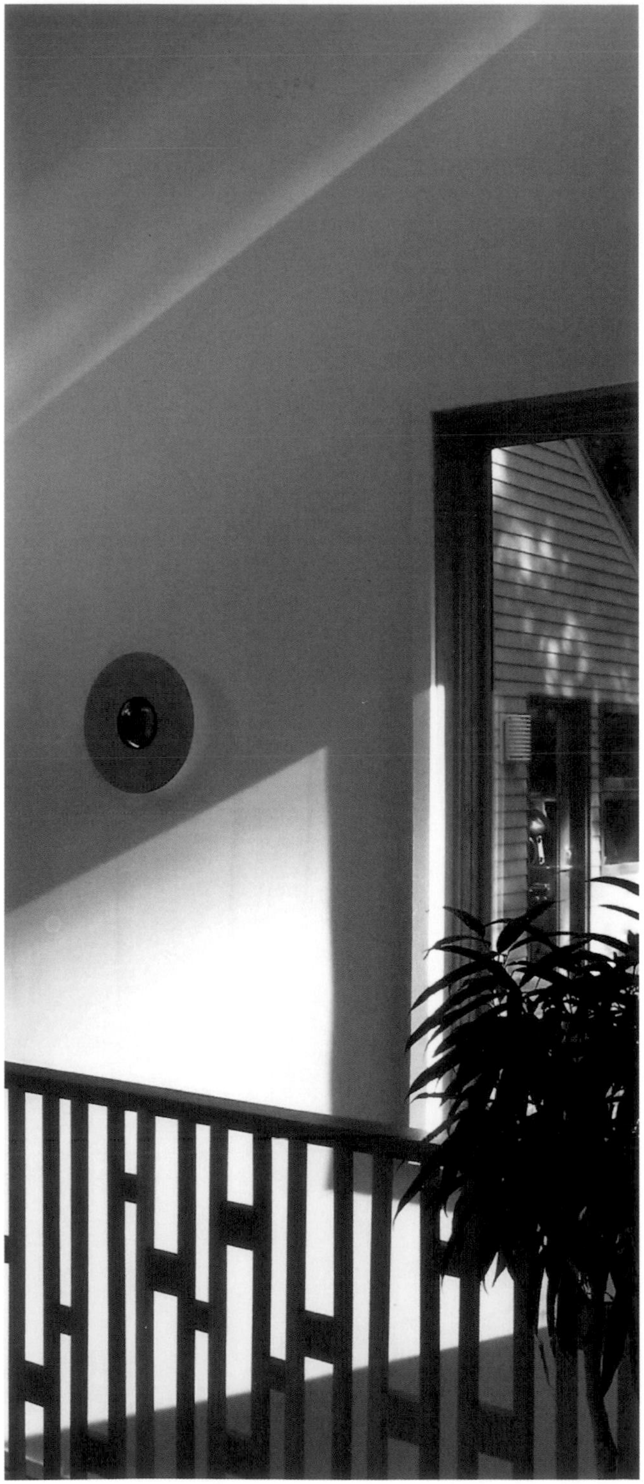

HEMMER CORRALES HOUSE

Sunderland,
Massachusetts
| 2018 – 2019 |

Bob Hemmer and Javier Corrales commissioned Miller Pollin to design a 2,400-square-foot contemporary home for them on a level site in Sunderland, Massachusetts. The property is skirted by a wooded wetland area and one neighboring residence. Looking west from the house is a beautiful view of nearby Sugarloaf Mountain. The first level contains a double-height living room open to a dining and kitchen area. The master bedroom suite is contiguous with the living room on the east side. Two guest rooms, bathrooms, a sauna and a study with a small view deck are located on the second level with a connecting hallway open to the living room below.

Miller Pollin designed the exterior massing to express the programmatic spaces of the house. She then used color to clarify and define the various volumes. There is a clear reference here to the color articulation found in the work of 20th-century Dutch architect and furniture designer, Gerrit Rietveld.

The home is designed to be energy efficient with super-insulation, dual-glazed windows able to withstand very cold winters and a high efficiency heating and cooling system. The roofs are south facing to accommodate future photovoltaic panels.

SITE PLAN

1. House Footprint
2. Driveway
3. Lawn
4. Bordering Vegetated Wetland

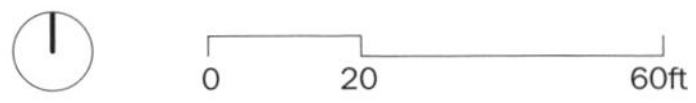

94
93
92
91
90
89
88
87
86
85
2
1
3
3
3
3
90
89
88
87
86
85
80
4

FIRST FLOOR

1. Entry
2. Living Room
3. Kitchen
4. Dining Room
5. Master Bedroom
6. Master Bathroom
7. Garage
8. Laundry / Powder Room

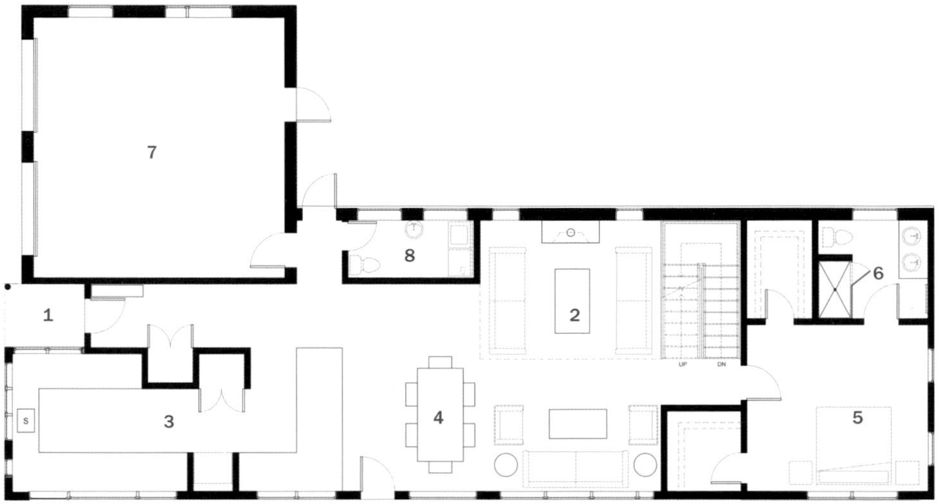

SECOND FLOOR

1. Open to Below
2. Bridge
3. Bedroom
4. Study
5. Bath
6. Sauna
7. Roof Terrace
8. Roof

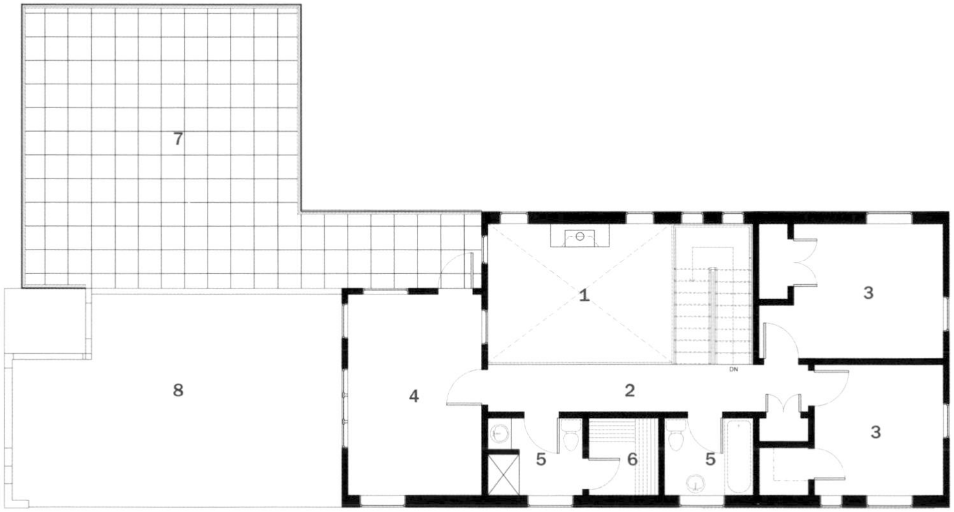

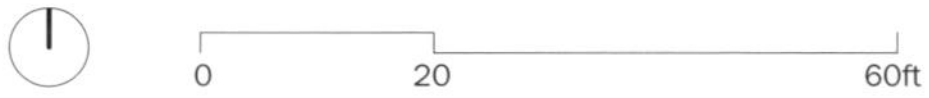

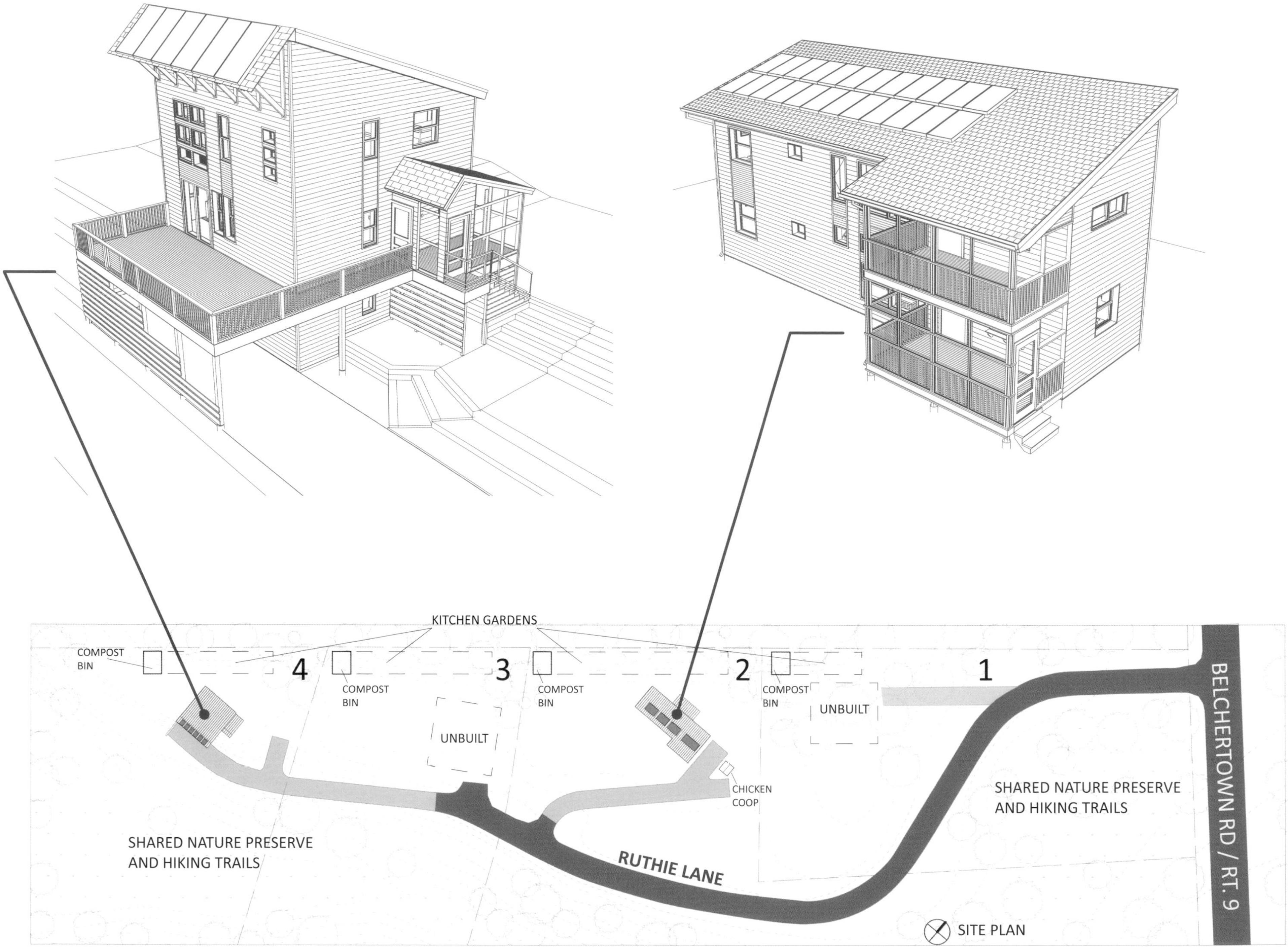
KITCHEN GARDENS
COMPOST BIN
4
COMPOST BIN
3
COMPOST BIN
2
COMPOST BIN
1
UNBUILT
UNBUILT
CHICKEN COOP
SHARED NATURE PRESERVE AND HIKING TRAILS
SHARED NATURE PRESERVE AND HIKING TRAILS
RUTHIE LANE
BELCHERTOWN RD / RT. 9
SITE PLAN

RUTHIE LANE

Amherst,
Massachusetts
| 2010 |

Two houses perch on a wooded lot on the edge of the town of Amherst. A shared driveway winds into the dense forest from the main road and into a sunny glade. These are compact, affordable, LEED Gold houses. Super-insulated and south facing, their technical efficiencies are coupled with vintage features such as root cellars for preserving locally grown fruits and vegetables, a chicken coop, and clotheslines. Each house has two porches for easy access to outdoor living and communal play spaces for children. Inside, the spaces are defined by colors and ceiling heights, typical of Miller Pollin's work on larger projects.

In the Red House, the southern exterior wall encloses a narrow double-height space adjacent to the master bedroom. Through operable interior windows, this space allows heat from the pellet stove to rise up to the bedroom level in winter and admit cool exterior breezes in summer. In the Yellow House, a lower ceiling height over the dining area breaks open into a double-height living room which circulates air and features a staircase with a vertical rhythm of slotted plank balusters.

These are modest three bedroom, 1,500-square-feet houses with a super-insulated, simple building envelope. Cues about interior spaces and functions are expressed by the varying window types and sizes designed to enhance air flow and solar gain. The houses are tied to a New England clapboard tradition, yet with a contemporary flair. The forest embraces the site—a sunny glade for the families that have made their homes here. Miller Pollin creates variety through color, crafted details, and carefully considered spaces.

FLOOR PLANS

1. Porch
2. Kitchen
3. Living/Dining
4. Flex Space
5. Chicken Coop
6. Study Area
7. Porch
8. Bedroom

SECOND LEVEL

FIRST LEVEL

SECTION A-A

1. Energy Star Asphalt Shingles
2. South Facing Photo-voltaic Panels
3. Operable Bedroom Vent for Air Circulation
4. Vent Windows for Summer Cooling
5. Energy-Star Ceiling Fan
6. Summer Sun (July 21)
7. Winter Sun (December 21)
8. Two Level Screen Porch
9. Cross-Ventilation
10. Pellet Stove
11. Ventilated Root Cellar
12. Energy-Star Instantaneous Hot Water
13. Heat Recovery Ventilation System (HRV)

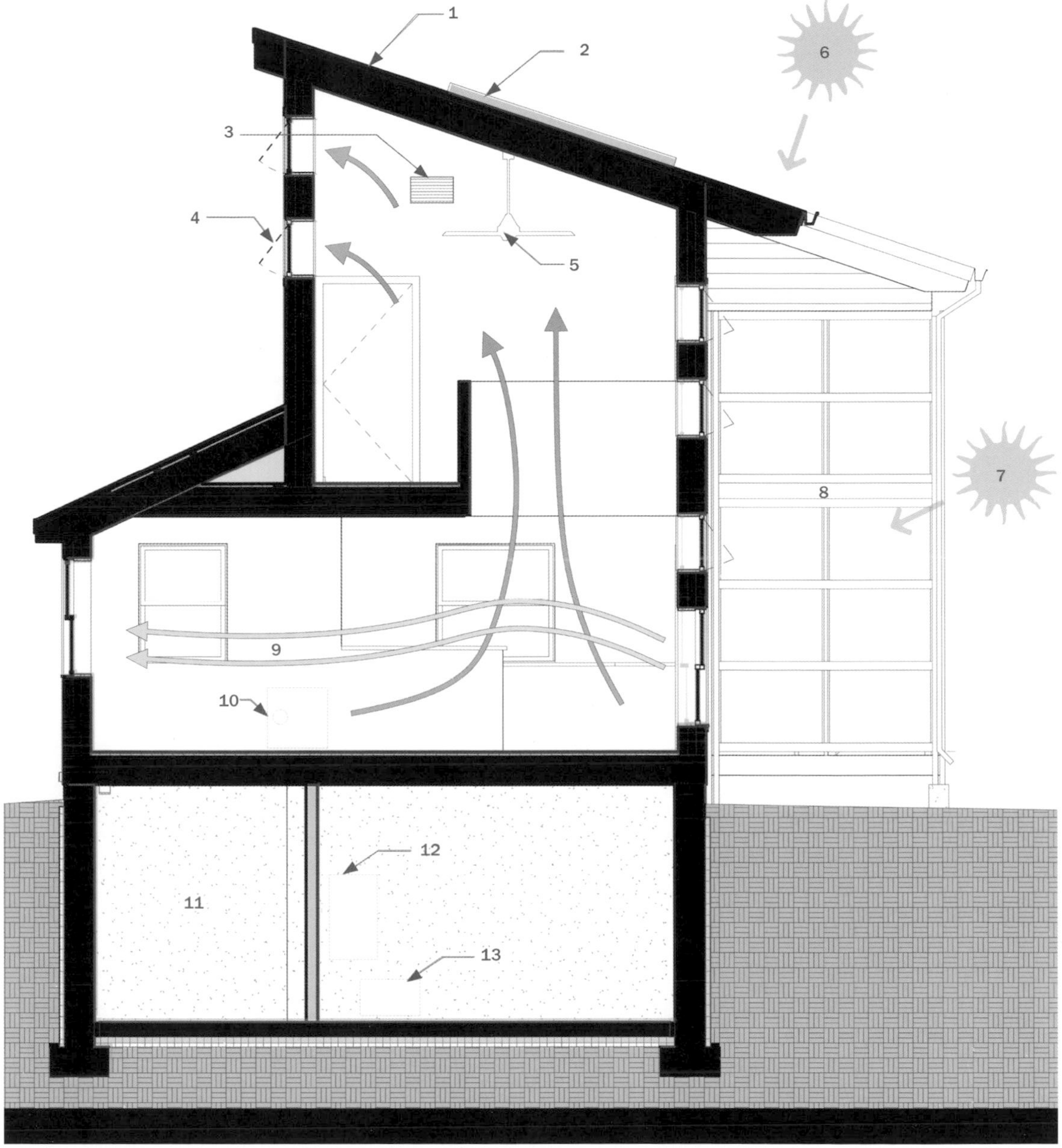

FLOOR PLANS

1. Root Cellar
2. Mechanical Room
3. Unfinished Expansion Space
4. Finished Entry
5. Carport
6. Porch
7. Kitchen
8. Living / Dining
9. Deck
10. Double-Height Space with Open Steel Grate
11. Bedroom

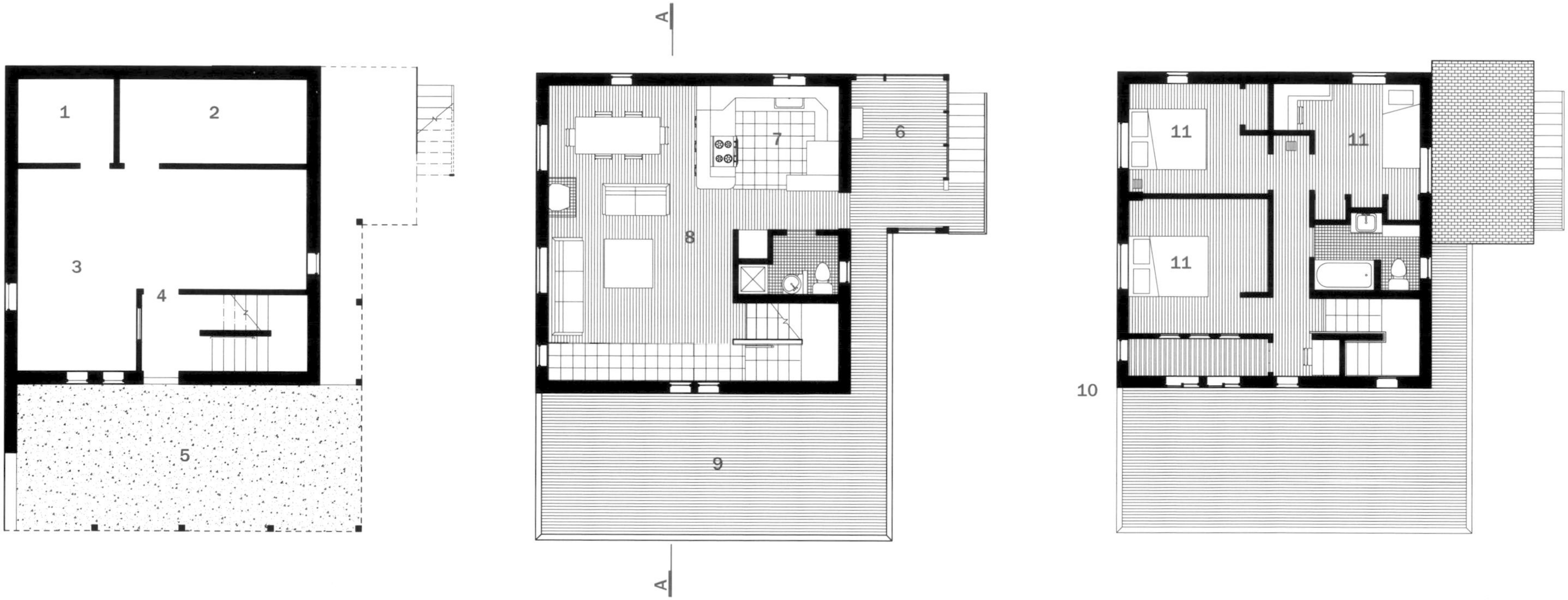

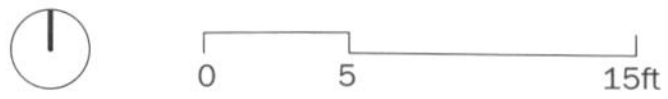

SECTION A-A

1. Summer Sun (July 21)
2. Winter Sun (December 21)
3. Solar Flat Plate Collector
4. Shade Sails Facing East and West
5. Storage (Ladder Access)
6. Operable Interior Windows
7. Cooling Air
8. Metal Grate
9. Cross Ventilation
10. Warm Air
11. Thermal Mass Tile Floor
12. Planters
13. Green Roof
14. Pellet Stove
15. Ventilated Root Cellar
16. Energy-Star Instantaneous Hot Water
17. Heat Recovery Ventilation System (HRV)
18. Car Port / Covered Patio

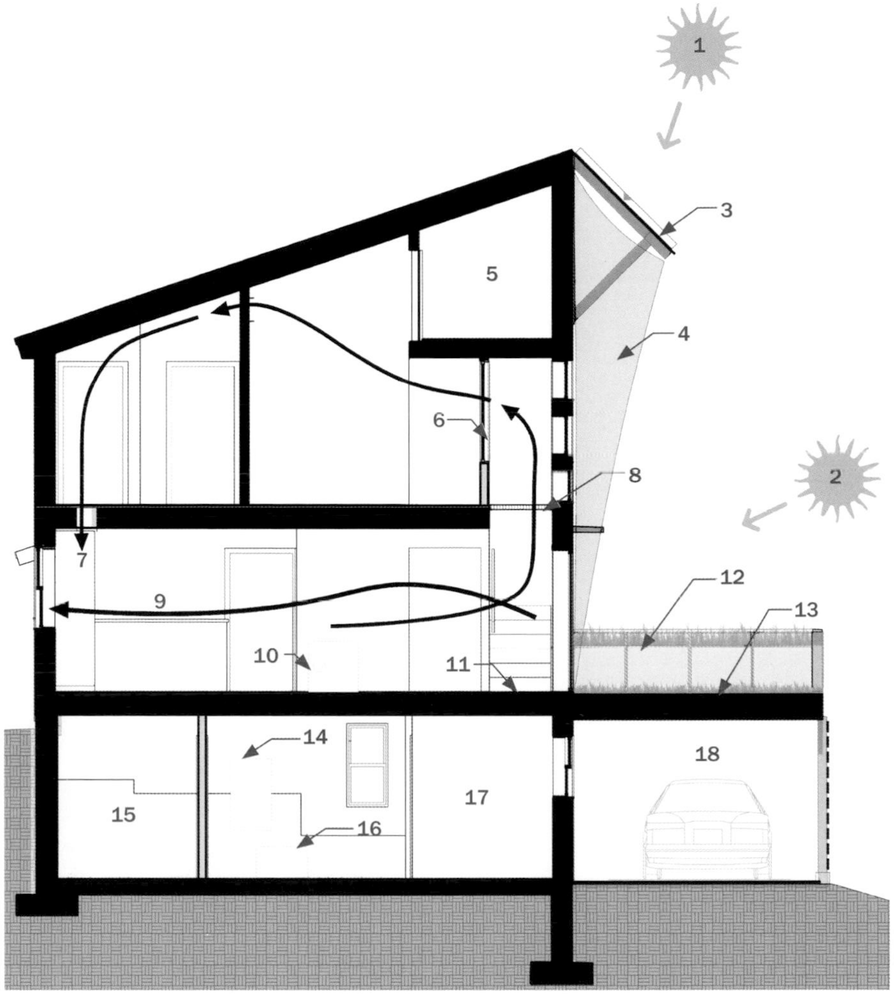

[TRANSFORMATIONS]

LORING BUILDING

UNIVERSITY PLACE

OPALINSKI HOUSE

RANSOHOFF HOUSE

COCKBURN HOUSE

LORING BUILDING

Riverside,
California
| 1987 |

Some of Miller Pollin's earliest commissions in California were with local developers in Riverside. One such project was the renovation of the Loring Building, the oldest structure on Main Street. The building was designed by A.C. Willard in 1890 in the Richardson Romanesque style. In 1918, G. Stanley Wilson remodeled the building, giving it a more restrained, Mission Style façade. By the time Miller Pollin was hired to renovate the building, the interior was in disrepair and needed seismic reinforcing and an attractive interior to entice tenants.

Though there was little left of the interior finishes, an antique birdcage elevator survived. Miller Pollin created an interior atrium space to feature it. She introduced a three-story curving wall that was engineered to carry lateral earthquake loads. An open, steel staircase followed the curve, providing access to new tenants' offices. The elevator became a central feature in this common space. The steel filigree of its screens echoed in the skylight Miller Pollin added. This is made of translucent panels in a grid-like frame. It brings muted daylight to the interior—light which penetrates the elevator cage.

Miller Pollin incorporated the curve of the seismic wall into her designs for the wall sconces that light the stairways. Their form was inspired by the Bird of Paradise, a dramatic flower common in California. The sconces are seven feet tall and made of copper, molded glass, and neon tubing. Like a sculptural relief, these fixtures are an assemblage of parts, the striated teal glass of one half, contrasting with the slivered arc on the other. Light filters through the molded glass and more directly through the openings in the arc. Like the cubist paintings of Braque and Picasso, a sinuous curved form at the top resembles the fractured body of a guitar.

These custom-made light fixtures, together with sophisticated engineering and warm wood paneling, further highlight the antique elevator in an inviting semi-public space.

STREET LEVEL PLAN

1. Pedestrian Mall
2. Atrium
3. Retail
4. Future Retail Lot
5. University Avenue

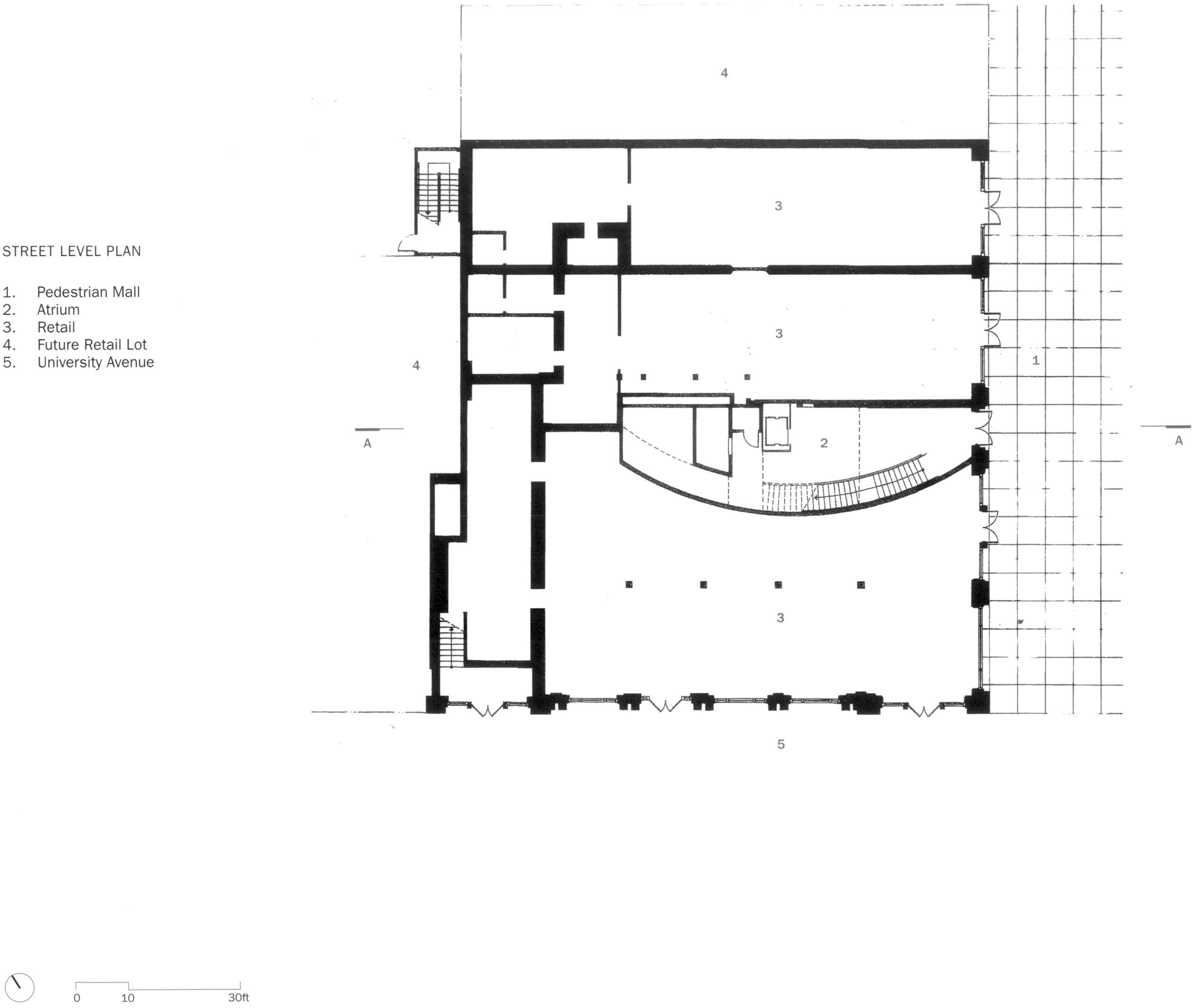

UPPER LEVEL PLAN

1. Open Office Space
2. Atrium

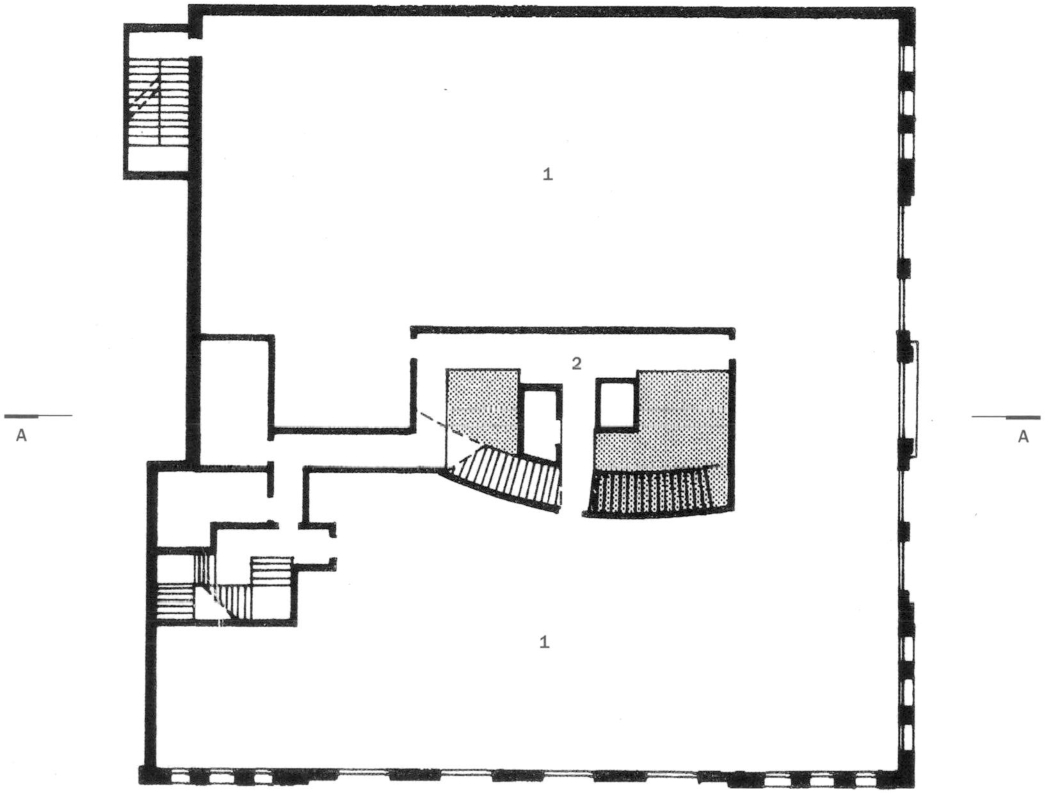

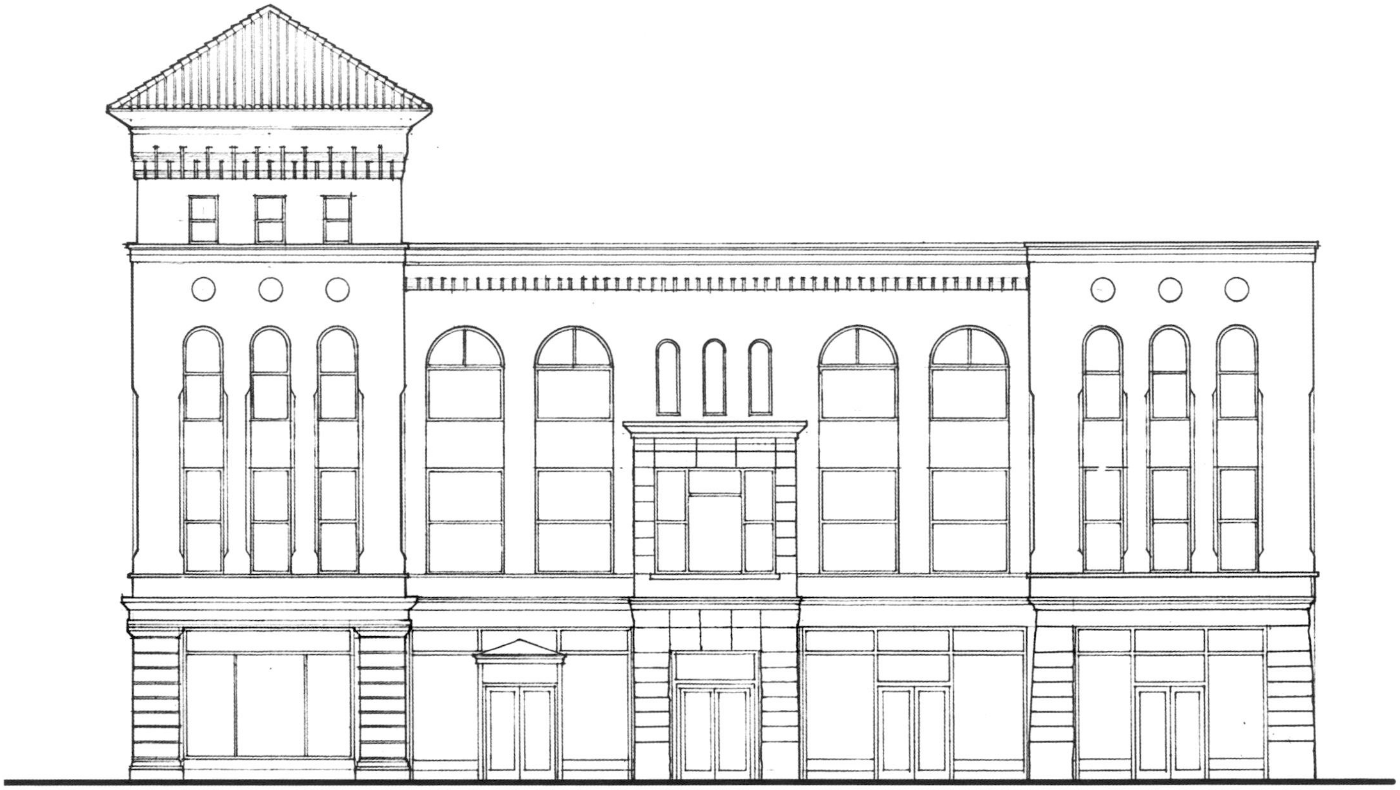

NORTH ELEVATION

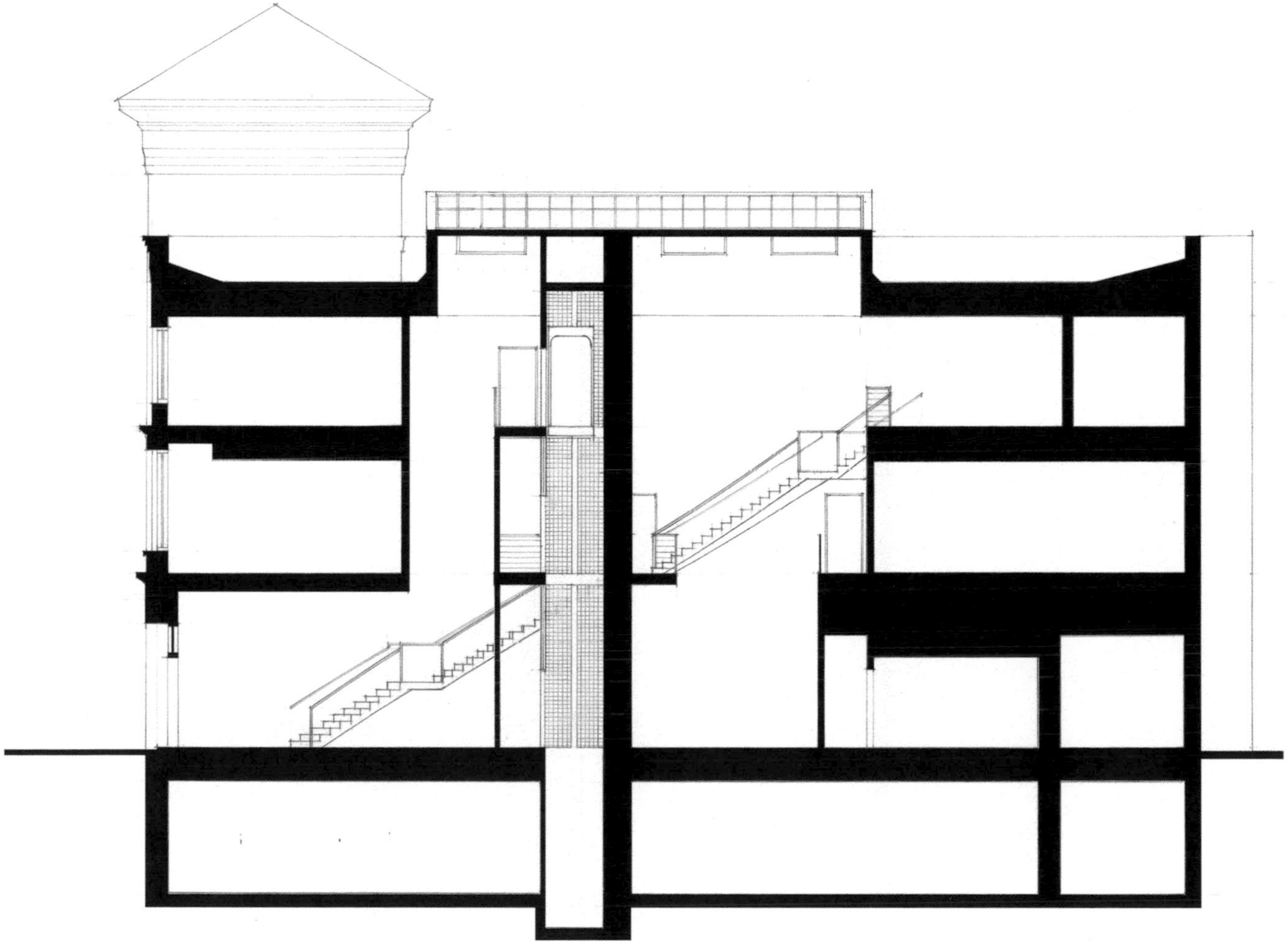

SECTION THROUGH LOBBY LOOKING SOUTH

UNIVERSITY PLACE
3560

UNIVERSITY PLACE

Riverside,
California
| 1985 |

The renovation of University Place in Riverside, California was another early project for Miller Pollin. Here, developers asked her to unify and modernize two single-story dilapidated commercial buildings in downtown Riverside. On a limited budget, Miller Pollin designed a central gallery space with a series of cross courts perpendicular to this main axis. These spaces provided appealing access to leasable tenant space. These common areas brought abundant natural light into what had been a very dark interior, and they created generous circulation deep into the joined buildings. Importantly, these spaces were to be built as the first phase of the renovation, allowing prospective tenants a chance to see the potential quality of the renovated spaces before leases were signed.

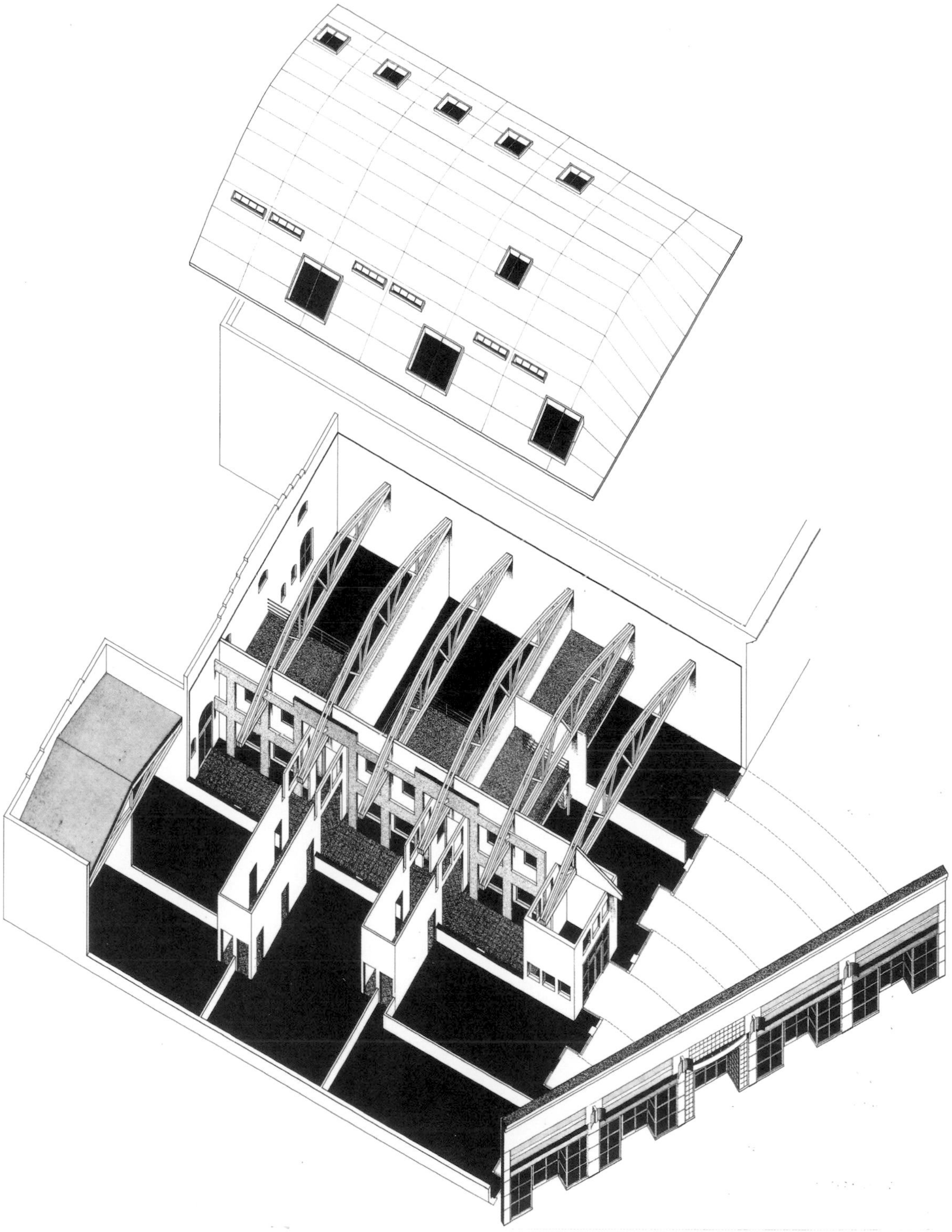

EXISTING CONDITIONS

1. Retail

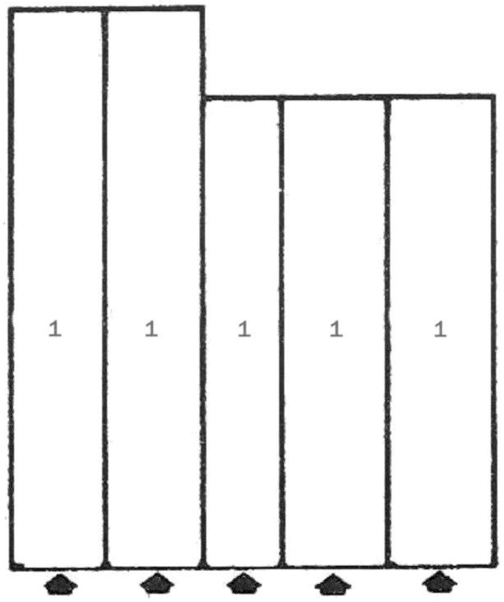

RENOVATION CONCEPT

1. Central Axis
2. Cross Courts
3. Retail Office
4. Flexible Office Space
5. Office Suites

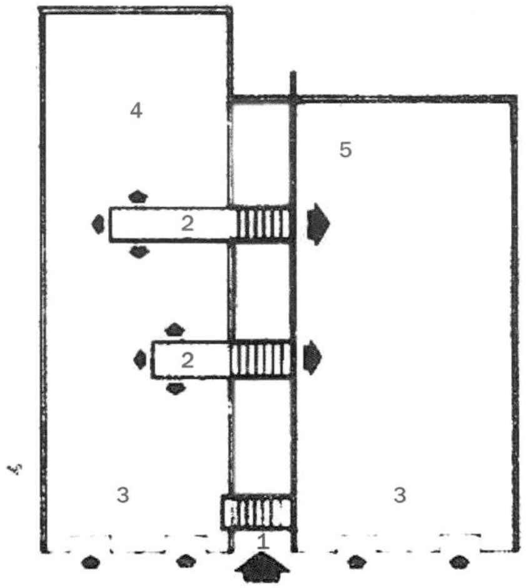

SITE PLAN

1. Ninth Street
2. Orange Street
3. Lemon Street
4. University Avenue
5. Vehicle Access
6. Parking

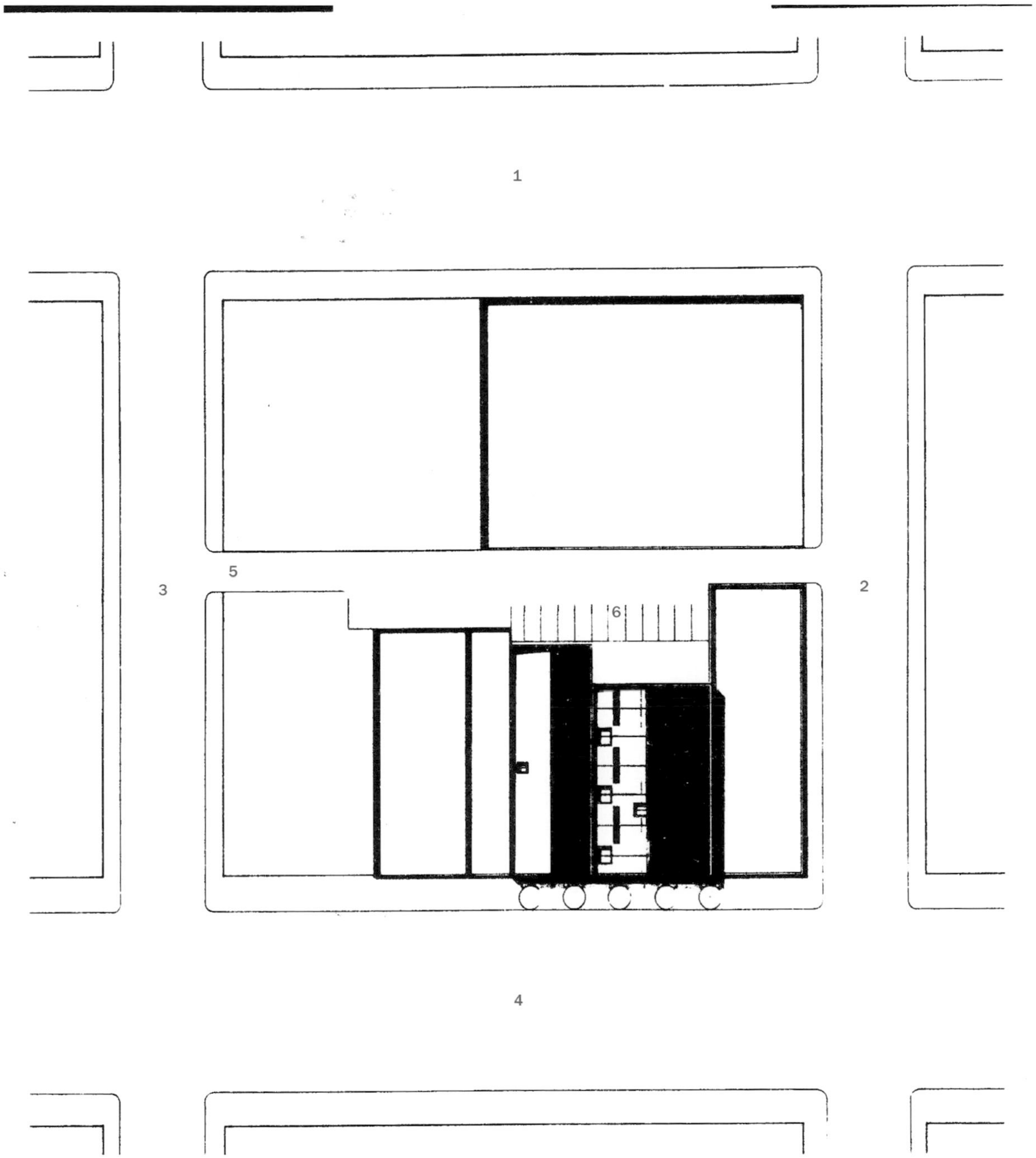

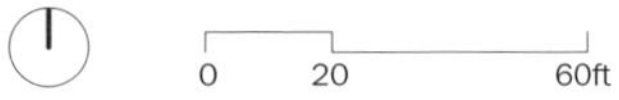

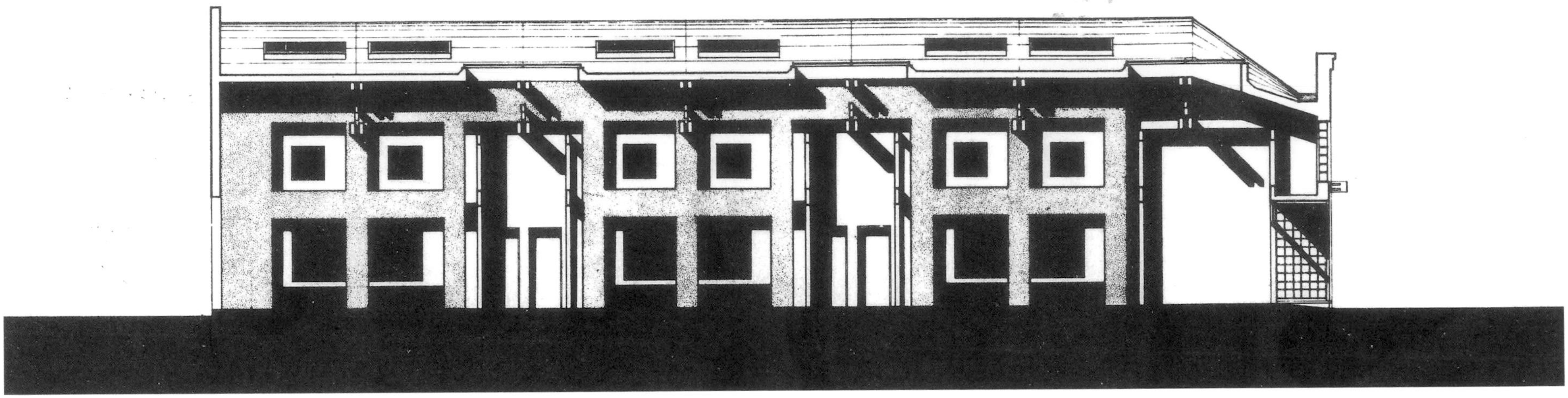

SECTION A-A

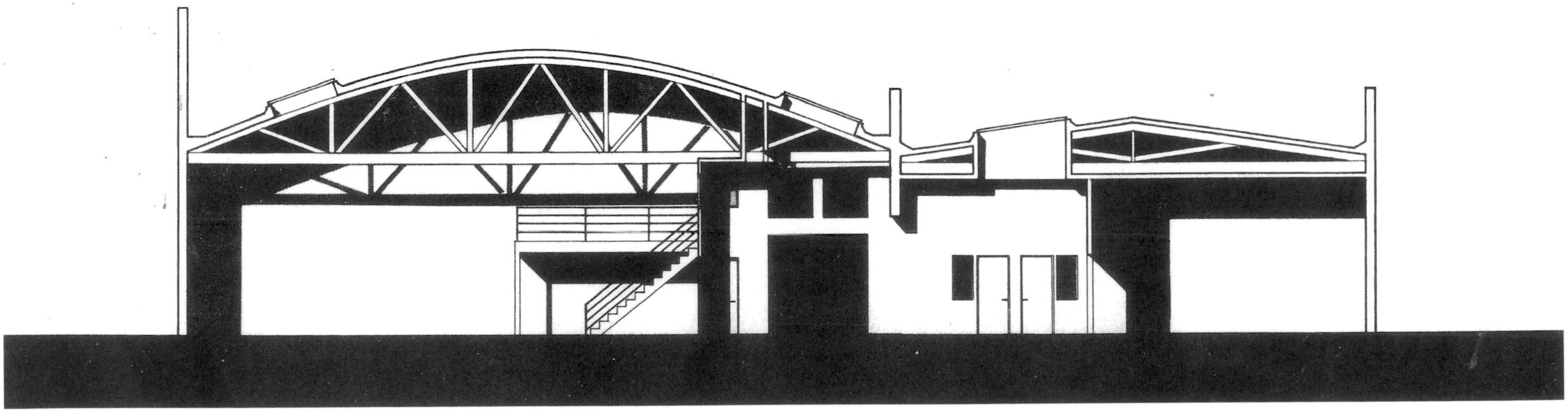

SECTION B-B

FLOOR PLAN

1. Leasable Office Space
2. Central Gallery
3. Cross-Courts

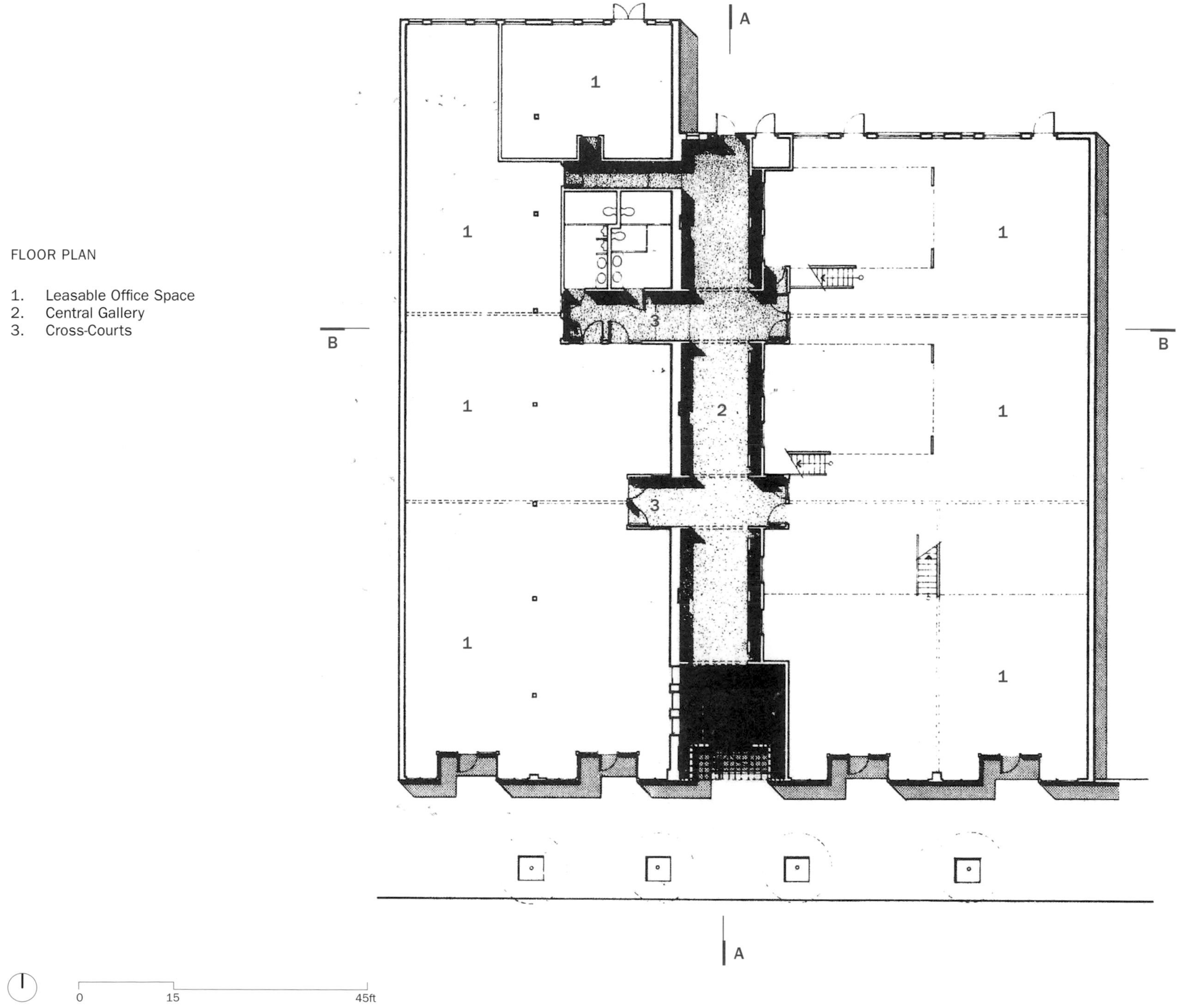

OPALINSKI HOUSE

Ware,
Massachusetts
| 2012 |

The Opalinski residence is located in Ware, Massachusetts, a former industrial town known for manufacturing shoes. The original brick ranch house, built in 1964, has a surprisingly elegant formality that is sharpened by its sprawling green lawn and the circular driveway leading to the front entrance. As visitors enter through the front door, the impeccably preserved aura of the 1960s that characterizes the exterior transforms magically at the entry threshold into a blend of brilliant white, warm wood and subtle lighting effects. Tracy and Paul Opalinski commissioned Miller Pollin to renovate the main level of this large, classic ranch.

The couple had inherited the house from an uncle, Edward J. Urban, a prominent Ware businessman and life-long resident. In 1959, Urban founded the American Athletic Shoe Company, one of the largest ice-skate manufacturers in the country. The house had changed little over the past fifty years. Indeed, the basement, an entertainment lair complete with yellow tufted leather bar, wood paneling, and poker table, is preserved as a historical snapshot of the 1960s. The new owners wanted their house to convey Zen-like calm. They also wanted a limited color palette and thoughtful storage solutions to reduce clutter. They shared these ideas with Miller Pollin. The result is a stunningly modern home with a surprising warmth. Entering the foyer, there is a disciplined whiteness, with a curving wall opposite the door, stark in its simplicity. A series of five white niches line one of the entry walls displaying Asian vases and a Buddha dramatically lit from above. White-paneled doors with no visible handles indicate a coat closet. On the opposite wall, a Shoji-like pocket-door slides open to reveal Tracy's office/yoga space. The room is empty save for a small built-in-desk, and white cabinets that conceal home office files. This room sets the tone for the rest of the residence.

Throughout, spaces flow into each other, providing vistas through and across the house. The influence of traditional Japanese architecture is clear as these larger spaces are easily divided by the sliding pocket-doors. These in turn, designed with translucent white Japanese rice paper, can define a space as needed while filtering light. The original windows remain but traditional interior frames were removed. Similarly, there are no baseboards or crown moldings. Instead, intersections of walls, floors, ceilings and windows are pared down for an unadorned simplicity. Such simplicity serves to better dramatize the spare use of smaller scale features such as wall niches. These appear in the foyer and are used to great effect above an L-shaped banquette. Lined with Brazilian Ipe wood, they set off six pieces of antique Czech crystal.

Small lights from above produce lacy patterns on the stark white walls, a delicate decorative touch against the pure modernism of the space. Similarly, inherited antique crystal wall sconces and a breakfast table chandelier create reflections on the white walls and ceiling. Open niches cut through a wall that partitions the breakfast table from the living room spaces. They frame views of the interior and landscape beyond. The public living spaces pivot around a central kitchen. The kitchen has no boundary walls. Two 13-foot islands

FLOOR PLAN

1. Entry
2. Family Room
3. Kitchen
4. Meditation Space
5. Master Bathroom
6. Master Bedroom
7. Bedroom
8. Bathroom
9. Screen Porch

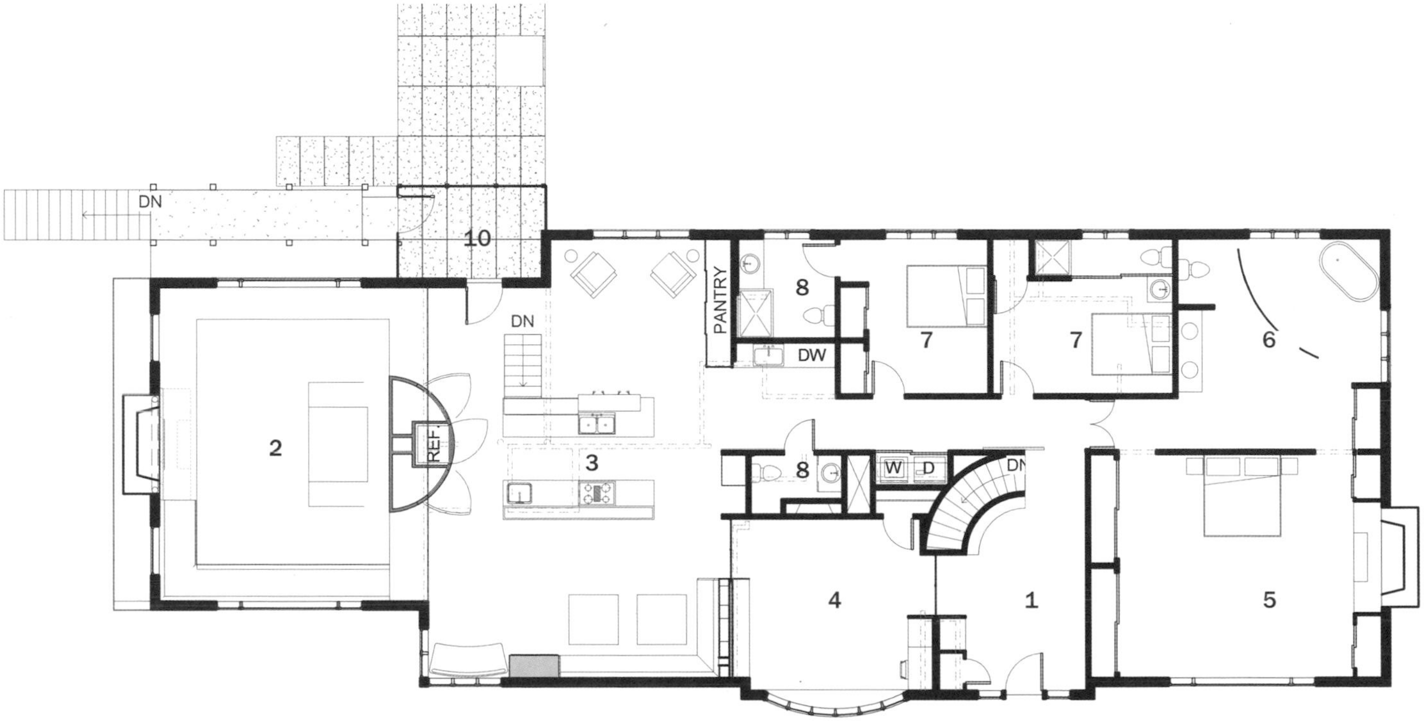

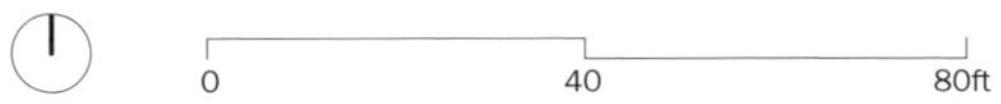

hold a sink, stove, and cabinets sheathed in maple. A beautifully tiled planter cantilevers out from one island, providing a screen of foliage that shields the kitchen work surfaces.

A staircase to the lower level is tucked beneath the south-facing kitchen island. A cubic volume on the island holds small appliances and separates the stair rail from the cooking space. The stairs are framed in a stainless-steel system of cables and railings which complements the overall openness and the largely orthogonal geometry of the house. Most dramatic of all is a full-height oval form located between the kitchen and living room. On the kitchen side, the elegant ovoid, clad in a dark polished Ipe, camouflages a refrigerator, freezer, pantry, and small closet. The form becomes a media center on the living room side. It is a study in uncluttered and streamlined functionality with remarkable sculptural beauty, and provides a fulcrum around which home life flows. In the living room, Miller Pollin stripped away the flat, traditional ceiling of textured plaster. In the manner of Wright at Fallingwater (an inspiration for the owners). She then also created varied ceiling heights.

Wooden mullions define translucent panels which provide muted, ambient lighting in the space. At Fallingwater, Wright set a flat ceiling within these horizontal panels. But here a shallow dome is centered above, lifting the ceiling into the roof rafters to create a greater sense of height.

The design of this ceiling yields an ethereal sense of space and height. While this project is a renovation of an existing structure, it still reflects many of Miller Pollin's architectural concerns. It was the product of a synergy between client and architect who, throughout the design process, shared a clear vision of modernist purity. Together they created peaceful and elegant spaces that elicit an interior calm.

Once again, Miller Pollin's knowledge of architectural history informed the design of areas such as the living room, with its reference to Wright. Yet Miller Pollin deftly handled this ceiling space to create a sense of height and mystery. Typical of Miller Pollin's work is the way in which she weaves past traditions into a new sensibility. In many ways, this is a modernist house, with its white walls and open floor plan, in the tradition of Le Corbusier. However, the ethereal white is grounded by the warm wood of the floors, cabinetry and oval Ipe multi-function form. The result is a home with a disciplined lack of clutter.

Aunt Jemima
Honey Nut
Cheerios

RANSOHOFF HOUSE

Los Angeles,
California
| 1998 |

In 1996, Sigrid's sister and brother-in-law, Lori and Steve Ransohoff, purchased a mid-century modern post and beam residence in the Brentwood area of Los Angeles. The original house, designed by Hap Gilman in 1960, was a single-level, three-bedroom home nestled in the foothills below what is now the Getty Center. This location was once the site of Greta Garbo's home and pool house. Garbo's house burned down in the Bel Air fires of November 1960, but the pool house remained.

With three children and several large dogs, the Ransohoffs wanted to create more living space—two new bedrooms, a larger kitchen, and dining area. They commissioned Miller Pollin to renovate the dining area and add a new kitchen, an upper level den, and two children's bedrooms. The challenge was clearly to maintain the integrity of the beautiful original post and beam structure while adding a significant amount of new space. Miller Pollin developed a scheme for a two-level addition. The stairs to the new second level combine polished stainless steel risers, clear Douglas fir treads, and screen wall planking. With many hours of homework ahead, the two children who would inhabit the second level needed places to study. The programmatic invention of a "crow's nest" was cantilevered from each of the two new bedrooms, providing a quiet study place overlooking the nearby mature live oak trees. The house and addition are largely clad in white stucco, but the studies are wrapped in weathering copper whose tone plays off of the hue of the redwood frame of the original house. Horizontal plaster reveals and window mullions on the addition harmonize with the horizontality of the Gilman design.

COCKBURN HOUSE

Petrolia,
California
| 1993 |

What follows is Miller Pollin's description of working with the renown political journalist, Alexander Cockburn (1941–2012), Scottish born and raised in Cork County, Ireland.

Alexander Cockburn was a colorful client full of ideas about the home he wanted in California. He constantly ran headlong into the next plan for the house—new bedroom, bathroom, light fixture, or piece of furniture. The images here cannot even begin to capture the absolutely engaging nature of working on design with Alex. When he decided to migrate from New York City to the West Coast, he drove his 1959 red Chevy Impala from Vermont to California. After an extensive exploration of various parts of Northern and Southern California, Alex set his sites on building a very small house on a hill in Big Sur overlooking one of the most spectacular views on the coast. I sketched a small structure for him that housed a kitchen, dining, and living space with a separate pod for sleeping and a bathroom with a wall that could rotate completely open, allowing a huge view from the "loo" of the Pacific. The house was intended to be like half of a ship's hull lodged into the hillside and punctuated at one end with a two-story viewing tower. The Big Sur project never came to fruition, but he would later revive ideas from it once he purchased a 1950s ranch house in Petrolia in northern California—another beautiful part of the California coast. The transformation of this ordinary ranch house developed out of Alex's vision of combining his desired architectural elements and aspects: the veranda, the conservatory, and the open modern floor plan.

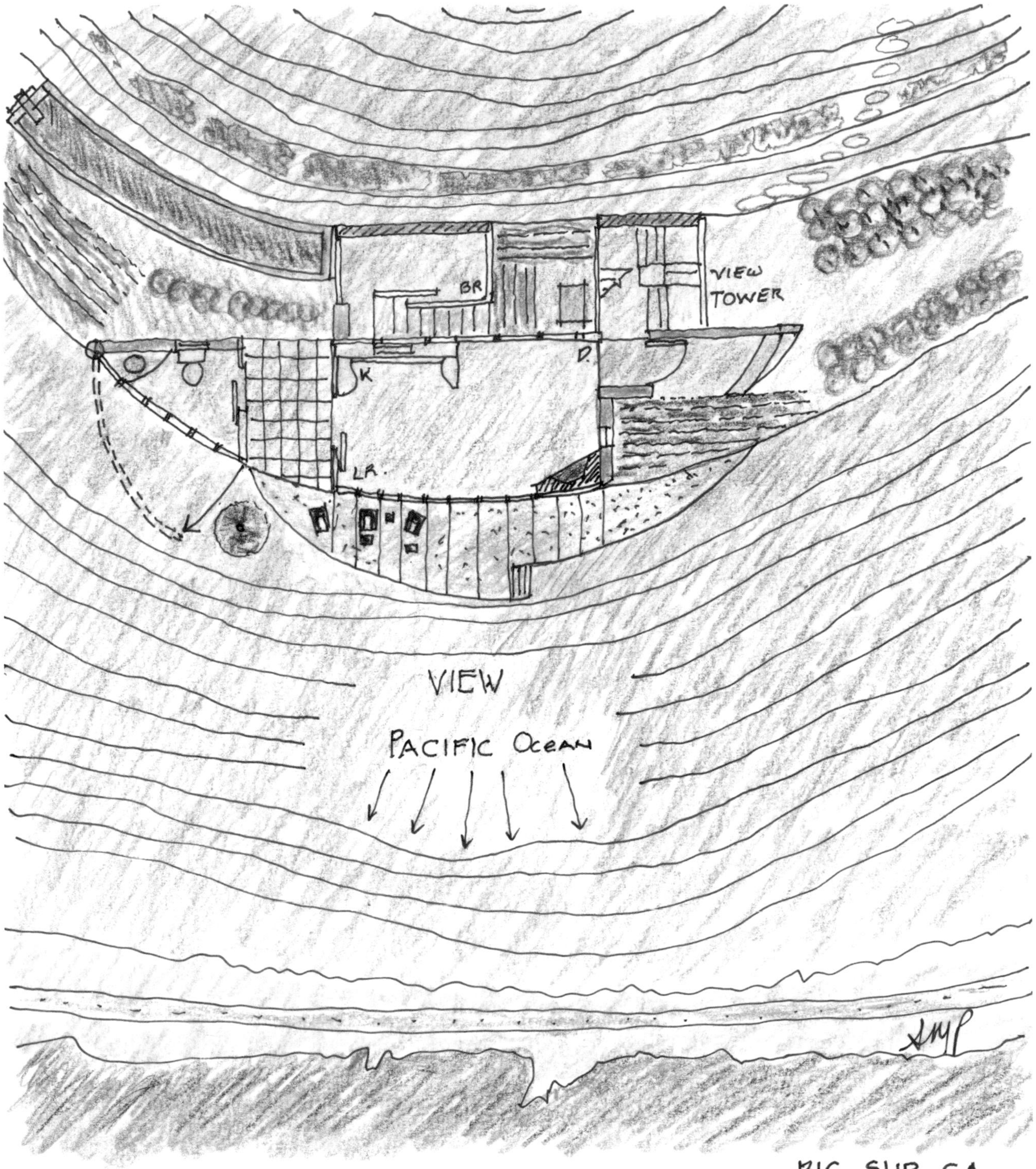

BIG SUR, CA.

Part of Alex Cockburn's plans for the renovation of this 1950s ranch house included two traditional architectural typologies: the conservatory (glass room often used as a greenhouse) and the veranda with its southern associations. Miller Pollin was tasked with reinterpreting these elements in the renovation in the spirit of rural, contemporary Northern California. This resulted in walls of redwood-framed glazing and gently pitched roofs. The window walls emphasized horizontality as a counterpoint to the vertical veranda posts. The red cedar and light filled interior spaces allow a visual connection with Cockburn's ever changing garden.

Miller Pollin kept some of the letters Alex dashed out on his portable typewriter. She explained that these letters set the tone for working with him.

"Having spent the last week or ten days looking through mullioned windows (not tiny Tudor horrors but ordinary six over sixes or twelve over twelve), I'm beginning to feel that my push for the unobstructed middle pane (sans the middle mullion) was unnecessary particularly with the door. Wrong, even. 'There's a lot to be said for the vista being seen long shot so to speak through the mullioned windows rather than the it's-my-view-and-I-own-it' bigger pane. I think extended veranda entry with three-beam (column) treatment. What do you think?"

“I’ll talk to you on the weekend. I think it’s working out very well and you had most elegant solutions under a very short deadline. (Which of course is what I think my work is all about!)”

“A big rain storm up here. My road is holding up, with assiduous water bar work. You do have to stay on top of it. I love surveying for the first insidious trickle, like sentries on the watch for subversion.”

“The bedroom of impending joy (formerly the bedroom of despair) is well along, but it would be nice if you could just sketch a style for the front of the bed platform, which should accommodate four drawers.”

[COMMUNITY HOUSING]

COLTON SENIOR HOUSING

AVALON EL SEGUNDO SENIOR HOUSING

SOUTH EAST STREET AFFORDABLE HOUSING

COLTON SENIOR HOUSING

International Competition
Colton, California
| 1989 |

In 1989, Miller Pollin submitted her designs and models to a competition for a senior housing complex in the City of Colton, California. This was an international competition, with over 130 entries from twenty-five states and seven countries. The program called for 100 apartments on a two-and-a-half-acre site in the center of Colton's historic district. The neighborhood is comprised of mostly modest single-family California bungalows, which feature front porches, sloped roofs, and clapboard siding. Miller Pollin was one of five architects chosen to compete in the second stage of the competition. She received the First Award of Honor for her scheme.

This scheme echoes the character and scale of the existing residences and locates most of the units along two street edges. It was important to hold the street edge to strengthen the pedestrian character of the neighborhood. Units are clustered together but individually articulated. Front porches face the street while secure entry is from the block interior. The configuration of the clusters forms a rich variety of common spaces on the site. A corner lathe house for growing shade-loving plants is connected diagonally to a small orchard, which, in turn, is linked to a hardscape piazza. The community center and mail room complete this diagonal chain of shared spaces. There are two landscaped mews that join the orchard space: one entered from a street fronting on a public park and the other from parking and a side street. These mews spaces provide shade and casual places to walk and socialize. Miller Pollin designed the piazza for evening events under the stars. As the model shows, each unit has direct access to green spaces and a variety of common areas.

This was the only two-story scheme in the second phase of the competition. It won the support of the community members because it demonstrated how this housing complex could both provide senior housing and revitalize a fragile historic neighborhood. Miller Pollin employed front porches and other architectural elements as fresh interpretations of the existing residential fabric. She respected the scale and rhythm of surrounding single-family residences. Wood siding and ground face block elevations harmonized with existing houses in scale, detail, and the inclusions of architectural elements such as dormers and porches. The submittal for the first phase referenced Irving Gill's Horatio Court in Santa Monica. This reference also set the stage for the second phase submittal. As part of her research for the competition, Miller Pollin consulted with renowned specialist Victor Regnier who has studied and written about senior housing for decades. As a result, she carefully factored in the needs of seniors in her design, as well as the contextual fabric of the neighborhood. This translation of the existing historic vernacular yielded a distinctly contemporary interpretation.

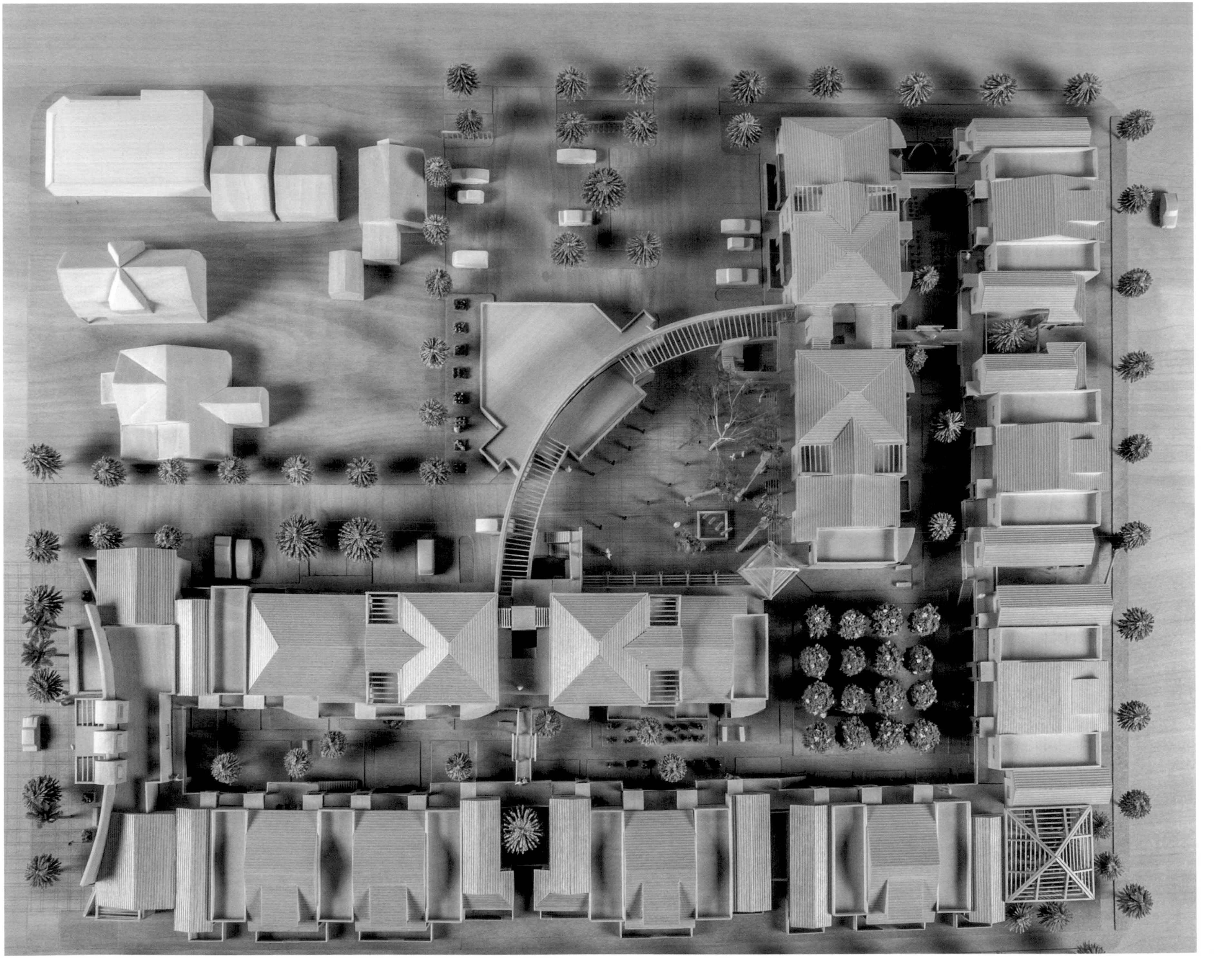

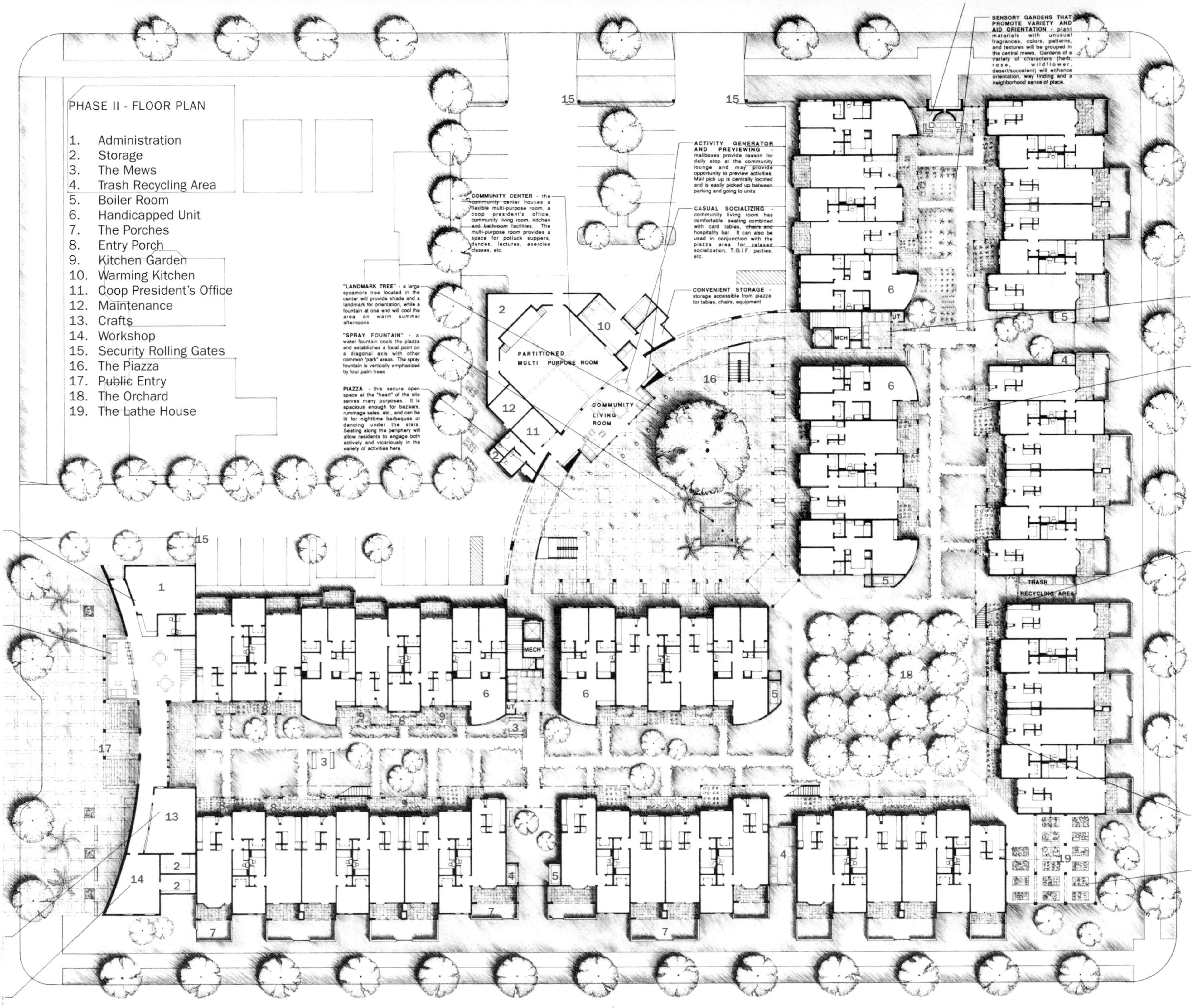
PHASE II - FLOOR PLAN
1. Administration
2. Storage
3. The Mews
4. Trash Recycling Area
5. Boiler Room
6. Handicapped Unit
7. The Porches
8. Entry Porch
9. Kitchen Garden
10. Warming Kitchen
11. Coop President's Office
12. Maintenance
13. Crafts
14. Workshop
15. Security Rolling Gates
16. The Piazza
17. Public Entry
18. The Orchard
19. The Lathe House
COMMUNITY CENTER - the community center houses a flexible multi-purpose room, a coop president's office, community living room, kitchen and bathroom facilities. The multi-purpose room provides a space for potluck suppers, dances, lectures, exercise classes, etc.
"LANDMARK TREE" - a large sycamore tree located in the center will provide shade and a landmark for orientation, while a fountain at one end will cool the area on warm summer afternoons.
"SPRAY FOUNTAIN" - a water fountain cools the piazza and establishes a focal point on a diagonal axis with other common "park" areas. The spray fountain is vertically emphasized by four palm trees
PIAZZA - this secure open space at the "heart" of the site serves many purposes. It is spacious enough for bazaars, rummage sales, etc., and can be lit for nighttime barbeques or dancing under the stars. Seating along the periphery will allow residents to engage both actively and vicariously in the variety of activities here.
ACTIVITY GENERATOR AND PREVIEWING - mailboxes provide reason for daily stop at the community lounge and may provide opportunity to preview activities. Mail pick up is centrally located and is easily picked up between parking and going to units
CASUAL SOCIALIZING - community living room has comfortable seating combined with card tables, chairs and hospitality bar. It can also be used in conjunction with the piazza area for relaxed socialization, T.G.I.F. parties, etc.
CONVENIENT STORAGE - storage accessible from piazza for tables, chairs, equipment
SENSORY GARDENS THAT PROMOTE VARIETY AND AID ORIENTATION - plant materials with unusual fragrances, colors, patterns, and textures will be grouped in the central mews. Gardens of a variety of characters (herb, rose, wildflower, desert/succelent) will enhance orientation, way finding and a neighborhood sense of place.
PARTITIONED MULTI PURPOSE ROOM
COMMUNITY LIVING ROOM
MCH
MECH
UT
TRASH RECYCLING AREA

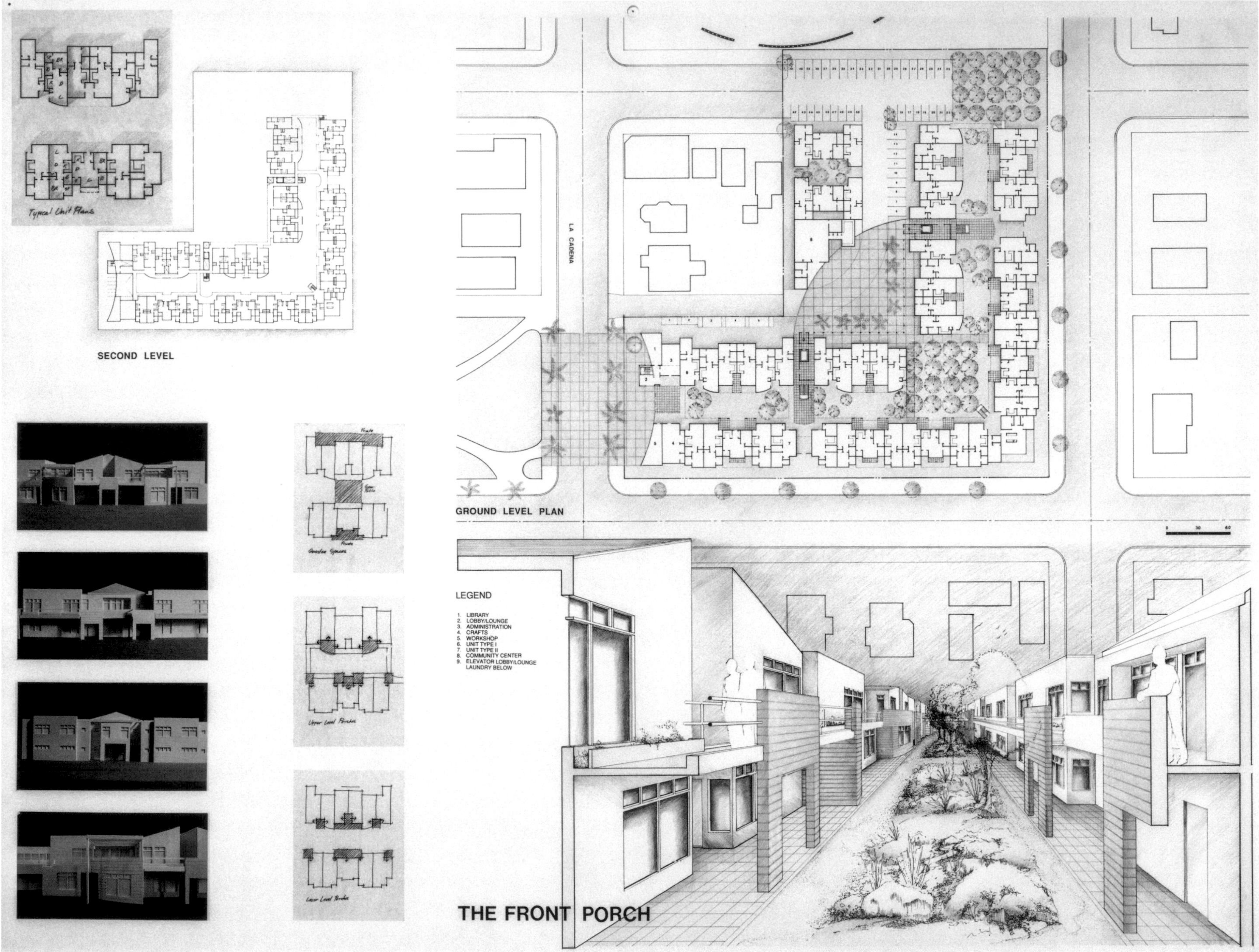
Typical Unit Plans
SECOND LEVEL
LA CADENA
GROUND LEVEL PLAN
0 30 60
LEGEND
1. LIBRARY
2. LOBBY/LOUNGE
3. ADMINISTRATION
4. CRAFTS
5. WORKSHOP
6. UNIT TYPE I
7. UNIT TYPE II
8. COMMUNITY CENTER
9. ELEVATOR LOBBY/LOUNGE
LAUNDRY BELOW
Upper Level Porches
Lower Level Porches
THE FRONT PORCH

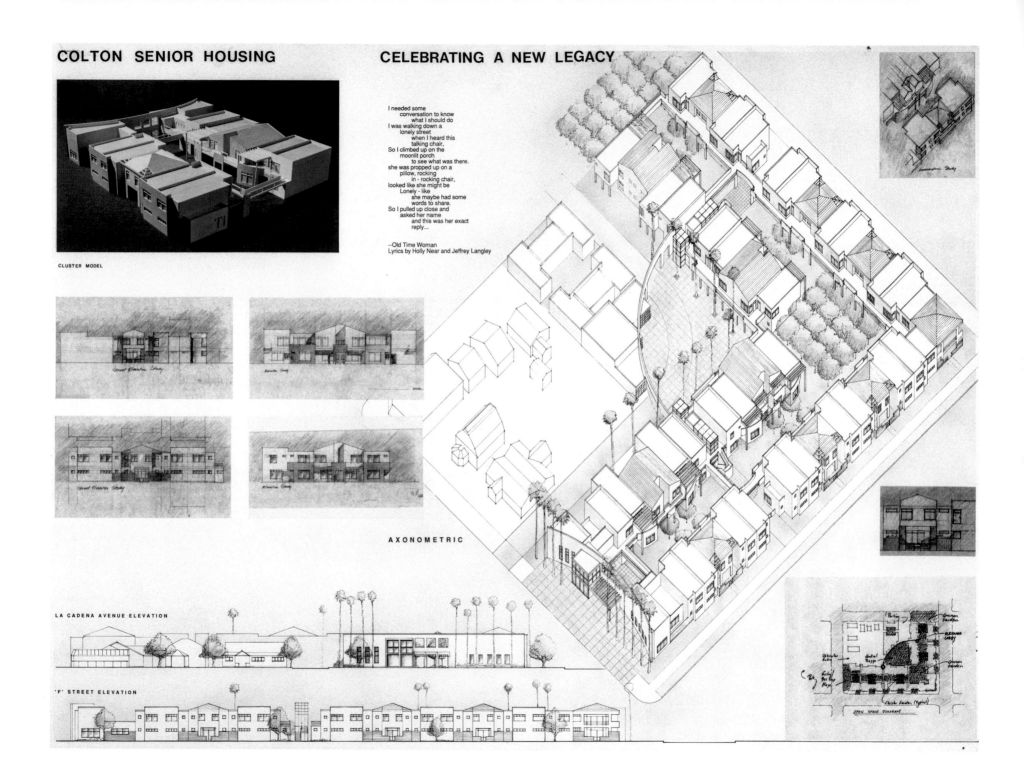

COLTON SENIOR HOUSING

CLUSTER MODEL

CELEBRATING A NEW LEGACY

I needed some
conversation to know
what I should do
I was walking down a
lonely street
when I heard this
talking chair,
So I climbed up on the
moonlit porch
to see what was there.
she was propped up on a
pillow, rocking
in - rocking chair,
looked like she might be
Lonely - like
she maybe had some
words to share.
So I pulled up close and
asked her name
and this was her exact
reply...

--Old Time Woman
Lyrics by Holly Near and Jeffrey Langley

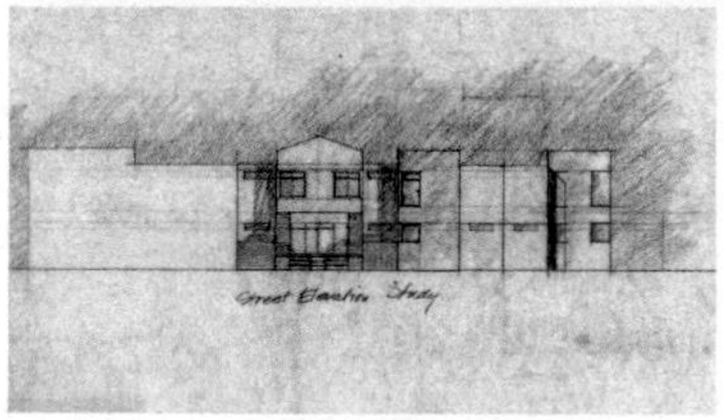

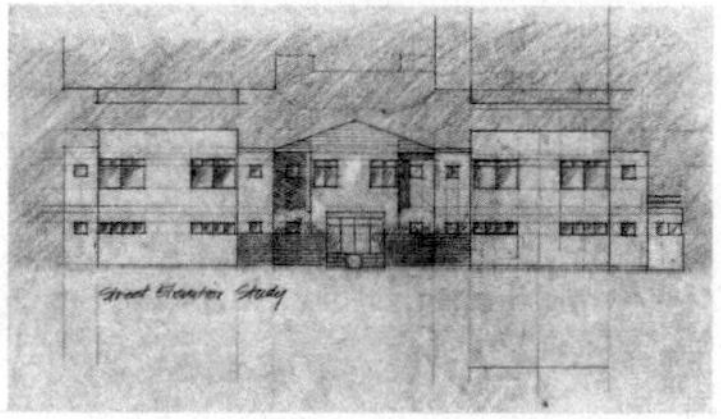

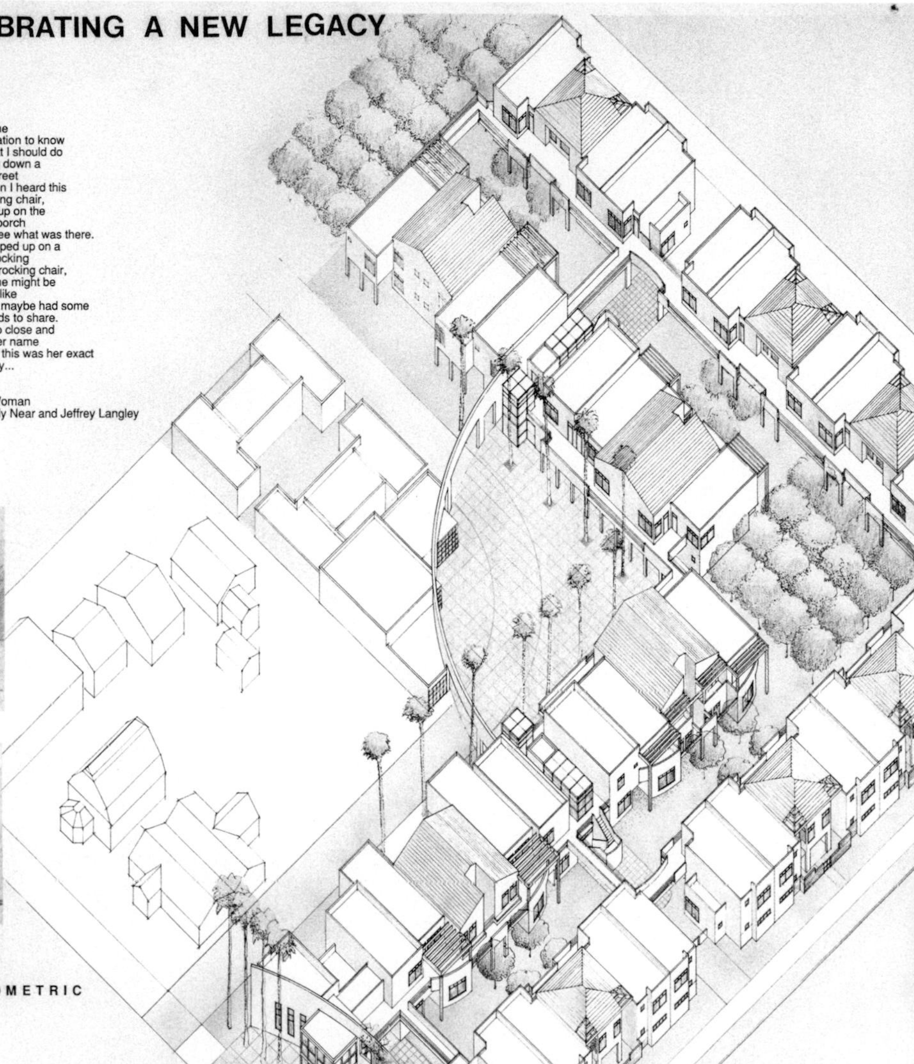

AXONOMETRIC

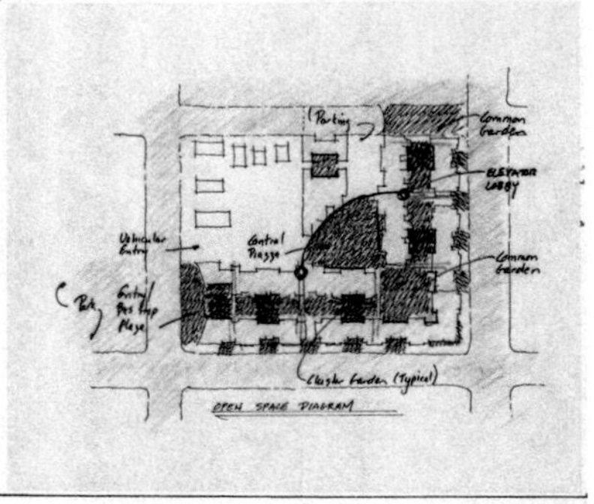

LA CADENA AVENUE ELEVATION

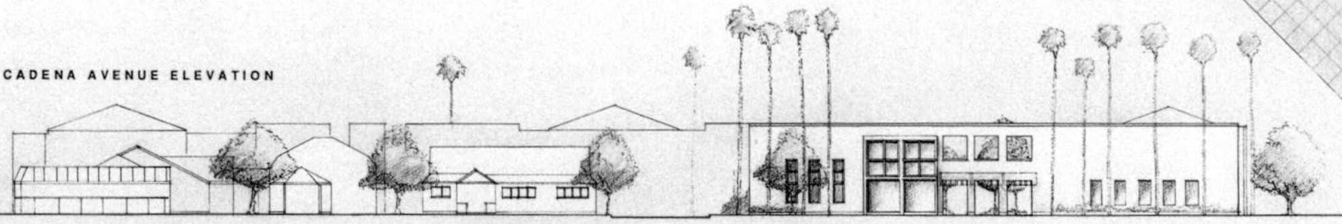

'F' STREET ELEVATION

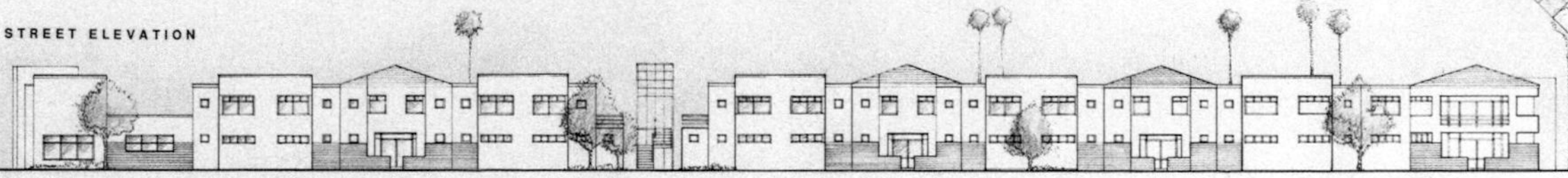

AVALON/EL SEGUNDO SENIOR HOUSING

Willowbrook District
Los Angeles, California
| 1997 |

In 1996 the Southern California, minority-owned development firm, Sustainable Housing Development, Inc., hired Miller Pollin to design forty-two housing units and a community center for low-income senior residents in the Willowbrook District of Los Angeles. During a series of community meetings with neighborhood residents, a number of priorities became clear. These included communal spaces, a common park area, private balconies, and universal accessibility. Miller Pollin added plenty of natural light in the units as well as kitchen gardens in the design process.

While the apartments are all contained within one large structure, Miller Pollin broke up the volume with an ell at each end. The main body of the building is in a soft yellow stucco. Individual units are articulated by porches on the ground floor. The balconies above are formed by darker yellow volumes pulled out from the basic closure walls and rising above the roofline. Moss green outdoor storage closets are housed in projecting vertical volumes that define one side of the balconies and visually partition the apartments. Steel slatted railings open up the balconies in contrast with the solid stucco surfaces. A spine-like corridor runs through the center of the building, providing access to the apartments and ensuring that each unit has access to the outdoors. The main entrance lobby is centrally placed in the middle of the long volume and articulated with a curved roof. Just beneath this roof is one of the common rooms with adjacent social hall with kitchen facilities, laundry and trash collection area. Planted gardens and trees offer shade and a green respite from the Southern California sun.

On a very tight budget, and with the needs of its senior residents in mind, Miller Pollin designed an apartment block with the feel of attached townhouses. The warm yellow of the stucco and the steel detailing of the porches and balconies, together with the contrasting colored wall-slabs that pull away from the body of the building, help to achieve a refined scale of individual units.

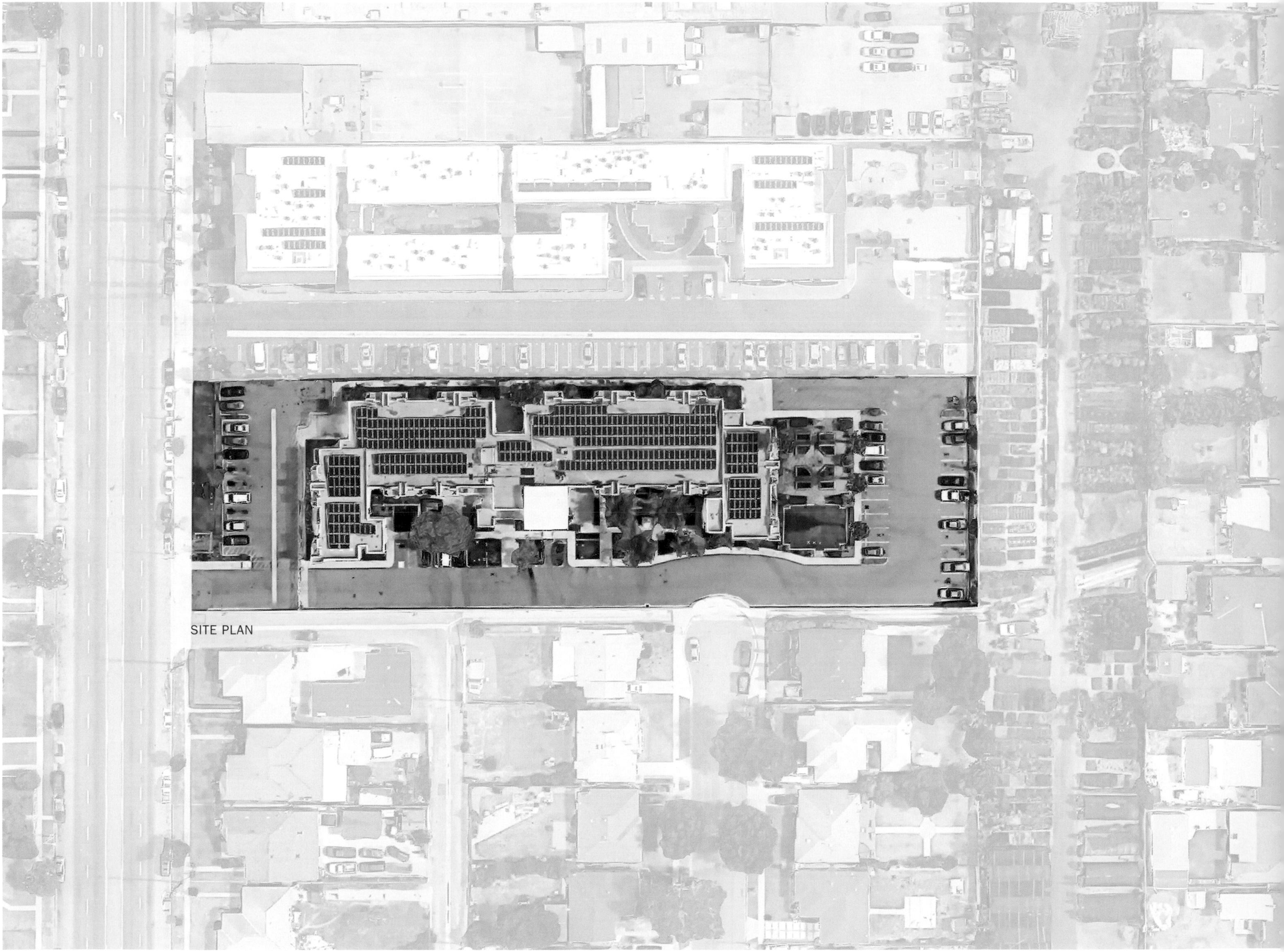

SITE PLAN

0 12 24 48 80ft

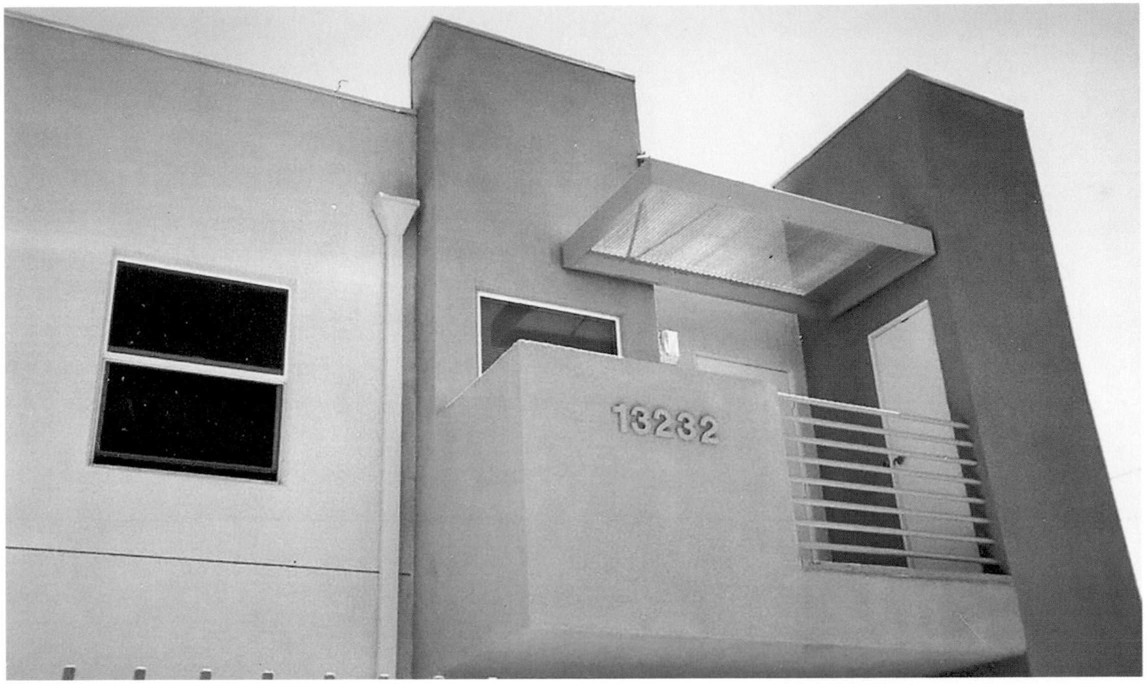
13232

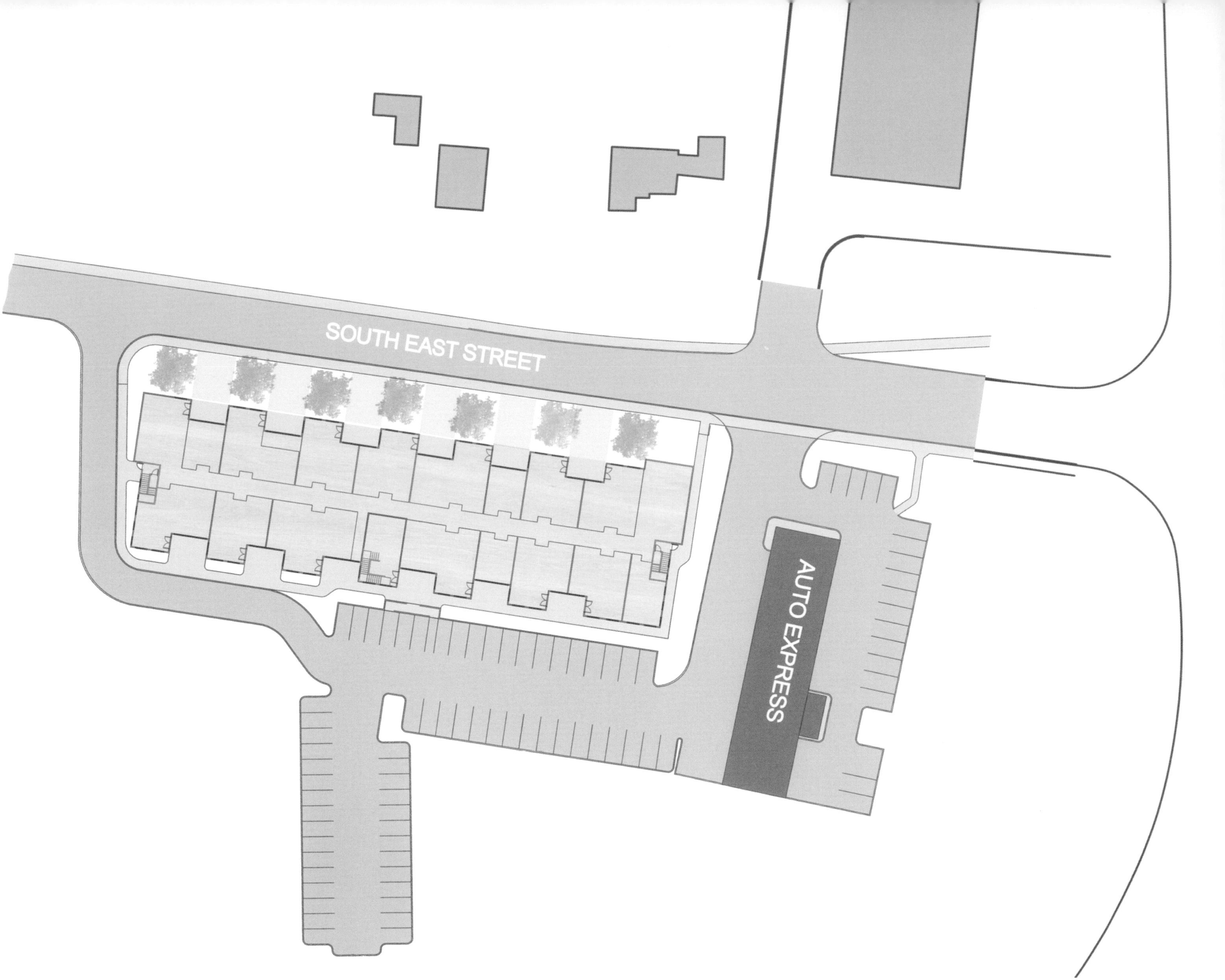
SOUTH EAST STREET
AUTO EXPRESS

SOUTH EAST STREET AFFORDABLE HOUSING
SCHEME 1

Amherst, Massachusetts
| 2005 | (Unbuilt)

Miller Pollin was commissioned by a local property owner to design 40 units of one- and two-bedroom affordable housing units in South Amherst. Scheme 1, located on the east side of the street, is comprised of interlocking townhouse units on three levels. The northern end of the building is designed for commercial use. These were included to generate income for the complex in order to make units more affordable. Optional ground level units could be leased for retail as well. All units have a small balcony. The exterior materials combine the traditional red brick found in the region with painted board and batten wood siding, which is also part of the regional vocabulary. Roofs are South facing and equipped with photovoltaic panels.

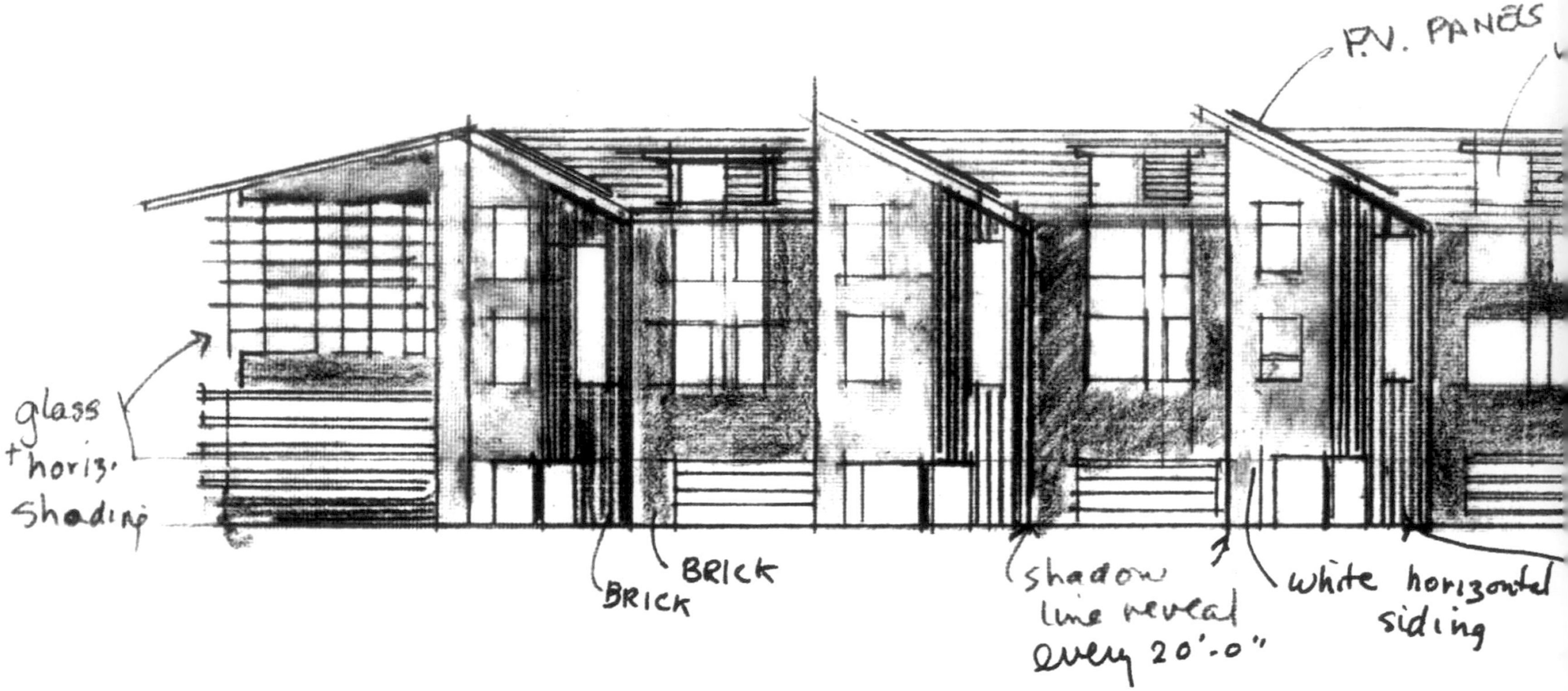

WEST / STREET ELEVATION

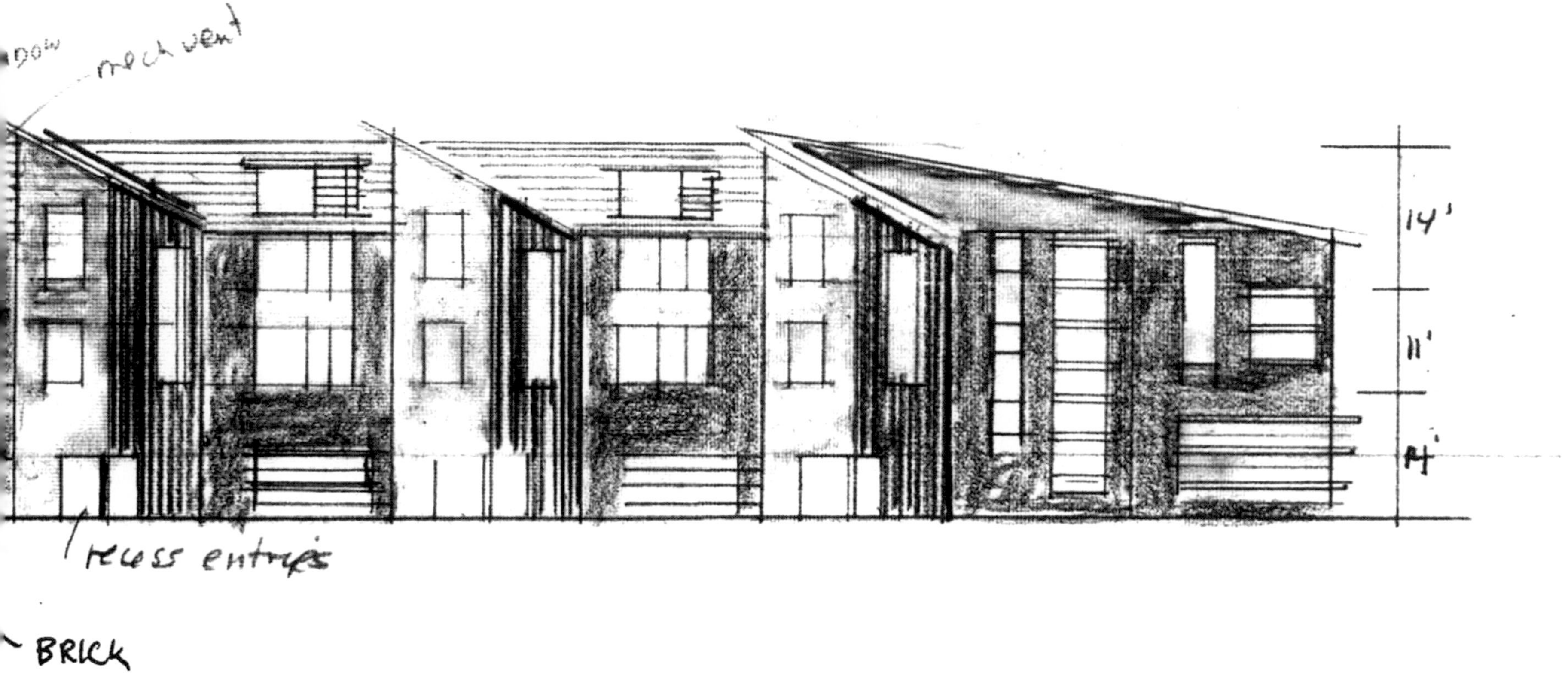
mech vent
14'
11'
recess entries
BRICK

IPODIA
DAHLIA
PRODUCTS

AMIR'S PASTRY

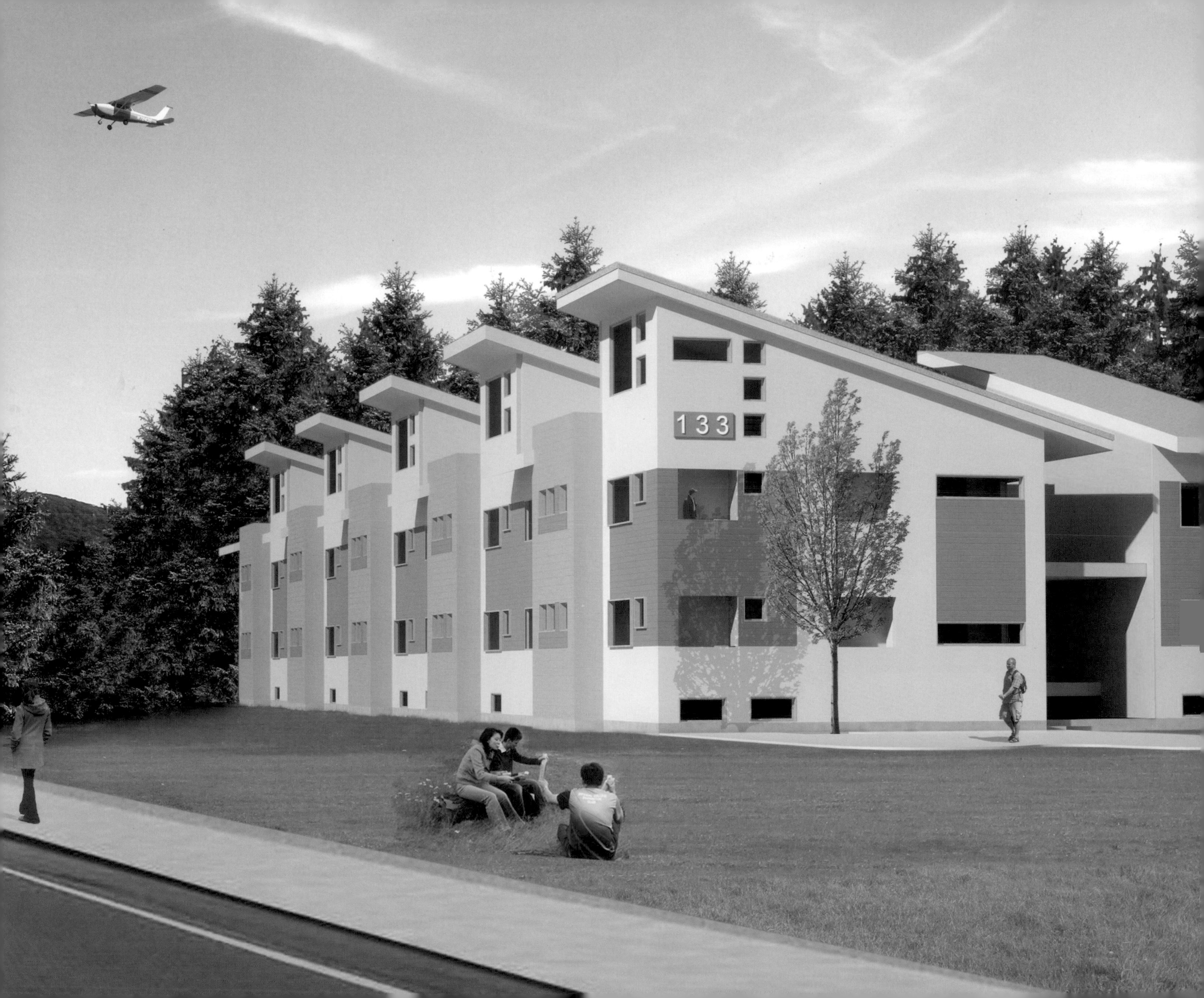
133

SOUTH EAST STREET AFFORDABLE HOUSING
SCHEME 2

Amherst, Massachusetts
| 2005 | (Unbuilt)

The property owner also asked Miller Pollin to design an alternative scheme for a site across the street on the west side. This scheme wraps around a rear parking area, keeping the parking area away from street view, an approach favored by town planners. The units are on two levels and a semi-underground level is designed to house storage and common space. The sloped roofs which alternate in direction and the white tones of the exterior give the structure a contemporary feel.

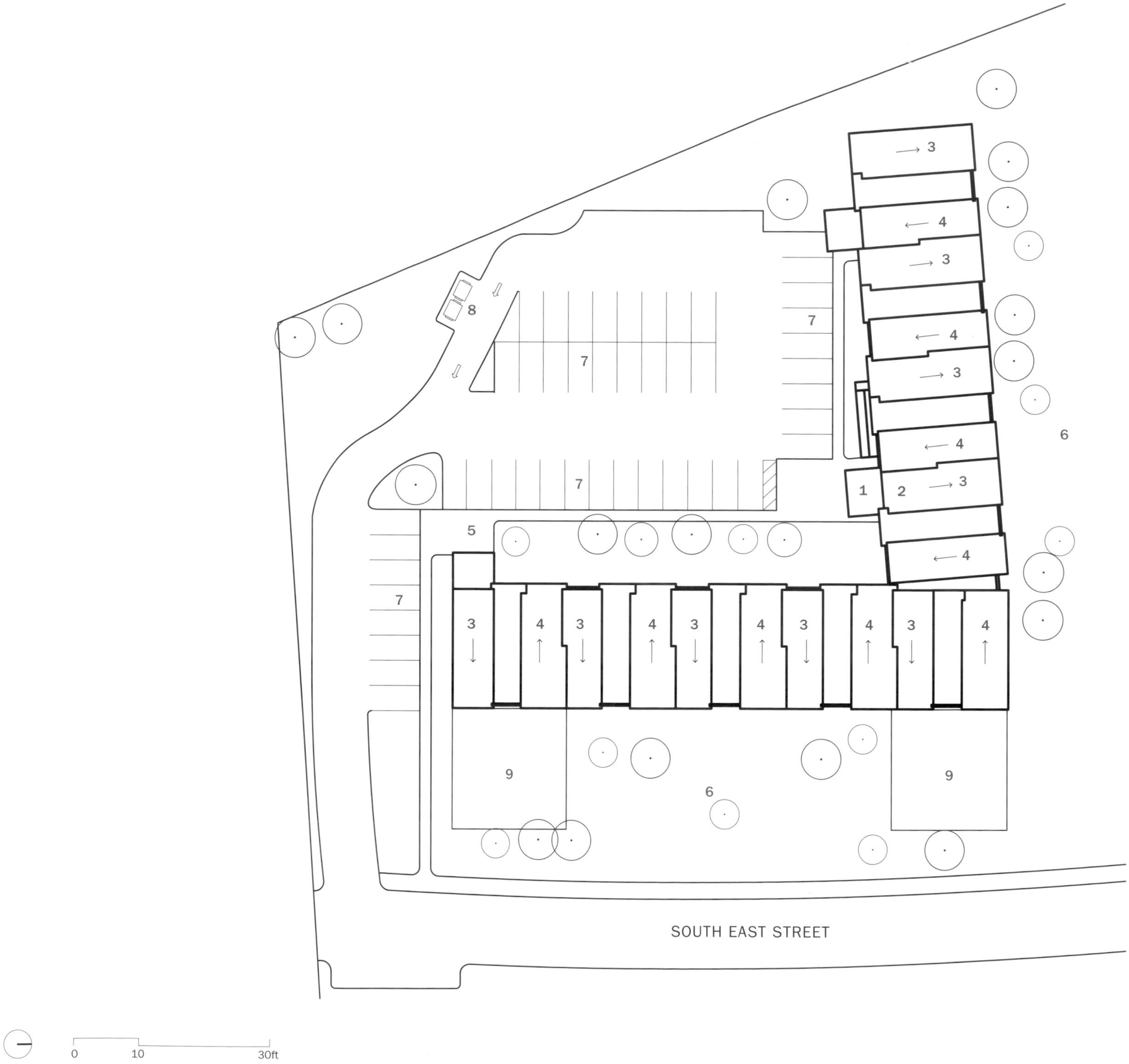
3
4
3
4
3
4
3
4
8
7
7
7
1
2
6
5
7
3
4
3
4
3
4
3
4
3
4
9
6
9
SOUTH EAST STREET
0
10
30ft

SITE PLAN

1. Main Entrance
2. Multi-Family Residential Building
3. Down-Slope
4. Up-Slope
5. Sidewalk
6. Lawn
7. Parking
8. Trash and Recycling
9. Patio

TYPICAL APARTMENT UNIT

1. Entry
2. Kitchen
3. Living Room
4. Bedroom
5. Bathroom
6. Porch

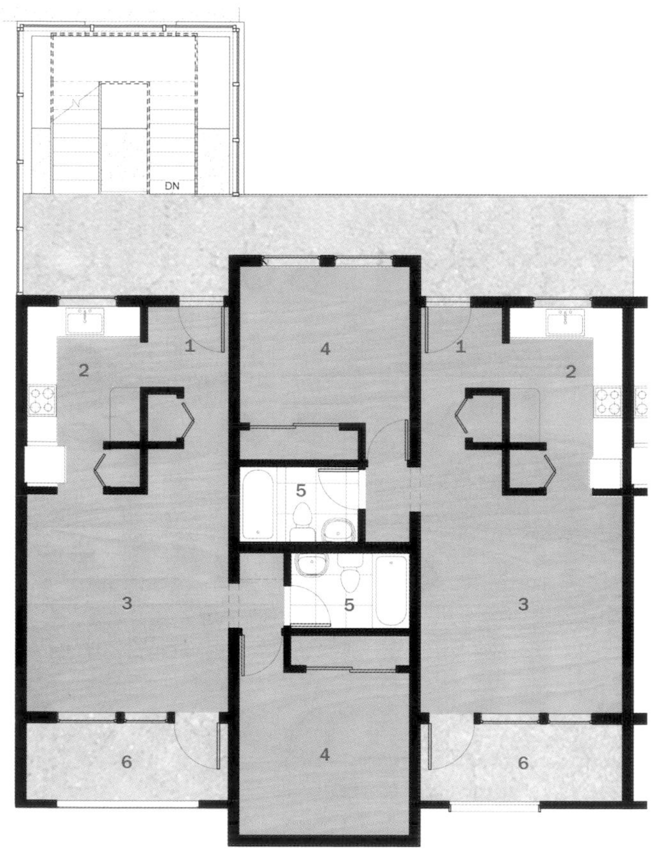

GROUND FLOOR UNIT - 610 SF EACH

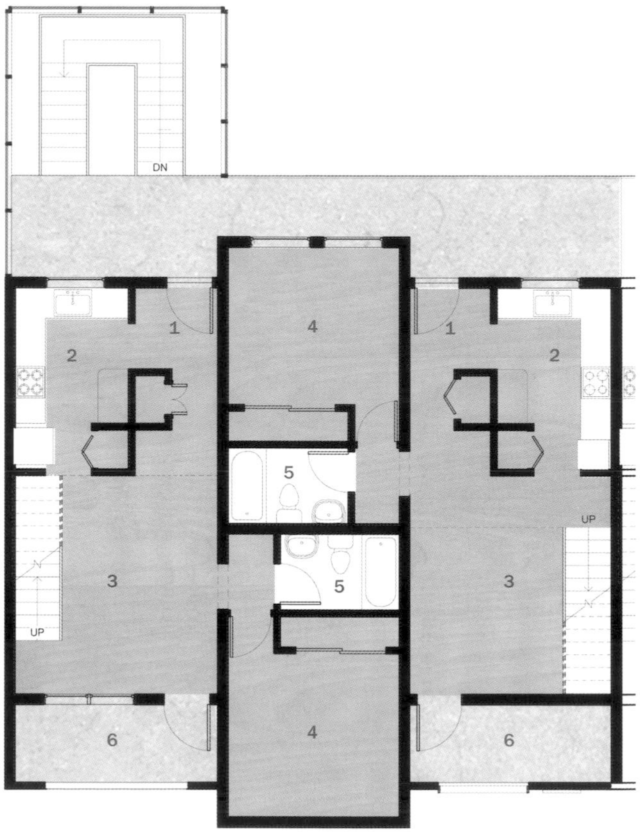

SECOND FLOOR UNIT WITH LOFT - 810 SF EACH

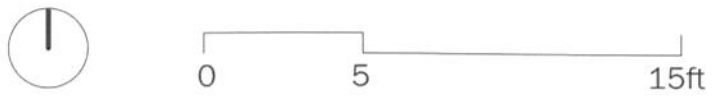

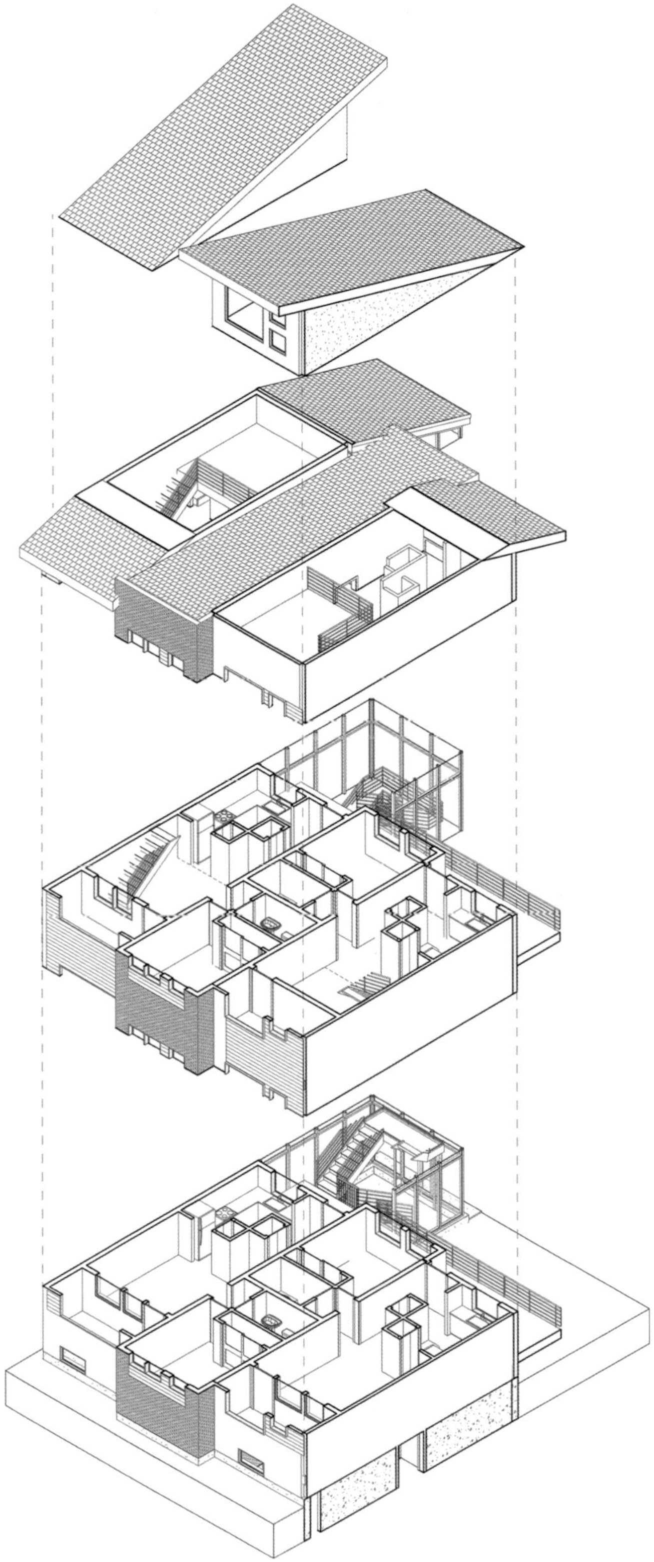

[QUESTIONS]

LANDSCAPE OF LEARNING

TOUCH-ME ARCHIFABRIC

CHAMELEONIC PYLONS

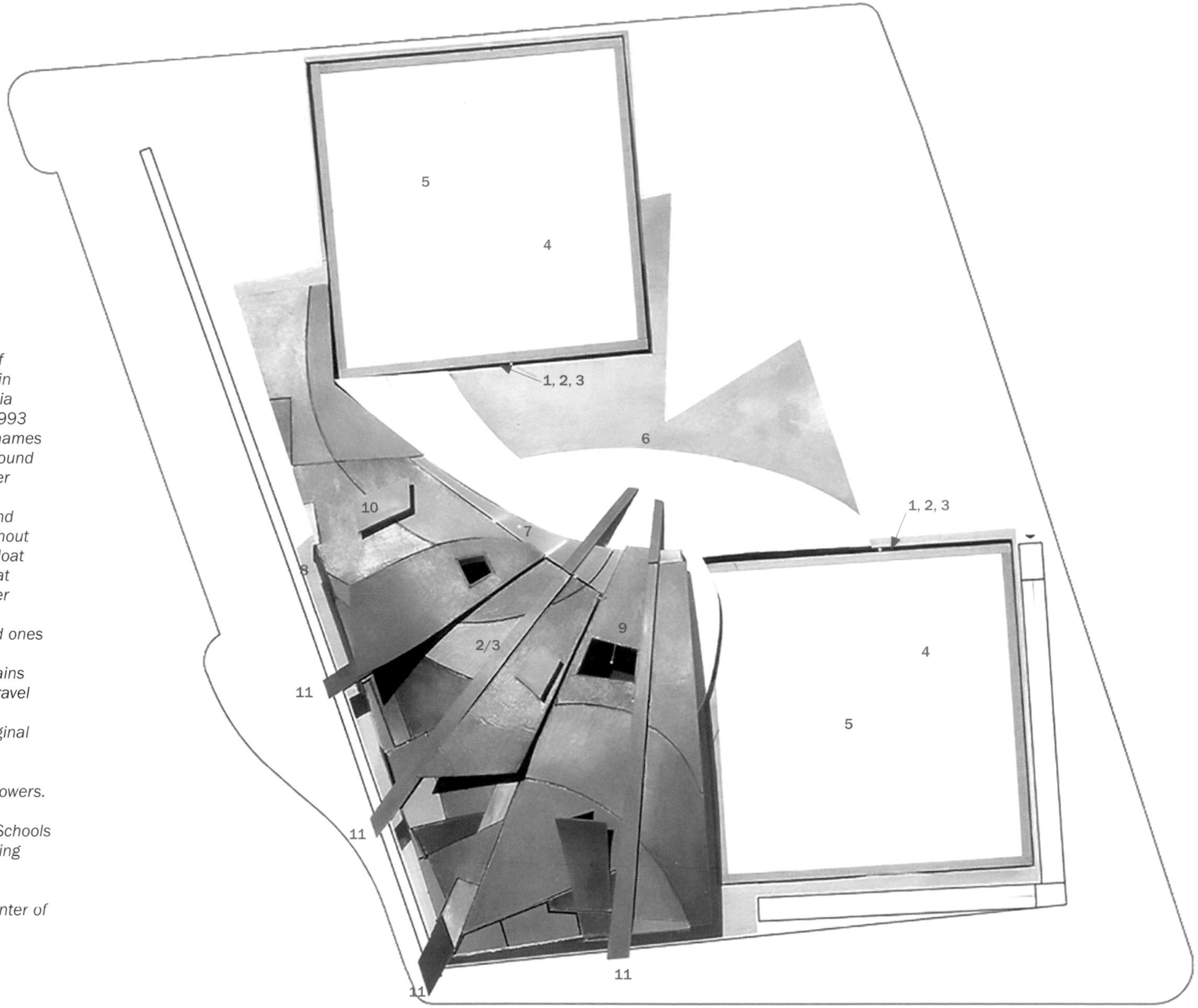

FLOOR PLAN

1. *Recognition of all victims of September 11, 2001 attacks in New York, Virginia, Pennsylvania and victims of February 26, 1993 terrorist bombing of WTC. All names will be listed alphabetically around the perimeter of the Twin Tower footprints.*
2. *Quiet areas for visitation and contemplation located throughout landscape membrane which float atop the learning center and at the perimeter of the WTC tower footprints.*
3. *Areas for families and loved ones of victims.*
4. *Final resting place for remains (buried below raked granite gravel bed).*
5. *Visible footprints of the original World Trade Center Towers.*
6. *Public Amphitheater*
7. *Connecting path between towers.*
8. *Visible existing slurry wall*
9. *Courtyards for NYC Public Schools Center for International Learning*
10. *Projecting skylights*
11. *Bridges and ramps from sidewalk to lower level and center of Memorial site.*

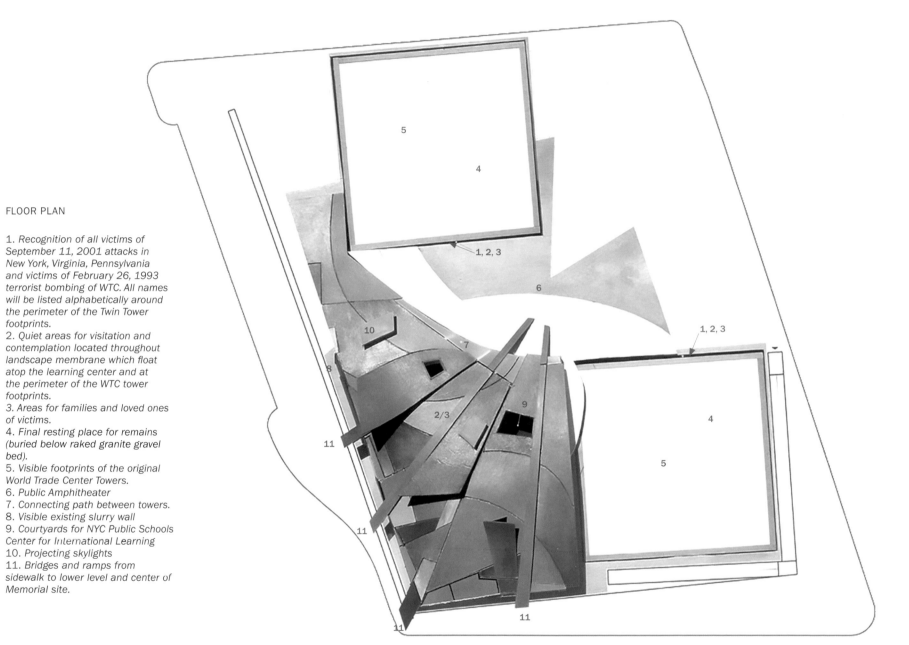

LANDSCAPE OF LEARNING

World Trade Center Competition
Miller Pollin Architecture with Professor Max Page
| 2004 |

In 2003 the Lower Manhattan Development Corporation announced an open competition for a memorial to the World Trade Center at the site where the Twin Towers were destroyed by terrorists on September 11, 2001. There were over 5,000 entries from sixty-three nations. The guidelines required that the footprints of the buildings remained untouched and that the memorial remember those who died, recognize the strength of those who survived, and the courage of those who came to the rescue. For their design of this profoundly moving site, Miller Pollin and UMass Amherst colleague Max Page envisioned an active exchange between the past and future. They presented the idea of a new school for international students of the five boroughs, set around the untouched footprints of the Twin Towers. They argued that such a school would celebrate the "human capital" of this great city. This "landscape of learning" would be set within a park-like setting of verdant green roofs housing classrooms, art and music studios, and courtyards and gardens. Gently sloping upturned roofs and glass walls would give visitors glimpses into the activities of the students as they walked toward the quieter, contemplative spaces to remember and honor those whose lives were lost. An amphitheater served as a bridge between the bustle of the school and the reflective spaces of the memorial. Red granite walls lined the tower outlines, etched with the names of those who lost their lives on that fateful day.

In their description of the project, Miller Pollin and Page cited the GI Bill enacted after World War II as an example of a memorial which honored the dead by investing in the living. They saw their designs in a similar light, as a means of bringing the past and the future together, with honor, reverence and optimism. The following text was submitted with the design proposal for the competition.

A LANDSCAPE OF LEARNING

Ground zero will soon be ringed by office towers, monuments to private capitalism. But down below, around the foundations of the Twin Towers, the public sphere should hold sway. New York should use the funds for a memorial to invest in what has always made New York great: not its private capital but its human capital. Instead of spending millions making a tourist destination and a lovely front lawn for financial firms, we propose a totally different memorial idea: invest in New York's future by creating a public school for international education, a landscape of learning at the site of Ground Zero.

We want to defy the New York State Appeals Court's recent decision that an eighth-grade education is all that New York City's young people need. Instead, we propose to create a public school designed to house after-school, weekend, and summer programs for New York City public school students to learn about the music, literature, and art of other cultures, to debate world politics, and learn from one another about the people of their remarkably diverse city, what E.B. White called "the greatest human concentration on earth, the poem whose magic is comprehensible to millions." Over the past three decades we have let that magic of New York—not the skyscrapers but the convulsive human life of the city—become

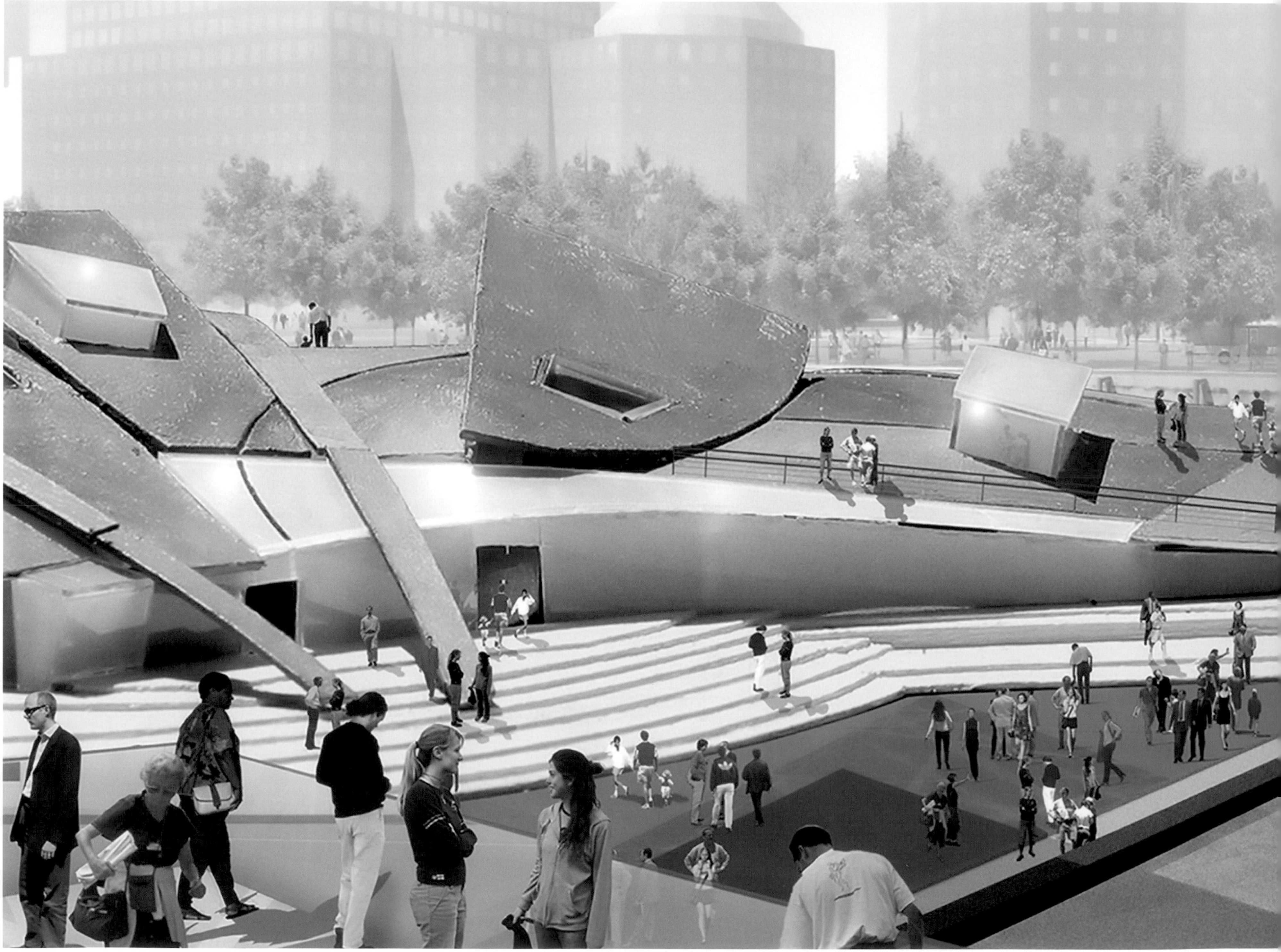

weakened by an unerring focus on building the monuments to finance and world trade. Now that it is time to rebuild the World Trade Center site, it should also be the time to affirm a new faith in public life.

We have done this before. After World War II, the country didn't build a triumphant physical memorial to the soldiers lost in battle (only now, fifty years later, are we building a memorial on the Mall in Washington). Instead, Congress passed the GI Bill and invested hundreds of millions of dollars in giving veterans access to education, loans, and decent housing. That helped launch the greatest expansion of the middle class the country has ever seen. Their living success was perhaps the finest memorial the dead could have asked for. So let us mark the anniversary of 9/11 by choosing to make New York's young people living memorials to those lost on September 11. Austrian writer Robert Musil famously wrote, "There is nothing in this world as invisible as a monument." But the sounds of young New Yorkers of every hue and tongue, laughing and learning at Ground Zero, would hardly be invisible. And it would be impossible to forget.

TOUCH-ME ARCHIFABRIC

D3 Nature Competition
Lower Manhattan, NYC
| 2012 |

Miller Pollin Architecture's entry into the 2012 D3 Nature Competition was an exploration of biomimicry in combination with a focus on the advanced technology of conductive ink. Conductive ink essentially results in a print or drawing that is capable of conducting electricity. The competition allowed entrants to select a site appropriate for their investigation. Miller Pollin selected a subway stop in Lower Manhattan at Greenwich Street and Trinity Place as a location for an above-ground passenger pavilion. The goal of the research and proposal was to create a closure membrane that could be responsive to the environment—open on a sunny day and closing in inclement weather. The team developed a scheme for a protective membrane composed of a large scale conductive ink drawing sandwiched between layers of translucent recycled plastic supported by steel arching frames. In the botanical aspect of the proposal, the team studied the Mimosa Pudica—a plant that responds to touch by closing up. The competition team translated the possibility for this kind of movement into the shelter membrane.

Touch-Me Archifabric is a protective membrane responsive in a range of ways to the environment. The membrane can be activated by touch, sound, or light. The conductive ink can be used to create a limitless range of imagery. The membrane's activation includes micro openings and macro openings depending on need. It can provide shelter from rain when all apertures are closed or allow natural ventilation when they are open. It is a smart skin that can allow an interior space to breathe in response to climatic conditions.

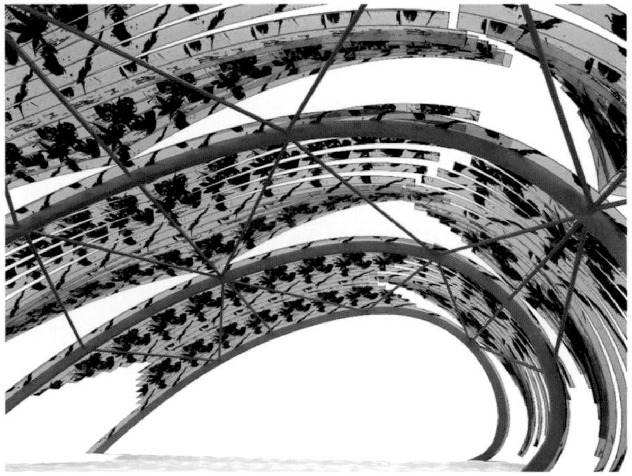

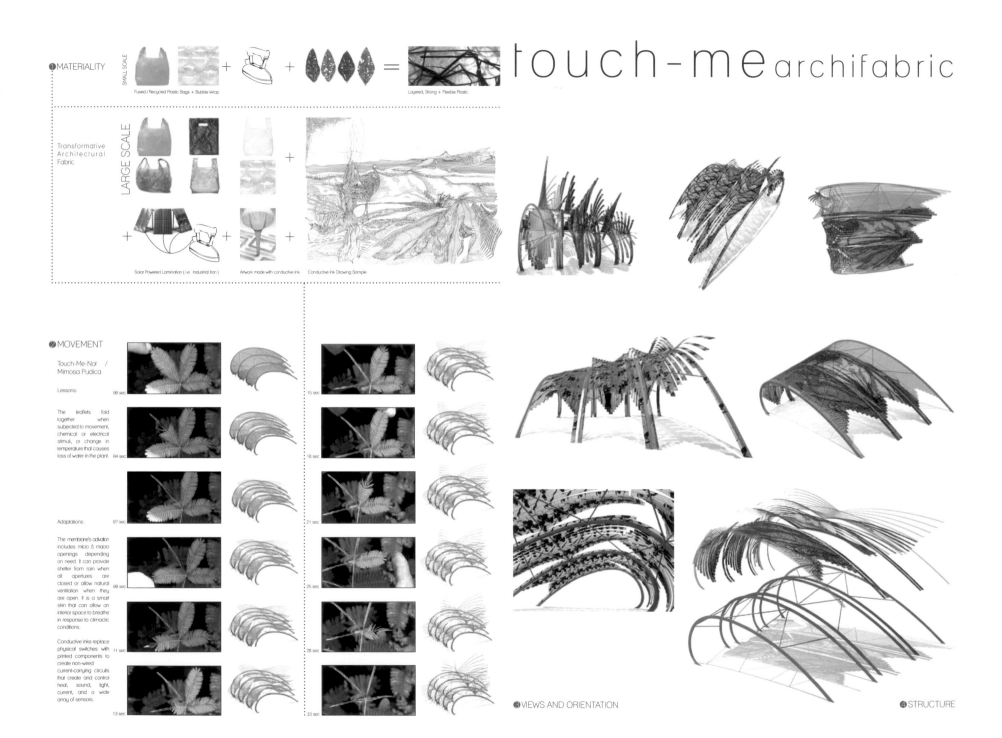

touch-me archifabric

1 MATERIALITY

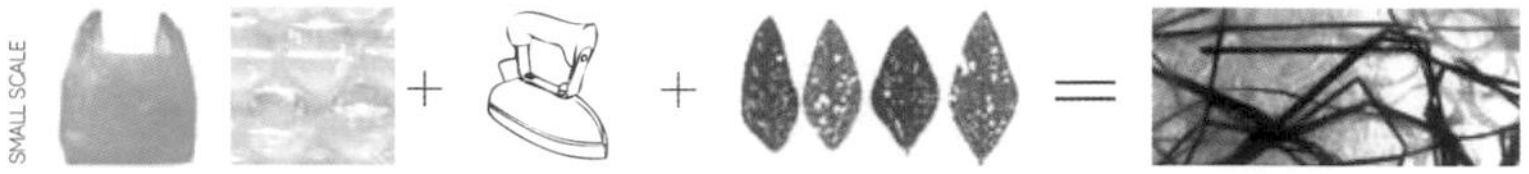

Fused / Recycled Plastic Bags + Bubble Wrap

Layered, Strong + Flexible Plastic

Transformative Architectural Fabric

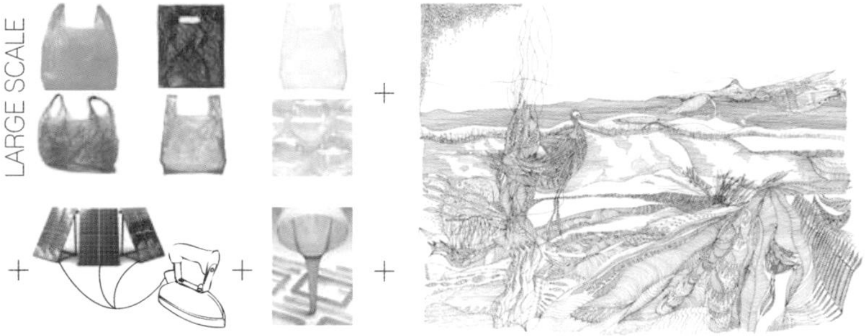

Solar Powered Lamination (i.e. Industrial Iron)

Artwork made with conductive ink

Conductive Ink Drawing Sample

2 MOVEMENT

Touch-Me-Not / Mimosa Pudica

Lessons:

The leaflets fold together when subjected to movement, chemical or electrical stimuli, or change in temperature that causes loss of water in the plant.

Adaptations:

The membrane's activation includes micro & macro openings depending on need. It can provide shelter from rain when all apertures are closed or allow natural ventilation when they are open. It is a smart skin that can allow an interior space to breathe in response to climactic conditions.

Conductive inks replace physical switches with printed components to create non-wired current-carrying circuits that create and control heat, sound, light, current, and a wide array of sensors.

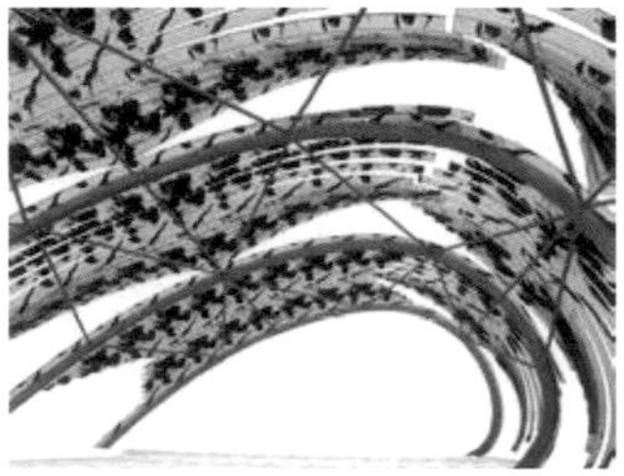

3 VIEWS AND ORIENTATION

4 STRUCTURE

touch-me archifabric

5 IMPLEMENTATION

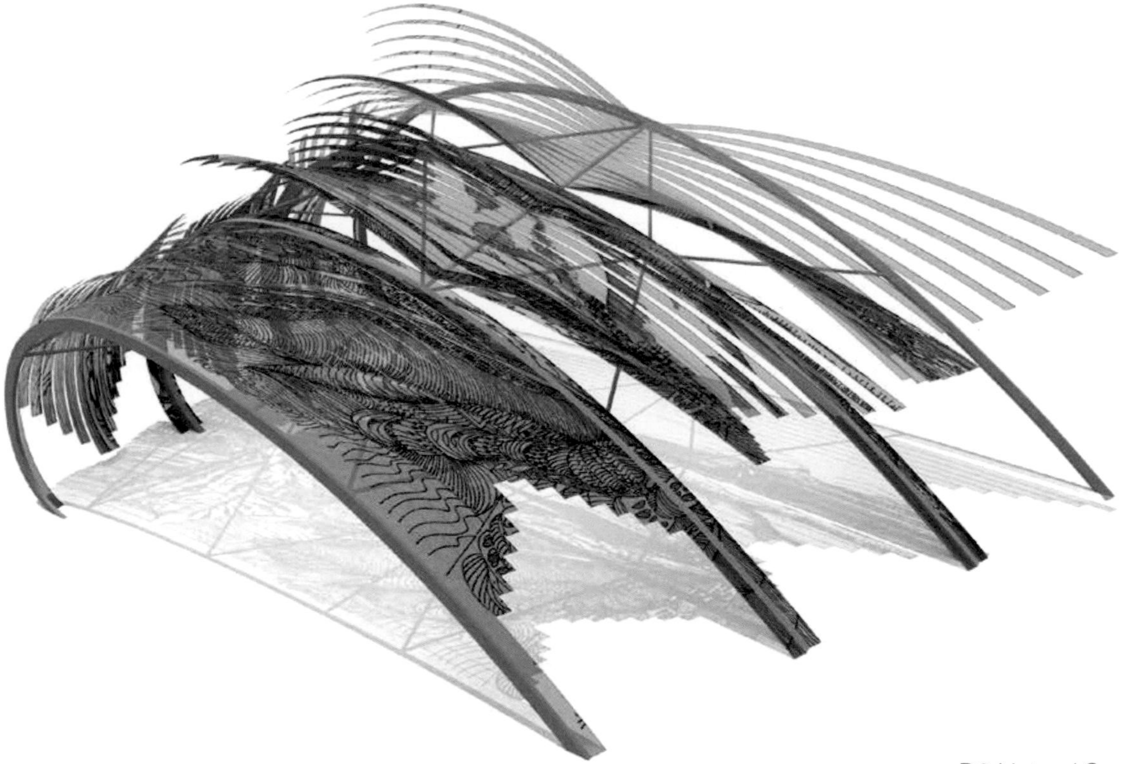

D3 Natural Systems

CHAMELEONIC PYLONS

Nano Tube Structural Configuration
| 2011 |

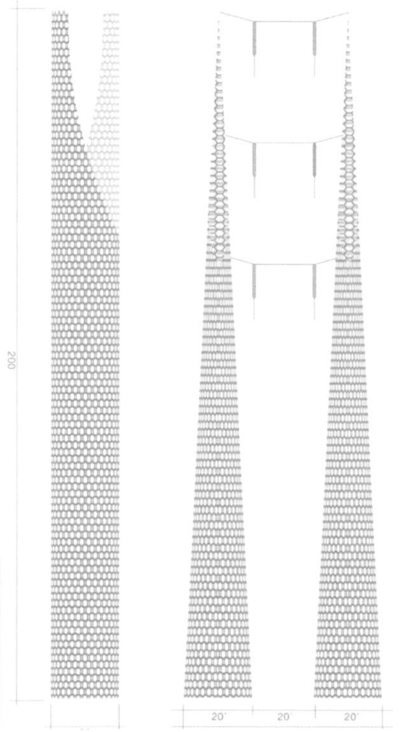

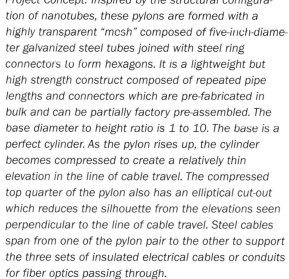

The brief presented by the Royal Institute of British Architects called for re-imagining the structure and appearance of high tension wire towers that dot the British countryside. The following is the text Miller Pollin submitted to the competition.

Project Concept: Inspired by the structural configuration of nanotubes, these pylons are formed with a highly transparent "mesh" composed of five-inch-diameter galvanized steel tubes joined with steel ring connectors to form hexagons. It is a lightweight but high strength construct composed of repeated pipe lengths and connectors which are pre-fabricated in bulk and can be partially factory pre-assembled. The base diameter to height ratio is 1 to 10. The base is a perfect cylinder. As the pylon rises up, the cylinder becomes compressed to create a relatively thin elevation in the line of cable travel. The compressed top quarter of the pylon also has an elliptical cut-out which reduces the silhouette from the elevations seen perpendicular to the line of cable travel. Steel cables span from one of the pylon pair to the other to support the three sets of insulated electrical cables or conduits for fiber optics passing through.

The steel mesh form can be painted to harmonize with the color palette of the landscape in a chameleonic manner. The pylons appear and disappear simultaneously depending on the color relationship to the landscape and skyscape. They are shown in the presented rendering with cloud white (near the base against green foliage), sky blue in the mid-portion and forest green at the top (against white clouds).

Like many architects with small practices and involvement in academia, Miller Pollin has participated in international competitions as a way of exploring ideas, technologies, and questions beyond the scope of client-based projects. This project and the previous one are part of this vein of the practice.

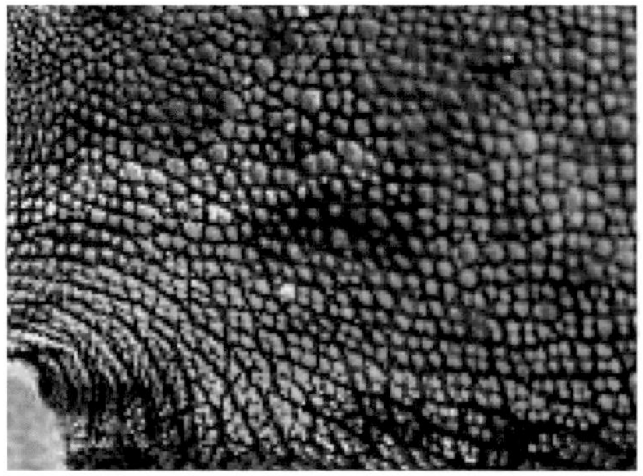

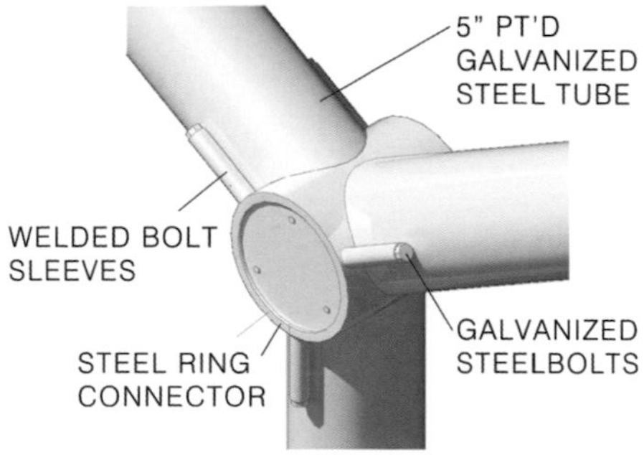

[LEARNING & PERFORMING]

RIVERSIDE SCHOOL FOR THE ARTS

AMERICAN MUSEUM OF TORT LAW

RIVERSIDE SCHOOL FOR THE ARTS

Riverside, California
| 2004 |

SCHEME I

In 2004, the President of Riverside Community College asked Miller Pollin to design a Center for the Performing Arts in downtown Riverside. This was envisioned as a cultural hub for the community college as well as a means of revitalizing the downtown. The concept revolved around bringing together art students from the community college, the University of California Riverside, and local high schools. The work was to be done in stages, and Miller Pollin developed a scheme with four phases of building. The first would feature a black-box theatre, an auditorium, and a gallery fronting University Avenue. Across a pedestrian plaza was a café and administration building. Phase II added to this another theatre, library, and bookstore. Across the plaza, also fronting University Avenue, were several more studios as part of Phase III. Phase IV planned for new student housing along the park side of the project.

SCHEME II

Disparate elements are tied together via an S-curve circulation spine. This continued over the pedestrian plaza, uniting both sides of this urban campus. As seen in the models and site plan, the curving form adds a unifying energy to the city grid.

Though the funding did not materialize for the project, it illustrates Miller Pollin's approach to larger-scale urban planning projects. Once again, she recognized the historic context of the City's grid, incorporated elements of this orthogonal approach, and then, with the swooping S curve, added an elegant circulation system which tied the whole together. Prior to this scheme, Miller Pollin Architecture produced several other schematic designs. They were to be sited in a single block near White Park in downtown Riverside.

The second scheme developed with two interactive elevations—one facing White Park with a variety of horizontal gallery windows and upper level terraces, and the other with its curvilinear fragmented façade incorporating digital screens for projecting outdoor films or art installations accessible to the public. It included a transformation of the traditional street arcade, providing a shaded sidewalk on the avenue.

FIRST LEVEL

1. Main Entrance Lounge
2. Card Control Entry
3. Information Wall
4. Lecture Hall
5. Projection / Control Room
6. Performance Lab
7. Prep Area
8. Green Room & Dressing Rooms
9. Gallery
10. Elevator Lobby
11. Toilet Rooms
12. Janitor's Closet
13. Storage
14. Mechanical Room
15. Service Drive

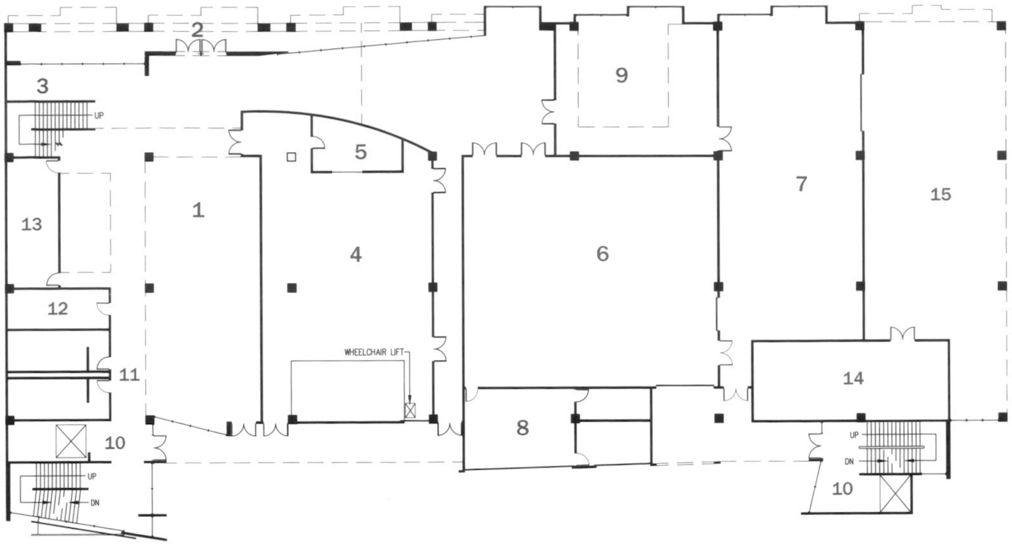

SECOND LEVEL

1. Lecture
2. Open to Below
3. Deans Office
4. Career office
5. Meeting Room
6. Computer Lab
7. Data Closet
8. Storage
9. Elevator Lobby
10. Toilet Rooms
11. AV/TV Room
12. Instr. Med.

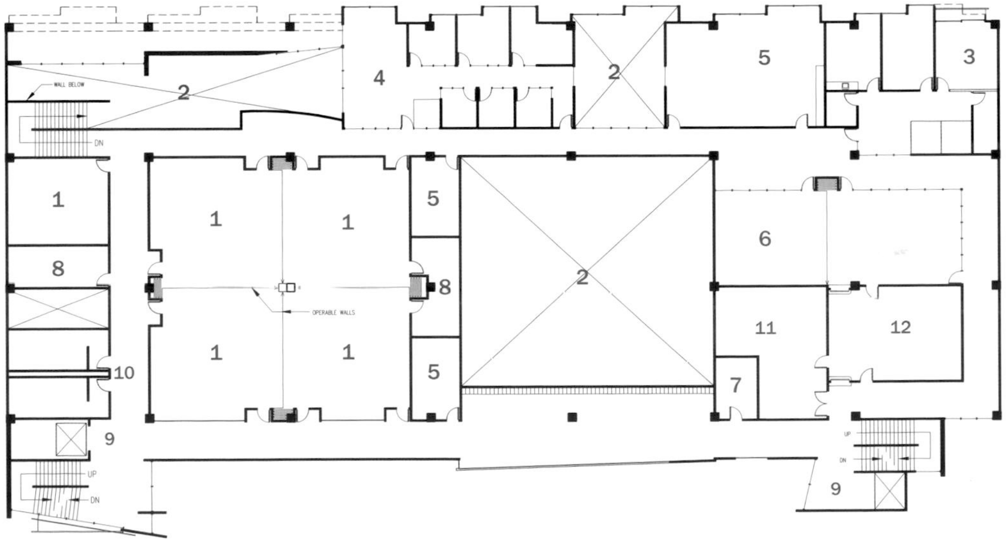

THIRD LEVEL

1. Performance
2. Common Performance
3. Visual Arts
4. Design Lab
5. Practice Rooms
6. Lecture
7. Balcony
8. Instrument Storage
9. Data Closet
10. Elevator Lobby
11. Toilet Rooms

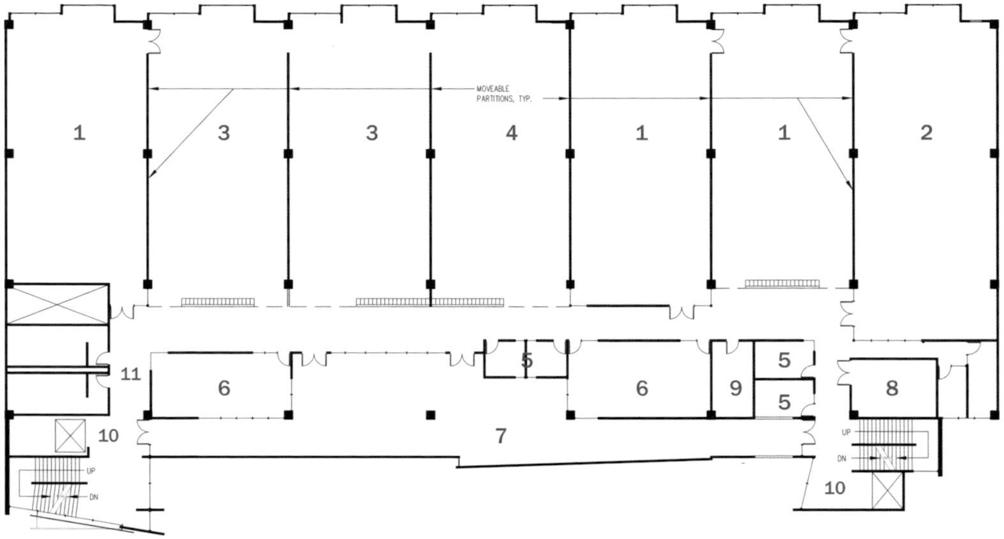

FOURTH LEVEL

1. Studios
2. Faculty Offices
3. Lecture
4. Meeting Room
5. Data
6. Storage
7. Open to Below
8. Deck
9. Elevator Lobby
10. Toilet Rooms

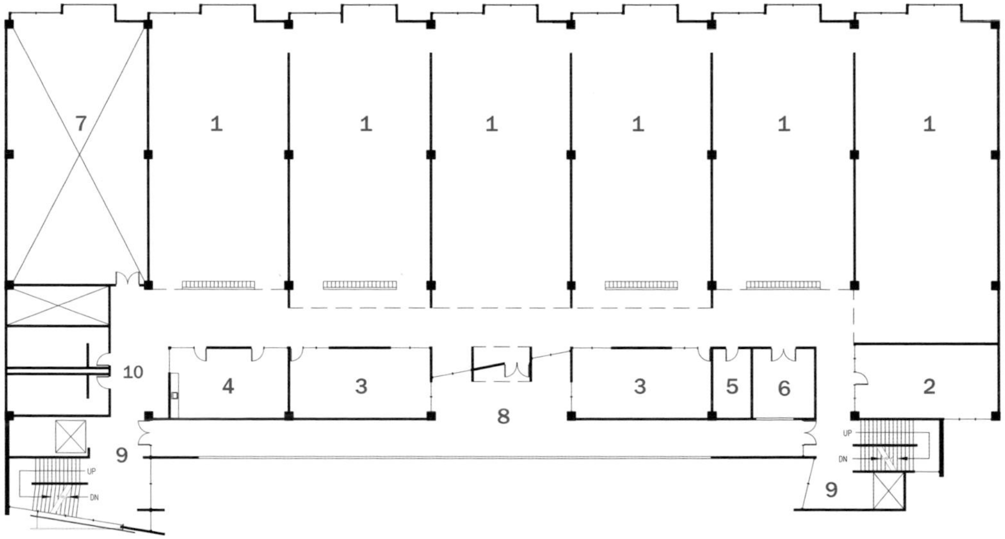

1
2
2
2
3

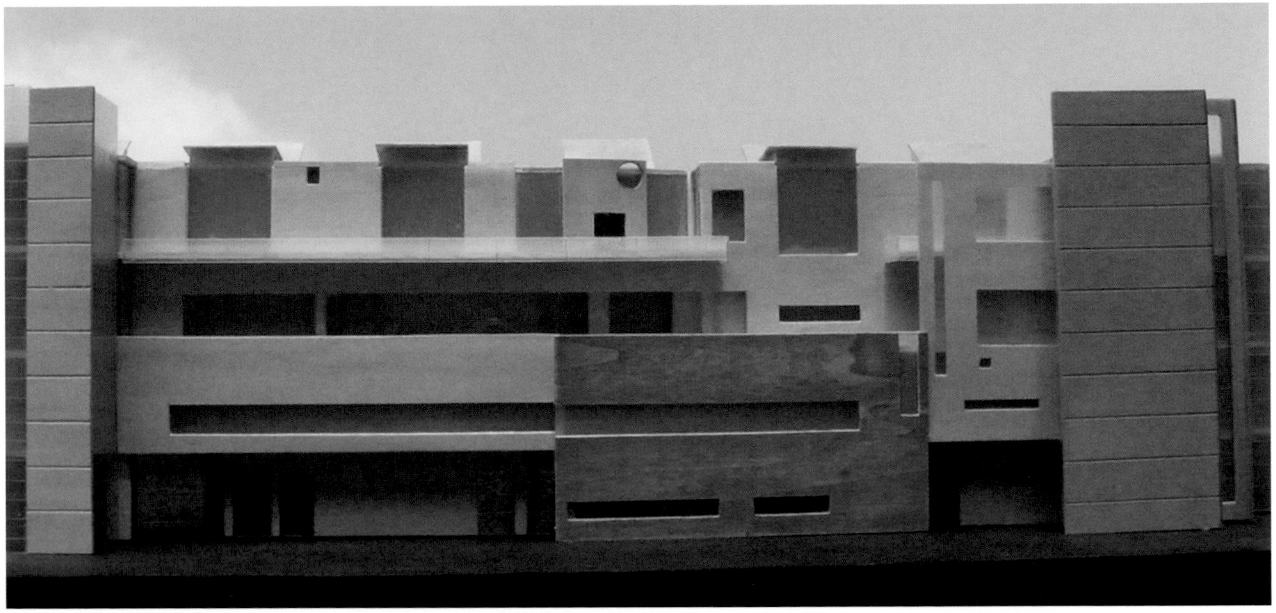

EXISTING SITE PLAN

1. Scheme 1
2. Scheme 2
3. White Park

<- RENDERING

1. Solar Panels
2. Digital Screens
3. Walkway / Arcade

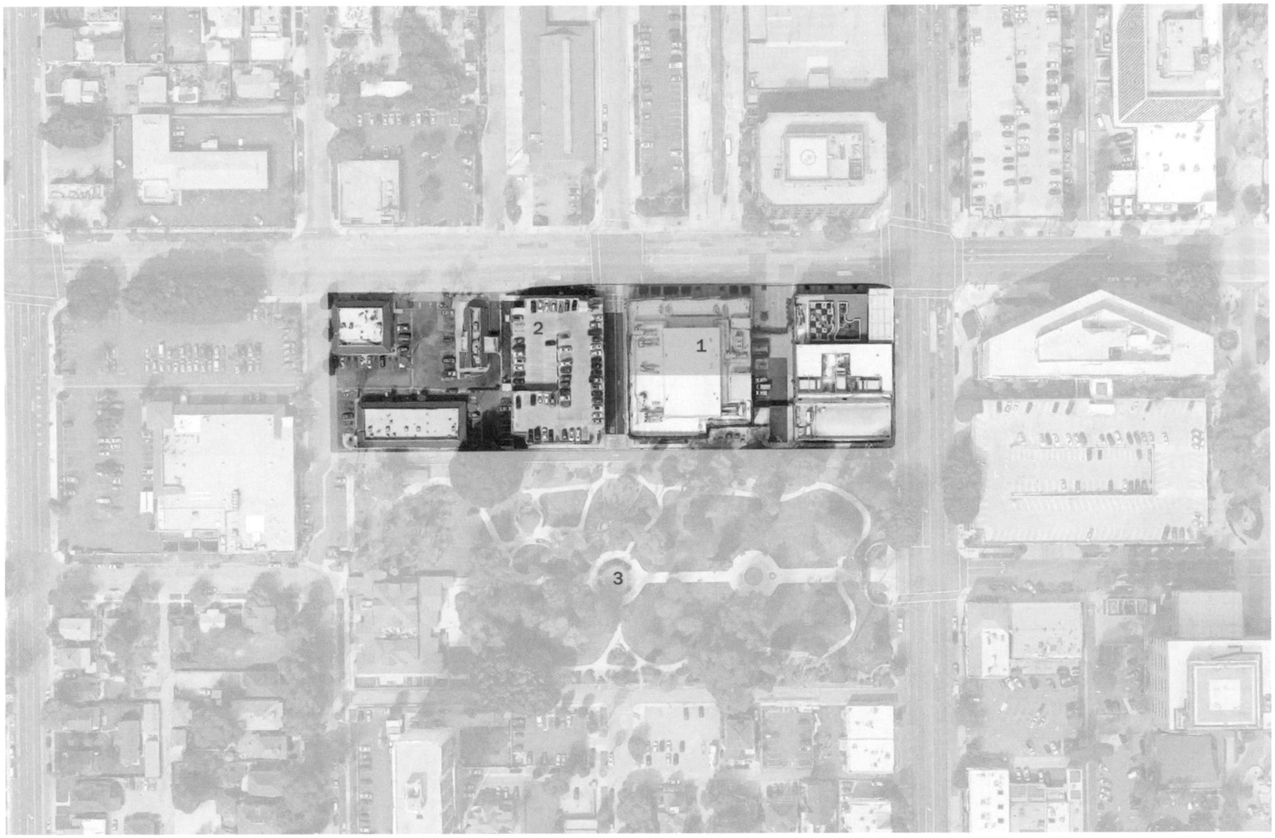

SITE PLAN

1. Auditorium
2. Art & Music Studios
3. Black Box Theater
4. Cafe
5. Administration Office
6. Lecture Hall
7. Student Residence
8. Circulation Spine

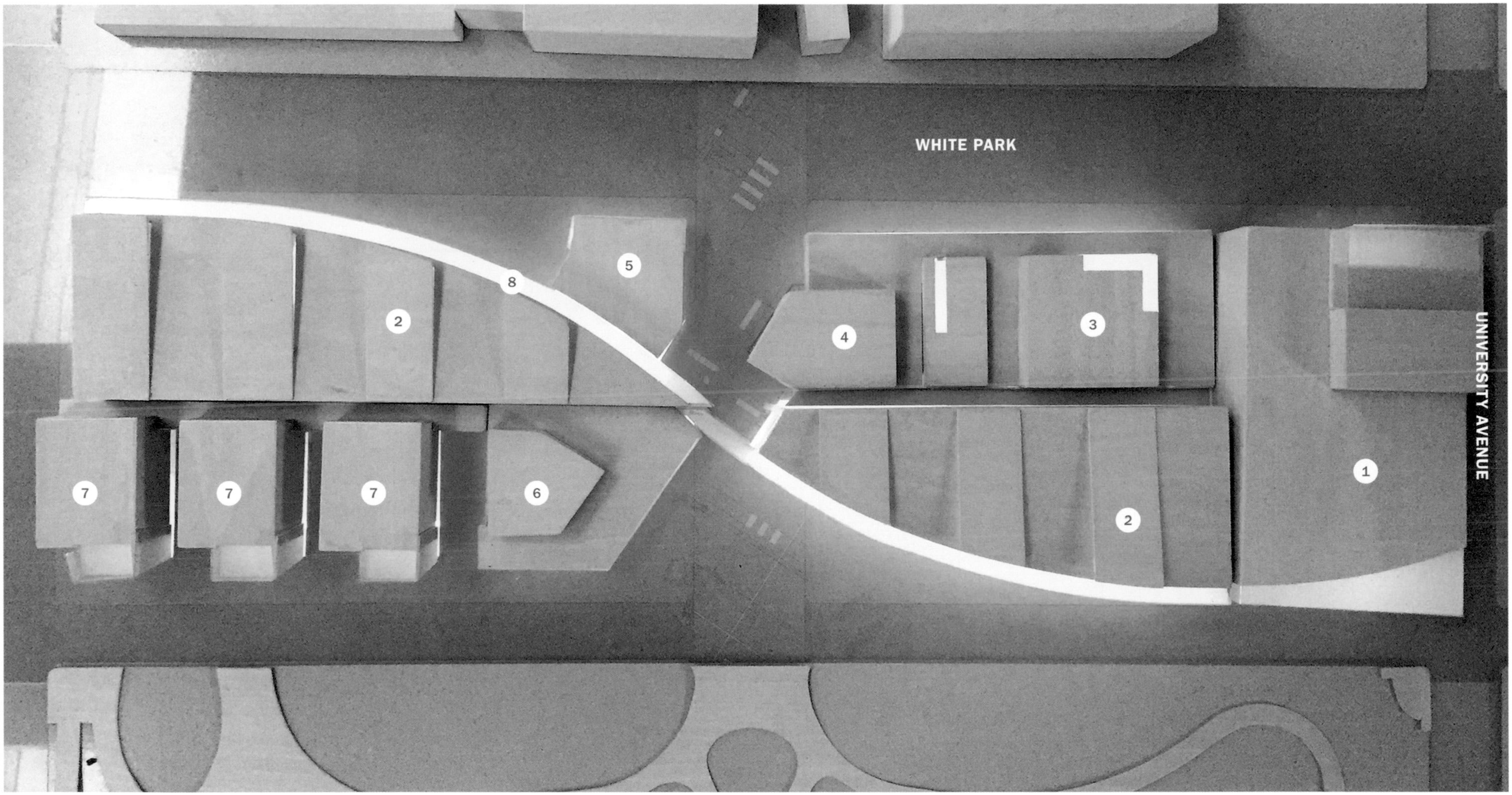

SCHEME II

AMERICAN MUSEUM of TORT LAW
American Museum of Tort Law

AMERICAN MUSEUM OF TORT LAW

Winsted, Connecticut
| 2018 |

The mission of this unique institution is to educate, inform, and inspire Americans about their legal system, with a focus on the right of trial by jury and the benefits of tort law. Through school group visits, self-guided tours, and quality curated programming, and its website, the museum has shown true dedication toward the fostering of greater civic knowledge and awareness (John B Larson, US House of Representatives, Congressional Record November 1, 2017).

The American Museum of Tort Law was founded by Ralph Nader in 2015 in Nader's hometown, Winsted, Connecticut. It is a non-profit, educational facility that raises awareness of the important role of tort law in the protection of personal freedom and safety.

In the beginning of the design process for a new addition to the museum, Ralph Nader and his museum board collaborated with Professors Sigrid Miller Pollin and Stephen Schreiber along with the University of Massachusetts Amherst Architecture Department undergraduate Design IV students in the Spring Semester, 2017. The students were charged with researching the history of Winsted, the site, the former bank building, its adaptive reuse program and the components of the anticipated new program. Each student designed an individual site plan and an architectural scheme incorporating the existing and requested program for a future expansion of the museum.

Following this phase Miller Pollin was commissioned to reassess the site and the 10,000-square-foot program in her professional practice. This assessment yielded the plans and renderings presented here.

Winsted is a small New England city in Litchfield County, Connecticut. The American Museum of Tort Law is now housed at 654 Main Street in the former Winsted Savings Bank building, a neo-classical structure faced in limestone. The specific location on the site for the new addition selected by Nader and his team working with Miller Pollin is adjacent to the south façade of the existing museum building.

Included in the proposed addition is a "Grand Courtroom:" a full-sized, amply equipped thinking-lab space that would be used as a public forum for "trials" of critical 21st-century issues such as liability with respect to autonomous cars. It would also function as a space for trial re-enactments, mock trials, and moot courts. It is anticipated that all events would be live-streamed around the country on the Museum's website. Other programmatic spaces would include a Citizens' Hall of Fame, archival storage, conference and meeting rooms, and a visitor's café.

FIRST FLOOR

1. Entry
2. Citizens' Hall of Fame
3. Courtroom
4. Meeting Room
5. Reception
6. Existing Museum

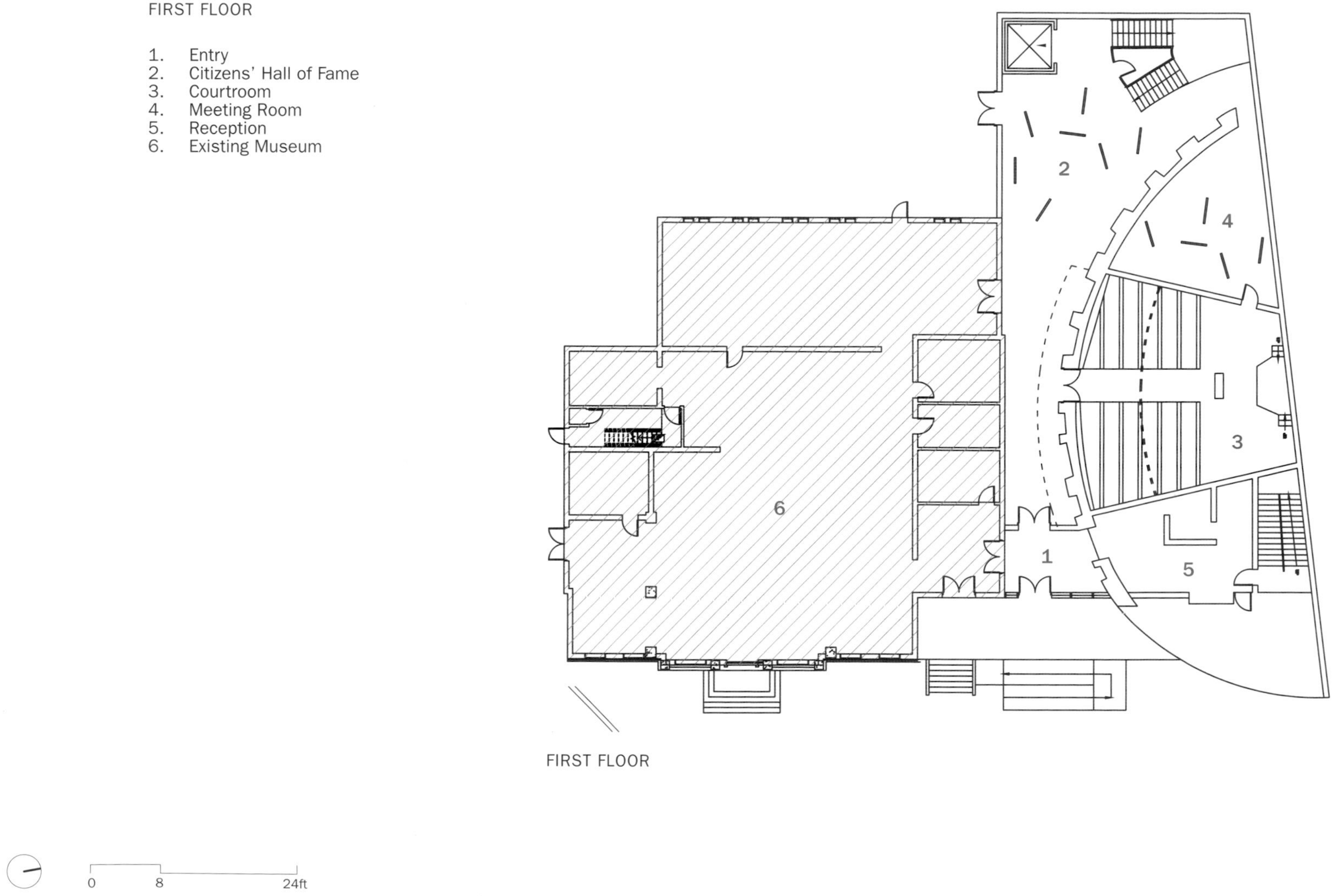

FIRST FLOOR

In the design proposal the visitor is introduced to a sweeping curved wall upon entry. This major design feature plays multiple roles in organizing the interior spaces. It is intended to be a steel truss wall that functions as an armature for exhibits for the Citizens' Hall of Fame, a circulation guide through the building, and as a closure element between activities of the new courtroom and the public exhibition areas.

The exterior stone veneer continues the light tone and solidity of the material of the existing bank building. The scale of the addition harmonizes with the existing museum. The clean, contemporary appearance of the new wing will add strength and definition to this location on Main Street.

SECOND FLOOR

1. Courtroom Balcony
2. Meeting Room
3. Archives
4. Media Room
5. Citizens' Hall of Fame
6. Existing Museum

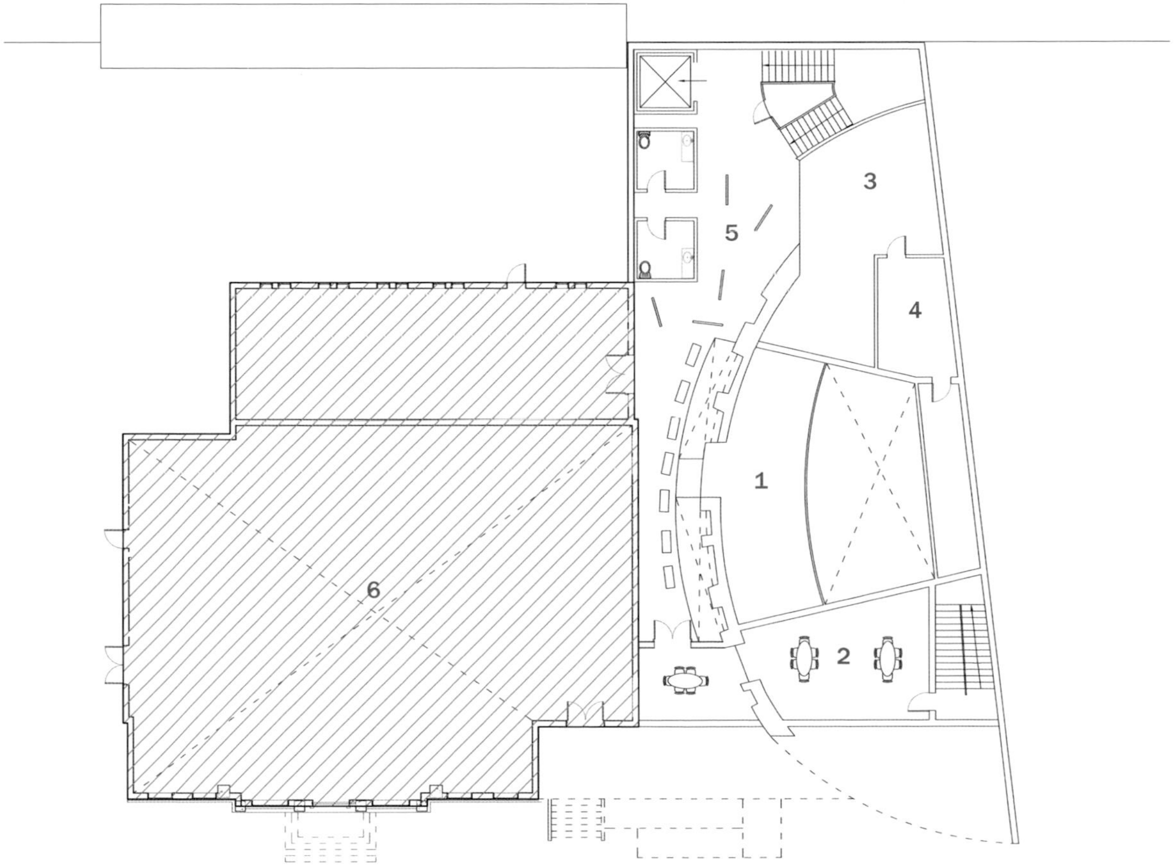

SECOND FLOOR

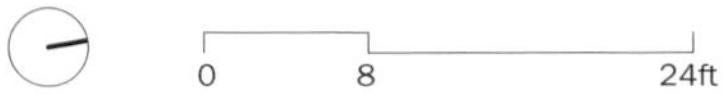

Citizens'
Hall of Fame
HILFIGER

[DRAWING & PAINTING]

RIVERSCAPES

CURTAIN SERIES

BAS RELIEF

CELL SERIES

PLANK DRAWINGS

TOPOGRAPHY DRAWINGS

RIVERSCAPES WITH FANTASY BIRDS

Ink on Paper
| 2012–2013 |

This series of drawings was inspired by spending time in Narragansett, Rhode Island on the Pettaquamscutt River. This river is, in part, a bird sanctuary with a wide variety of plant life. These intricate images combine elements of the visual reality of this riverscape with fantasy visions of aquatic and avian life in this delicate ecosystem. Here birds are impromptu designs. Miller Pollin began these drawings with a desire for intricacy that would offer a counterpoint or pause from her architectural drawings. These drawings, which began in 2012, were followed by the "Curtain Series," which looks outward to an inland landscape from within an interior space.

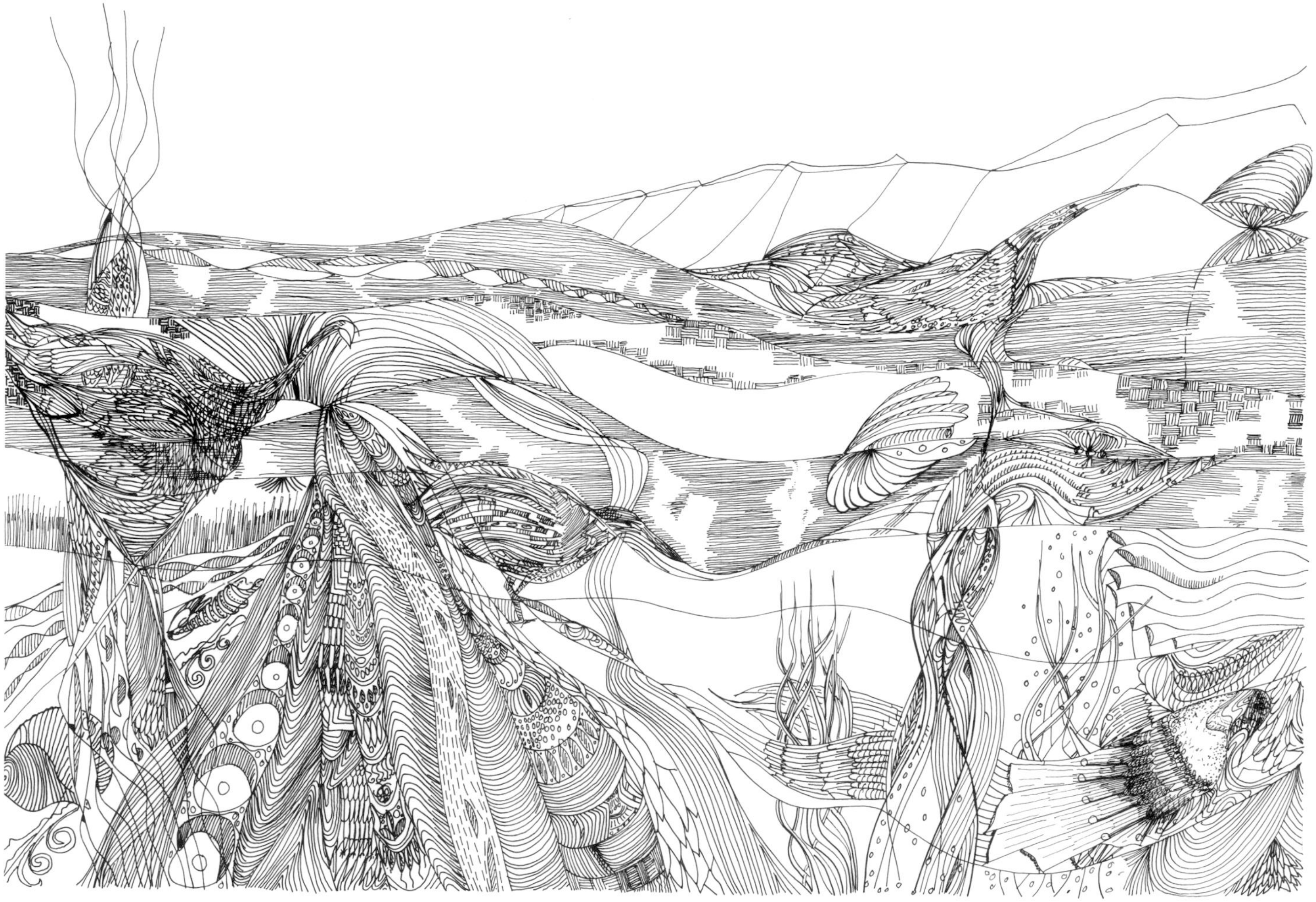

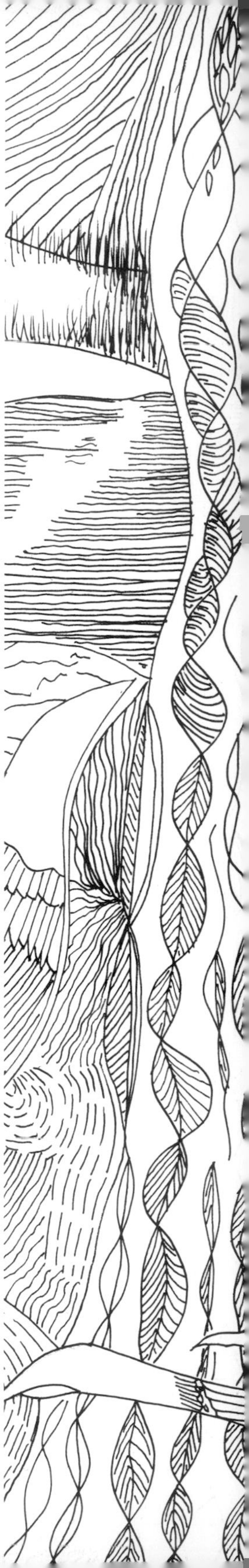

CURTAIN SERIES

| 2014 |

This Miller Pollin drawing series focuses us outward to a broad landscape from an interior perspective. In these intricate pen and ink drawings, we gaze through patterned, breeze-blown curtains to the patterns and perspective of the natural landscape.

The curtain motifs are derived from a range of sources, including traditional Japanese fabric designs and Western lace stitching. Miller Pollin takes cues from repetitions historically associated with feminine fabric and embroidery.

The imagery pairs the vastness of the landscape with intimate glimpses through invented curtains. In all of the drawings a fanciful "bird-plant" tassel floats through the curtain openings, animating the fore-ground. Through complex line work, the drawings often take on the qualities of traditional plate etching.

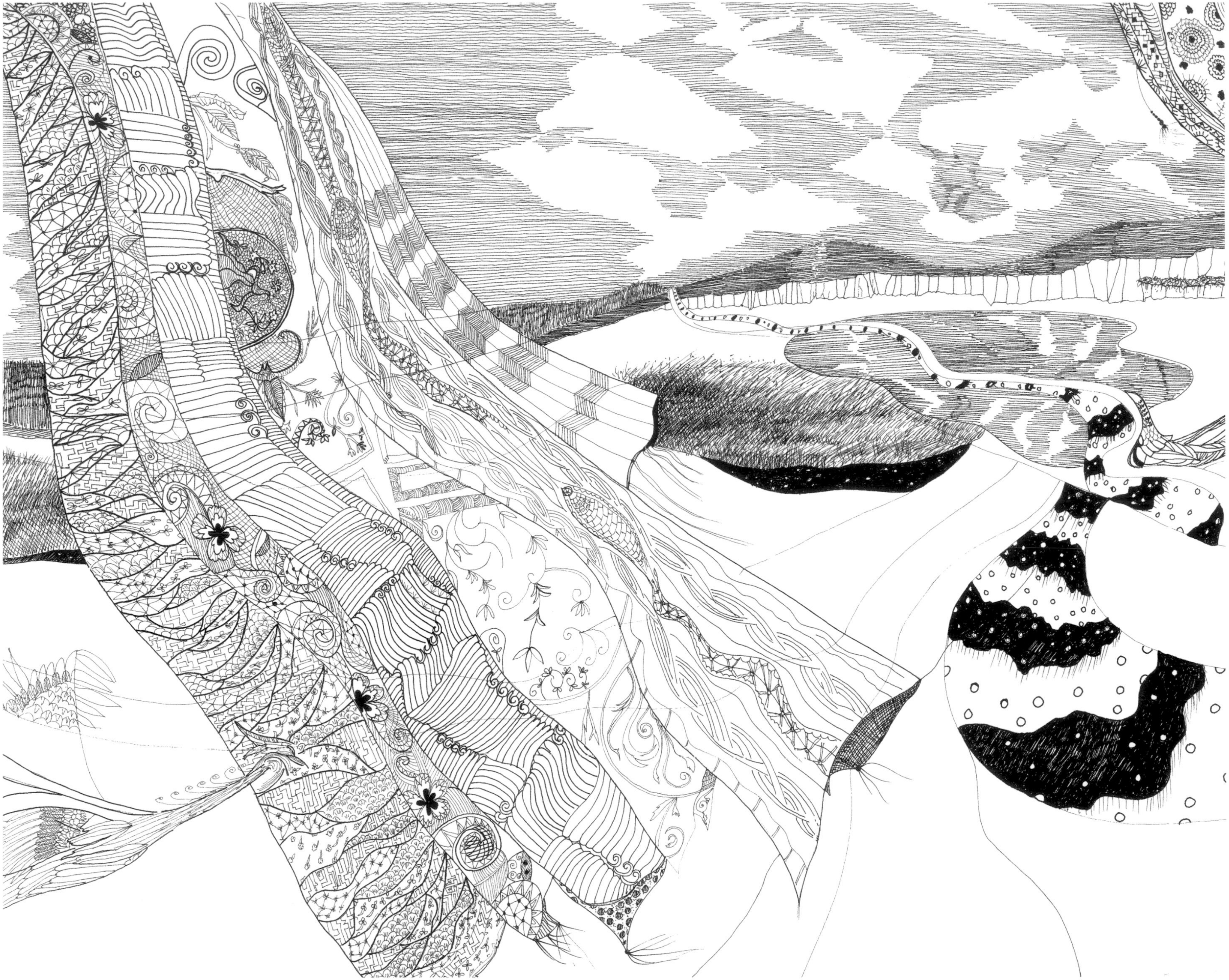

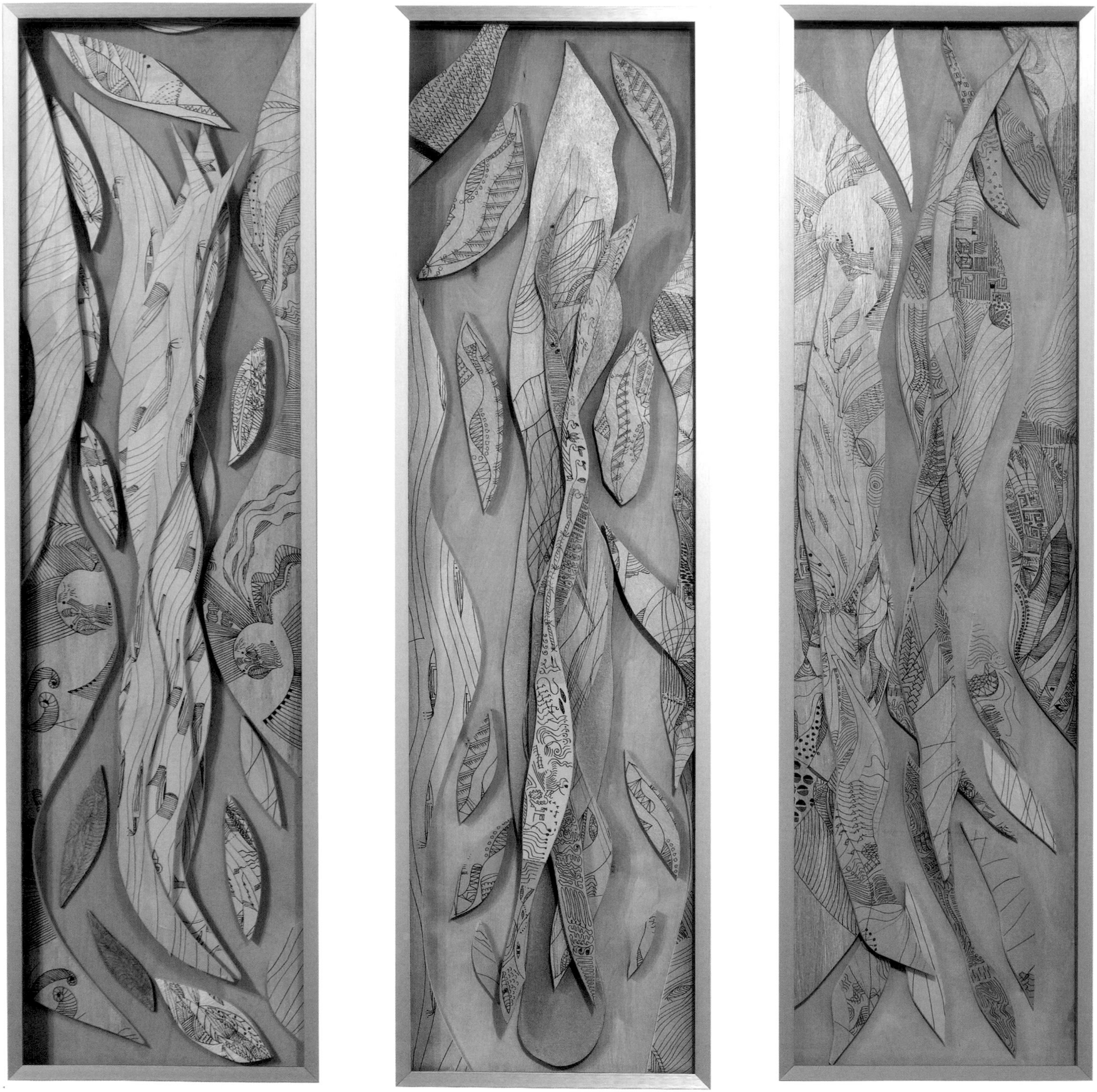

BAS RELIEFS

Acrylic and Ink on Basswood
River Islands | 2011 |

Inspired by leisure time spent on the Pettaquamscutt and Narrow Rivers in Southern Rhode Island, slender island shapes are cut from basswood, collaged onto a basswood background, painted in luminous acrylics and finished with pen and ink drawing. These are plan views of the river and its shores, framed in aluminum that echoes the metallic finish of parts of the bas reliefs.

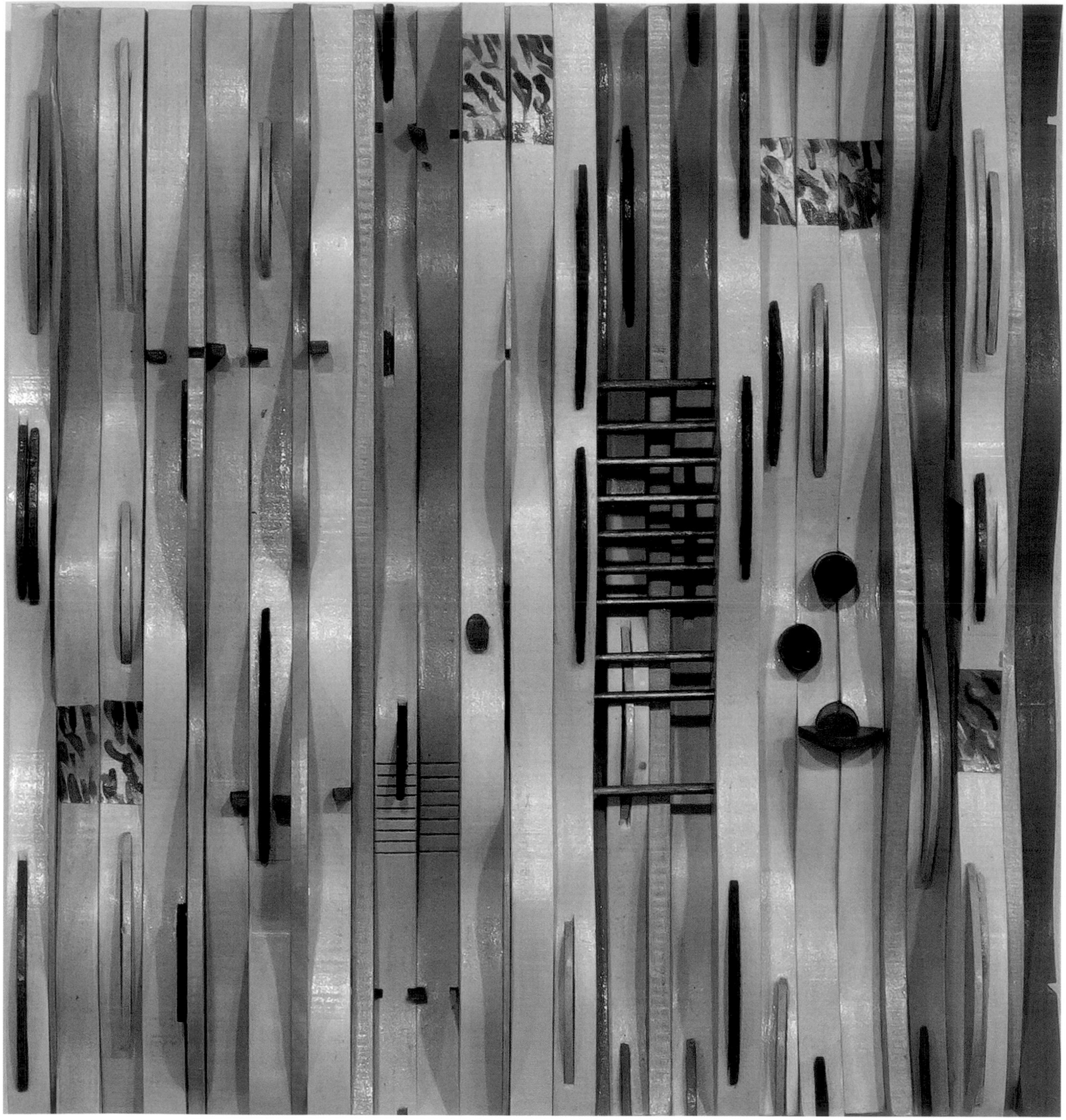

Blue Tears in Pastel Valleys
| 2013 |

A bas relief of curving basswood pieces laminated together to form a square of topography punctuated by small painted wood dowels was made shortly after Miller Pollin's father-in-law passed away. It is an expression of sadness and the joy that Abe Pollin brought into her family life.

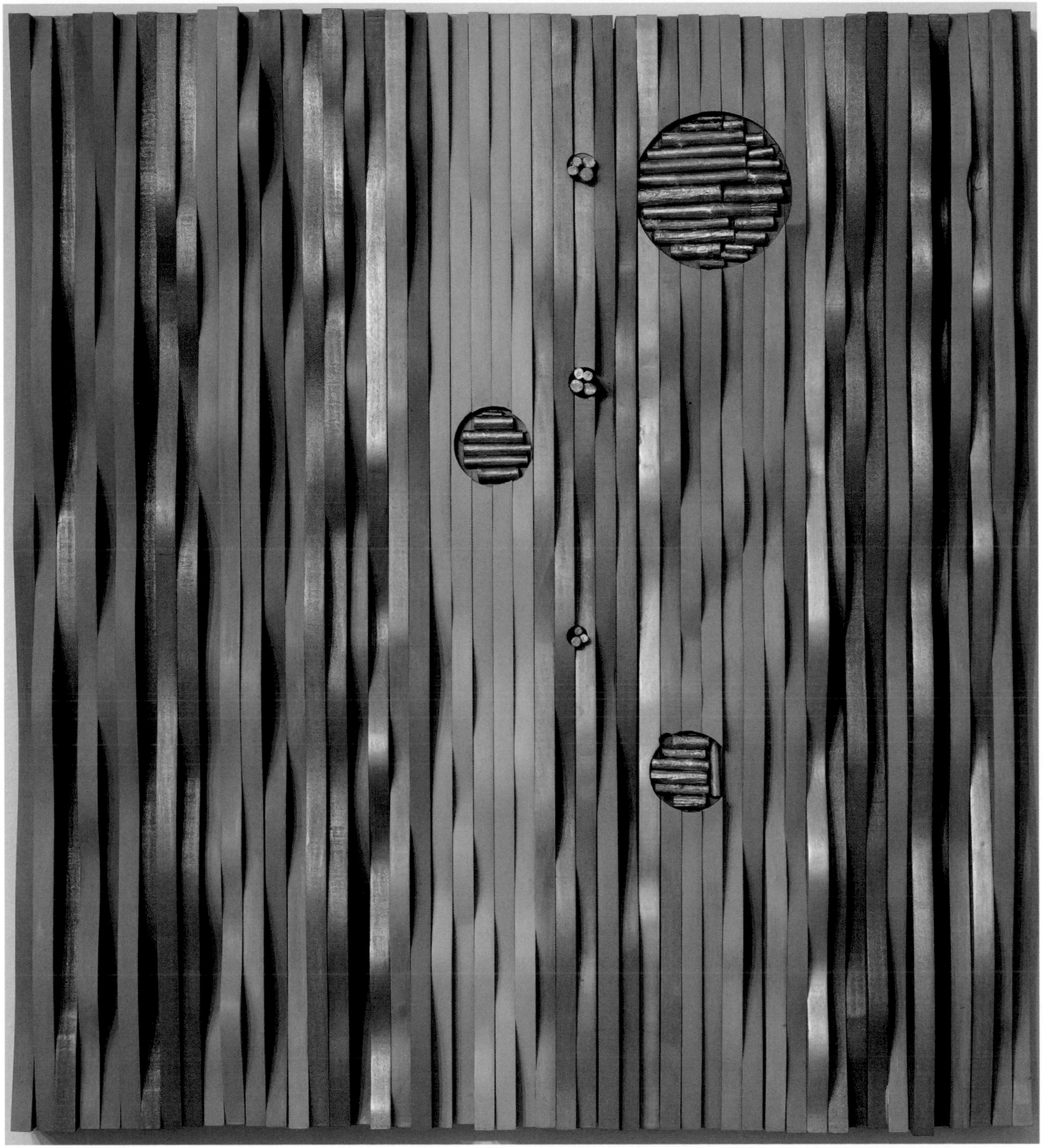

Golden Sun
| 2013 |

This bas relief, also constructed with curved, laminated basswood painted with brilliant yellows and golds, is a portrait of summer sun in New England. Small disk cut-outs are inlaid with painted twigs from Miller Pollin's garden.

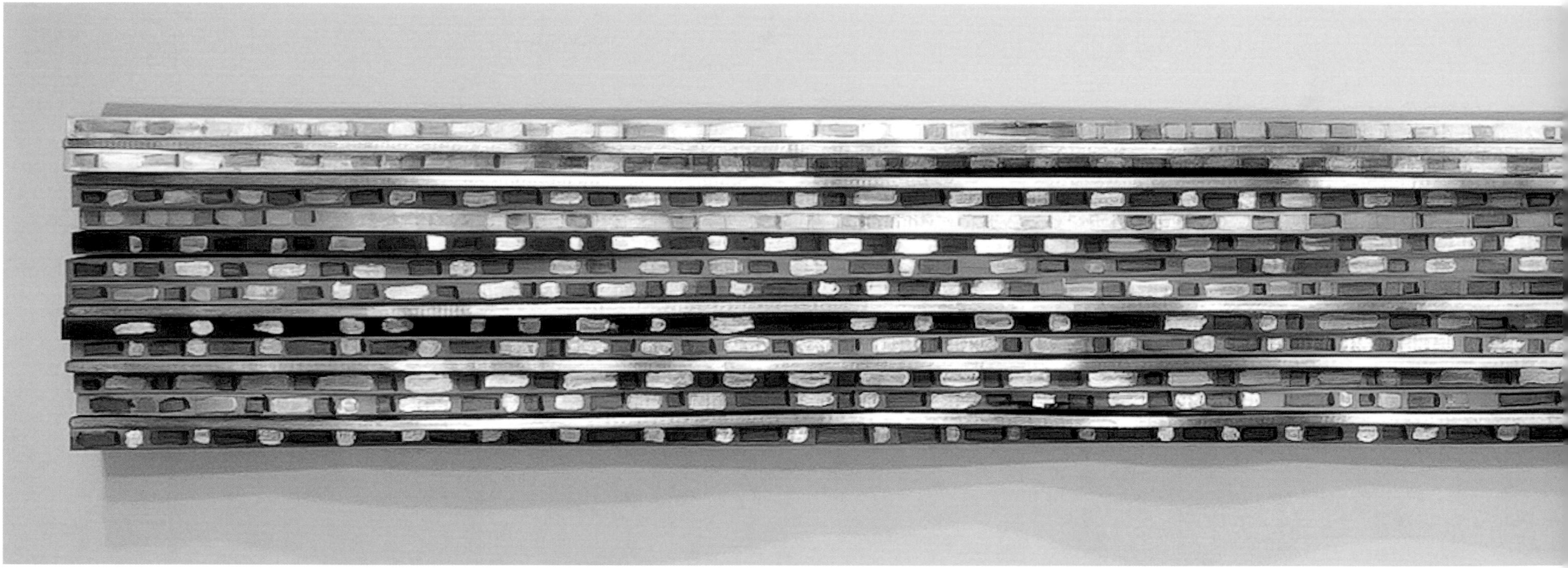

Ribbon Candy | 2013

This long, narrow piece is 9"(H) x 68"(W) long and composed of curved, laminated basswood painted with acrylic colors reminiscent of youthful memories of ribbon candy.

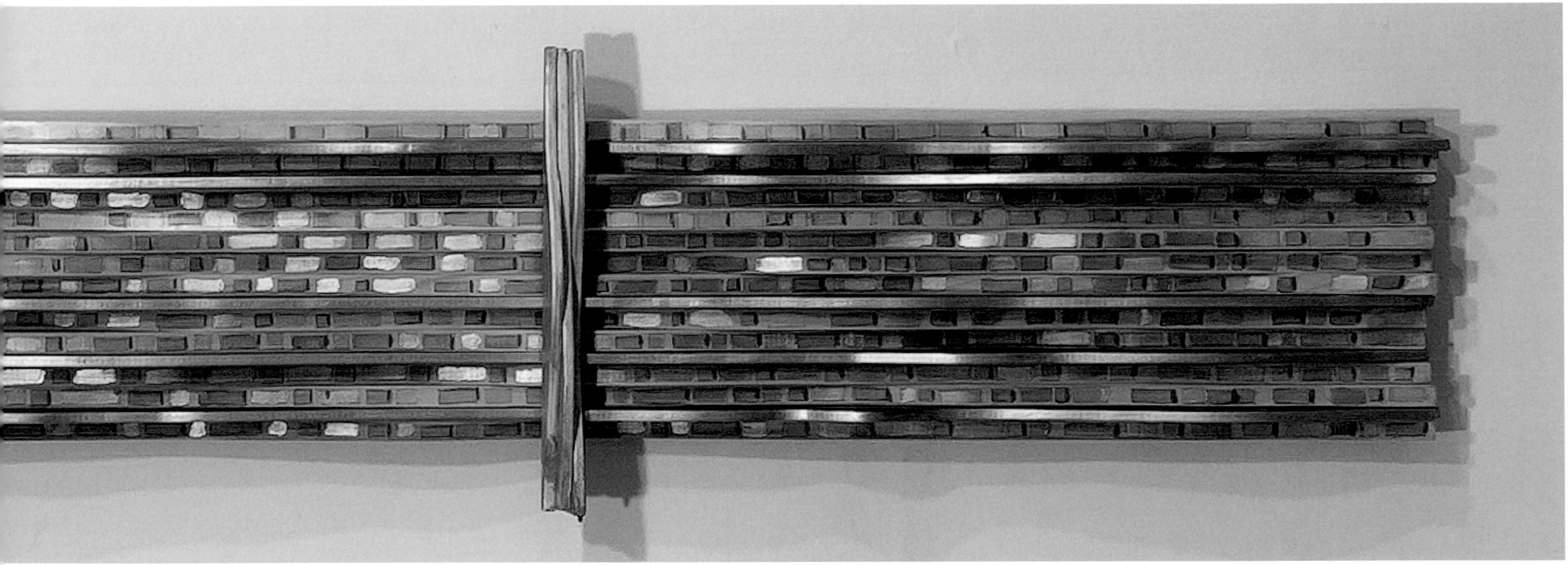

Pettaquamscutt Riverscape
16"(H) x 37"(W) | 2013

PLANK DRAWINGS

Ink on Basswood | 2014

These pieces are composed with ¼"-thick basswood planks mounted on and floated off of painted sheets of basswood. Interference and iridescent acrylic paints coat opaque acrylic colors yielding surfaces that reflect light and change color depending on the viewing angle. Pen and ink drawings of fantasy riverscapes, kites, and an array of images overlay the acrylics.

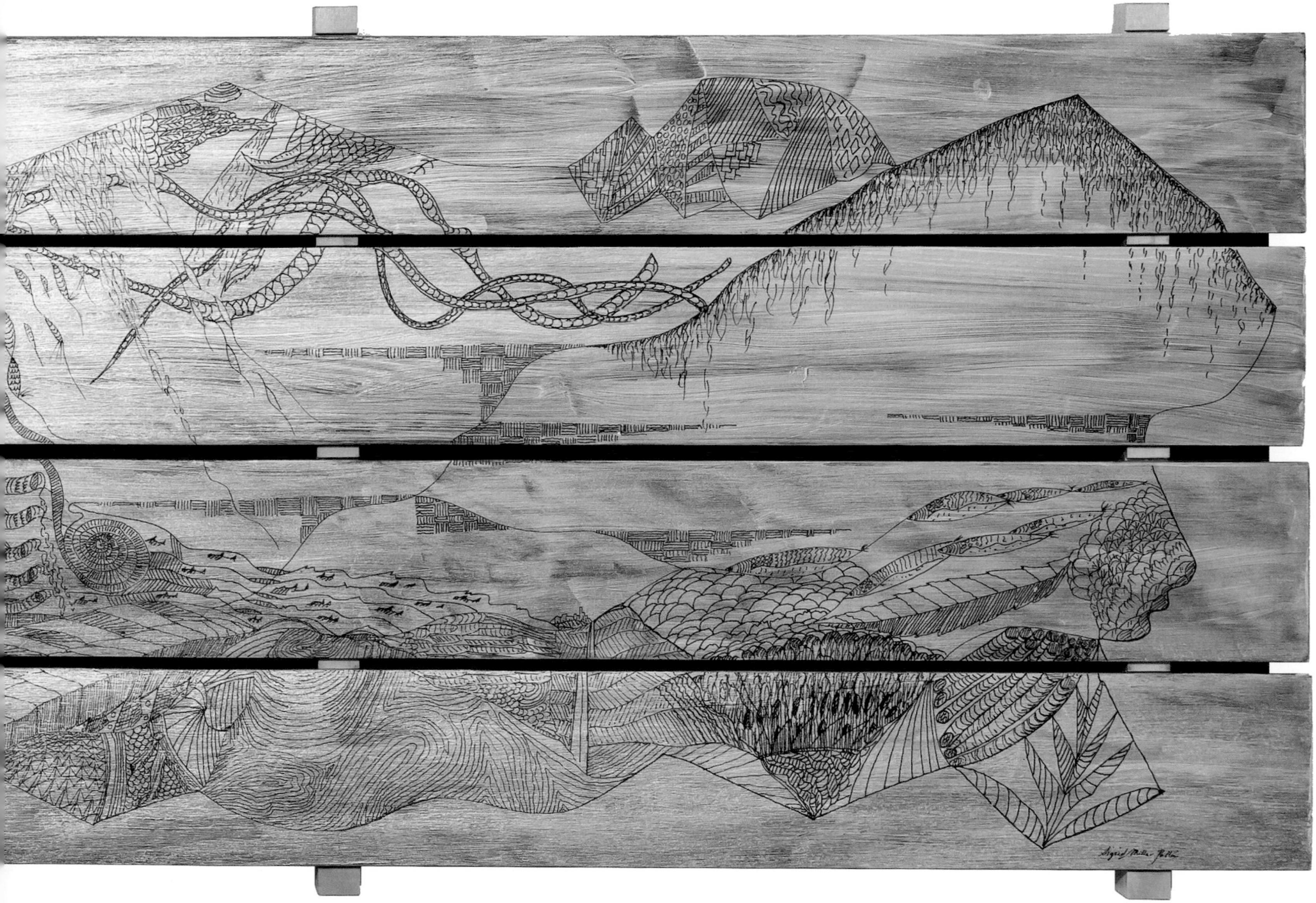

Pettaquamscutt Riverscape II
16"(H) x 37"(W) | 2013

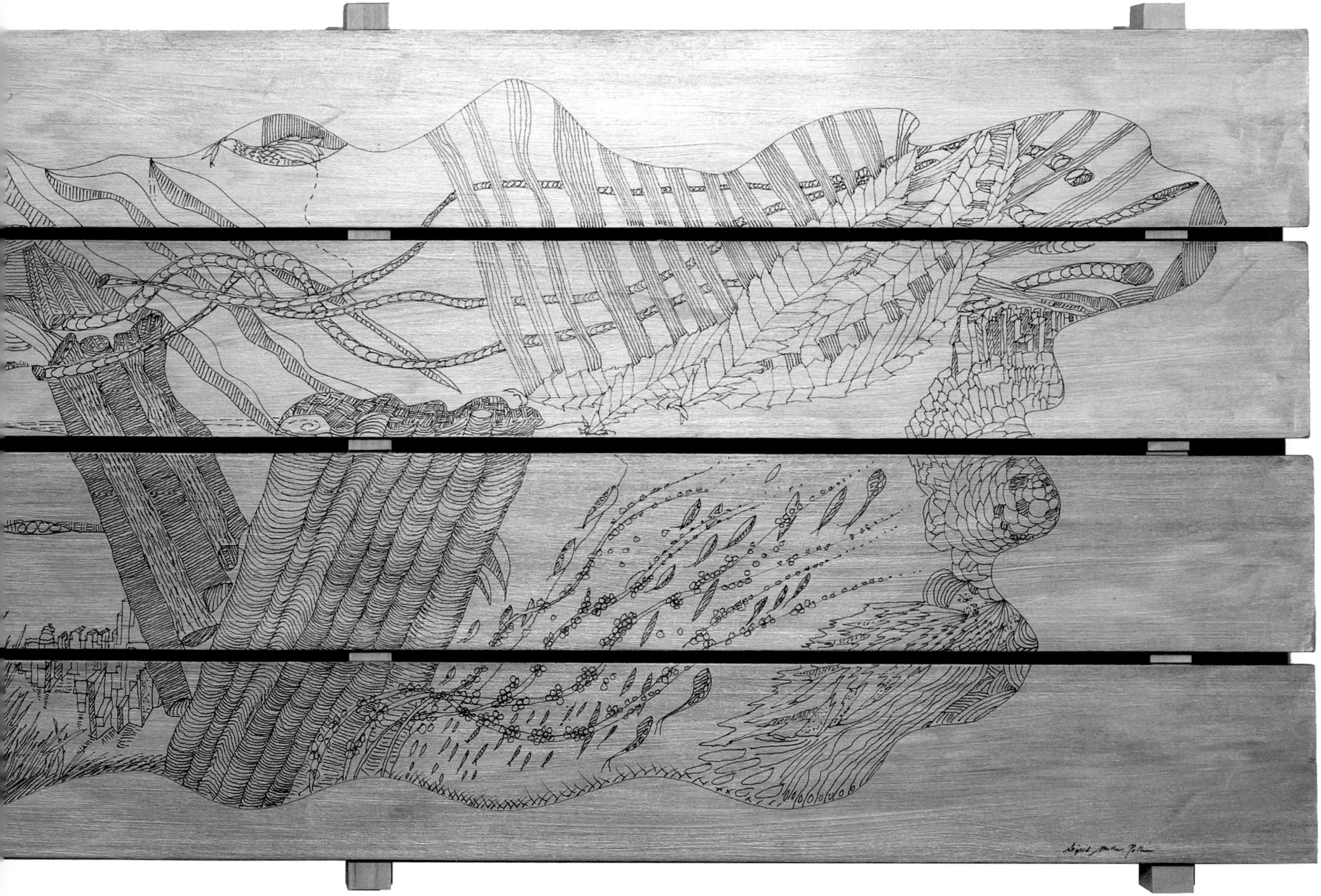

Underwater Fishes and Forms
16"(H) x 37"(W) | 2013

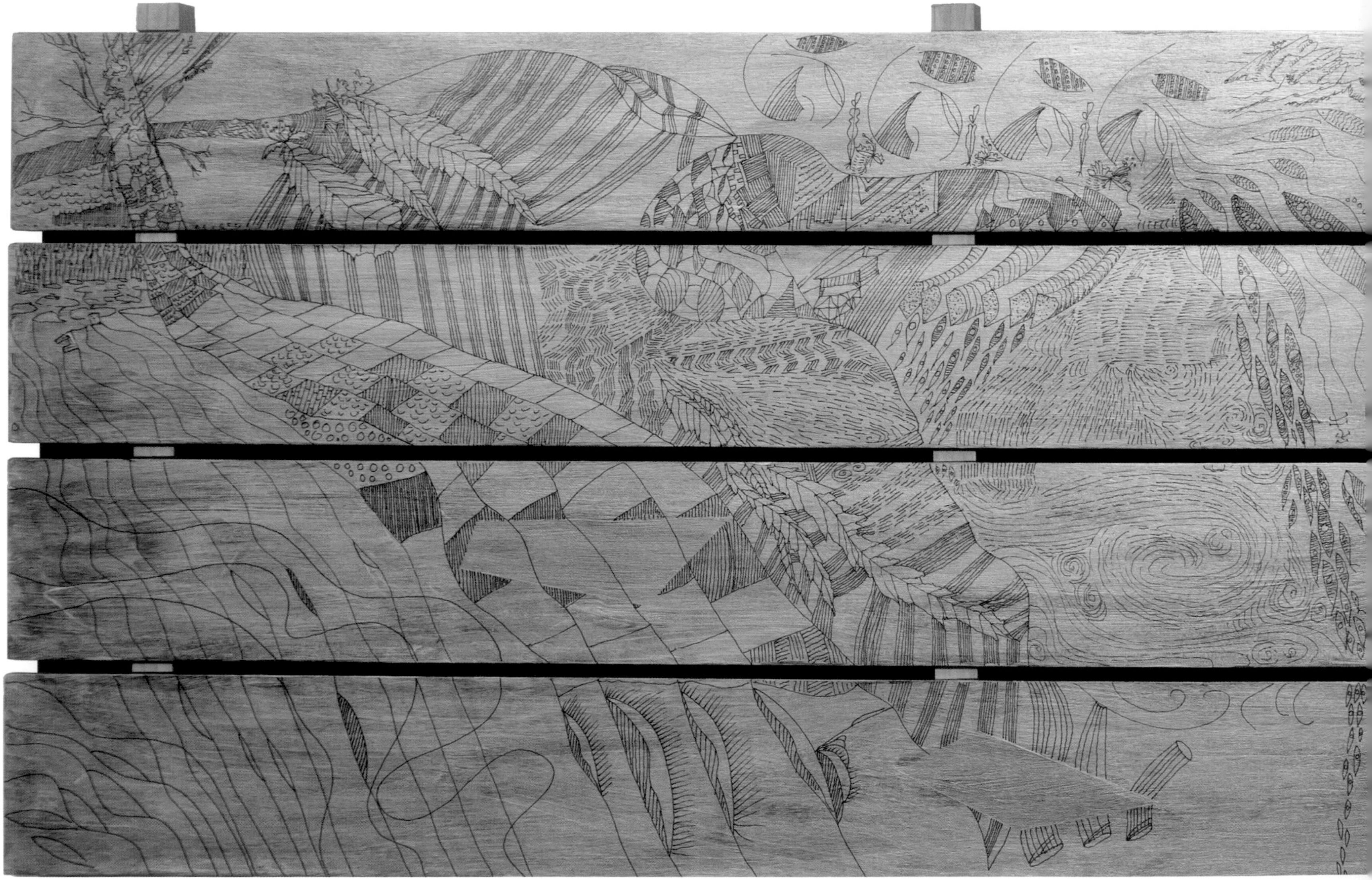

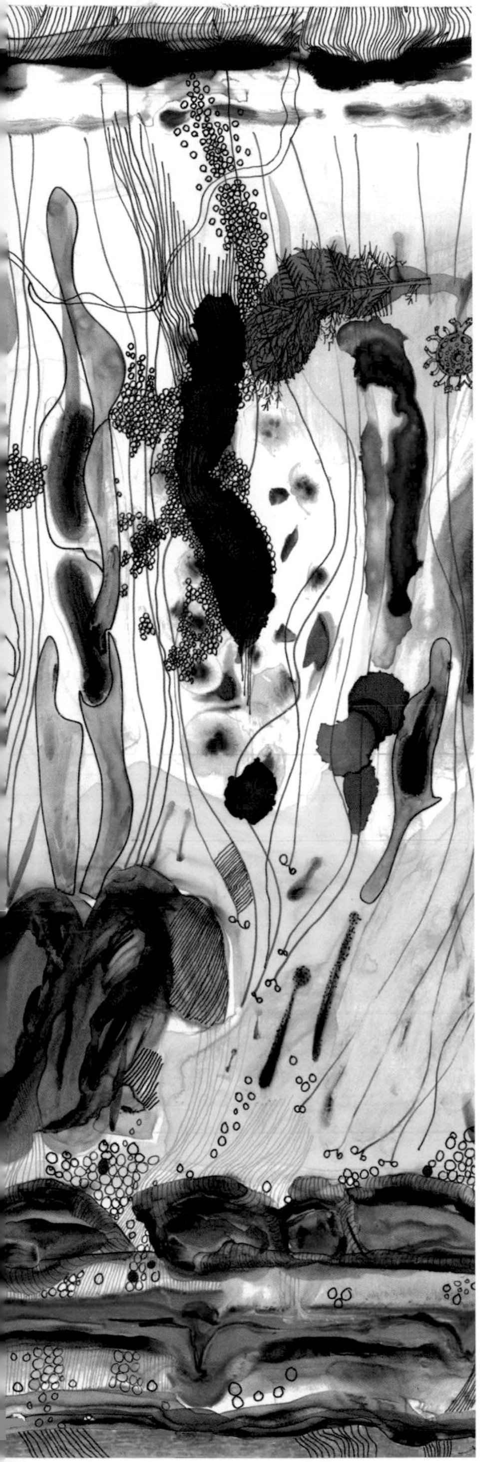

CELL SERIES

2018 | Water Color and Ink on Yupo Paper
| 30"(H) x 60"(W)

These water color and ink images are inspired by microscopic images of plant cells. The shapes and intricacies of cells are sectional in nature, taken from cuts through slices of various plant materials ranging from basswood (linden tree) to wheat rust. Miller Pollin first studied the microscopic images and made a series of small mixed-media sketches, which then transform into larger images on Yupo paper seen here.

These works began with thoughts about traveling inward, into the elements that surround us rather than traveling to distant places. The idea of exploring that which is close to us in our landscapes and our local settings has long been a theme in Miller Pollin's artwork.

The following essay on Miller Pollin's Cell Series was written by New York- and Virginia-based artist and curator Jeanette Cole. Cole's essay was part of a 2018 exhibit of Miller Pollin's recent art work, along with works by artists Paula Elliott and Joan Weber. The exhibit entitled *[Containing] Great Space* was held at The Hampden Gallery University of Massachusetts Amherst.

Cell Structure 1 | 2017

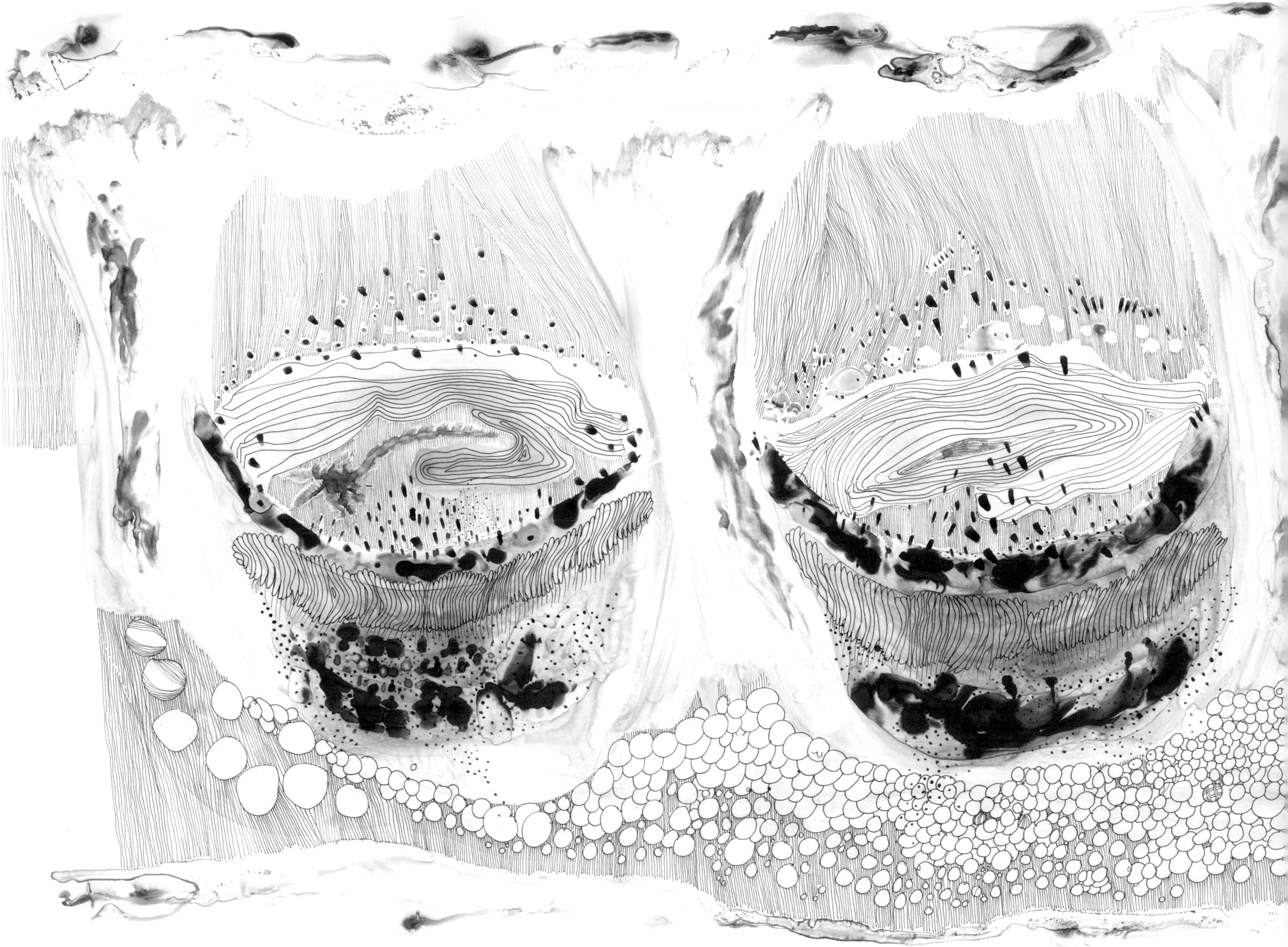

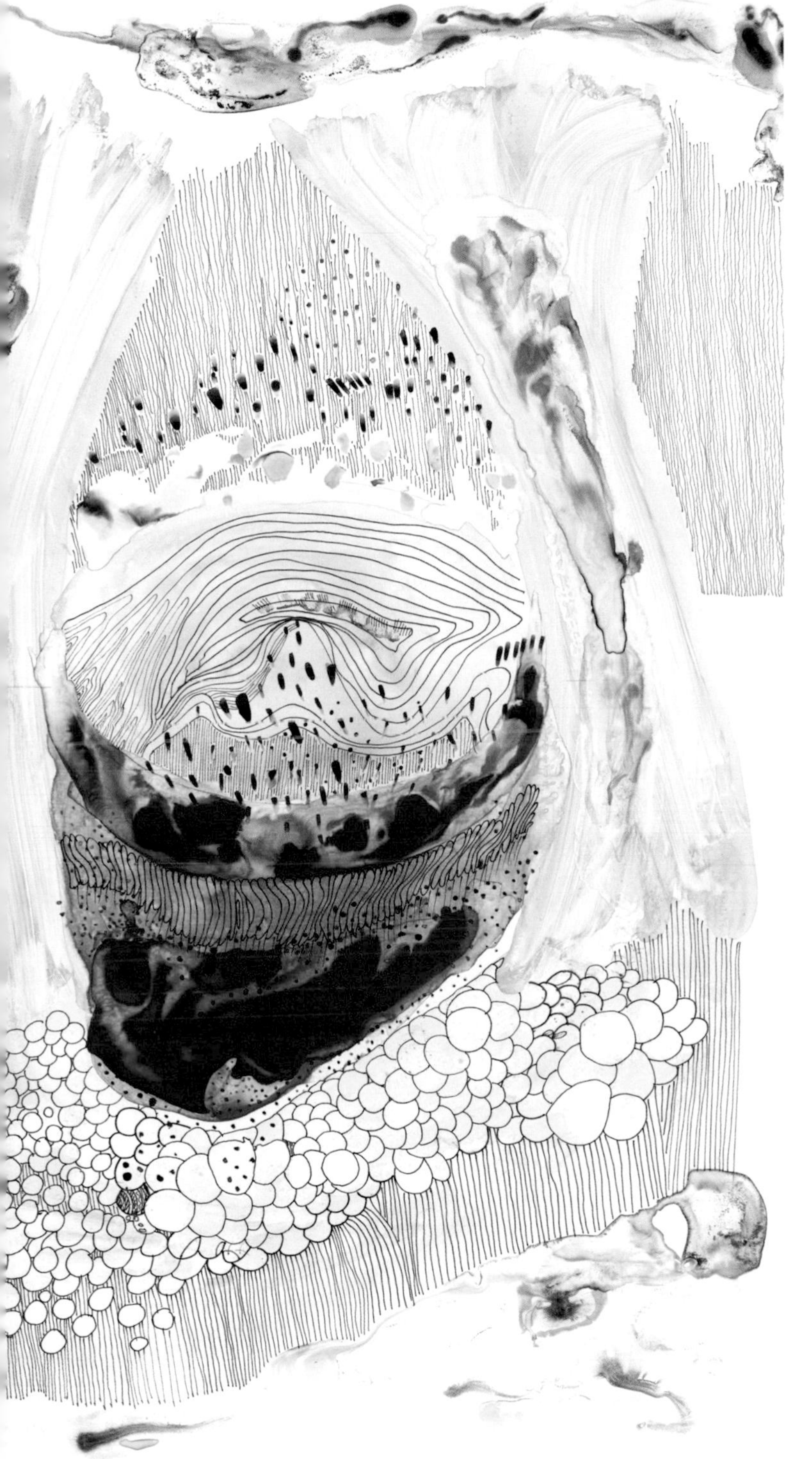

Inspired by the microscopic world of botanical cells, and their structure as rendered by 19th-Century naturalists, Sigrid Miller Pollin draws a world as imagined and observed inside them. She treats her subject as if she is orchestrating a visual jazz festival whose chief instruments consist of mechanical pen lines and colored, radiant ink blobs. She starts with the structure of a cell as conceived by a matter-of-fact scientific explanation. A practicing architect, she brings various elements of that discipline to these images. The architectural cross section, flat in rendering, brings volume to a floor plan. It is this basic operation that forms the structure by which these drawings are generated. Cell Structure-1 from basswood (linden tree) gives us the ground line at the bottom of the image, built with blue and red horizontal ink block-like forms. At the top, though narrower, a complementing band is laid across the top of the page. These layers at the top and bottom of the page represent the cell wall. Both horizontal elements are then connected with vertical forms. Envision the classic Greek temple structure base, column and entablature elements. After the initial setup, she engages with pulsing fluids of cellular life processes. The ink, as she applies it, is at once precise and precarious.

The concept of the cell and an examination of its inner workings is the core impetus of this work. Miller Pollin takes us inward, not as an act of turning away from the outside world but as a way of scrutinizing dispassionately the full force of the inner life. This work, unlike much contemporary art, is not about an emotional self-disclosure or overwrought identity politics. It is about a microscopic inner world that expands into a great space of awe and wonderment. The structure of the cell is a containment device for infinite subdivision and consequently expansion.

Cell Structure 2 | 2017

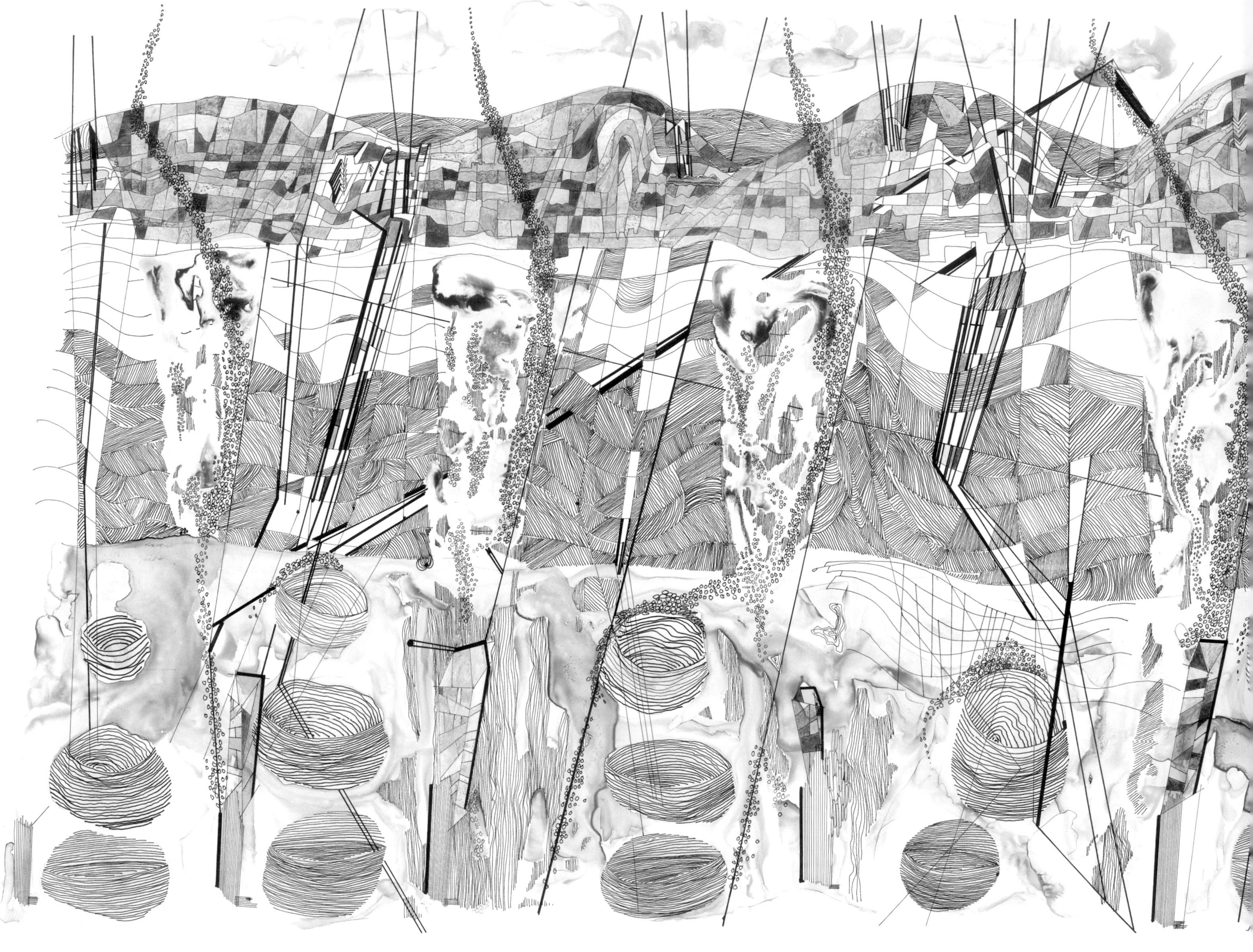

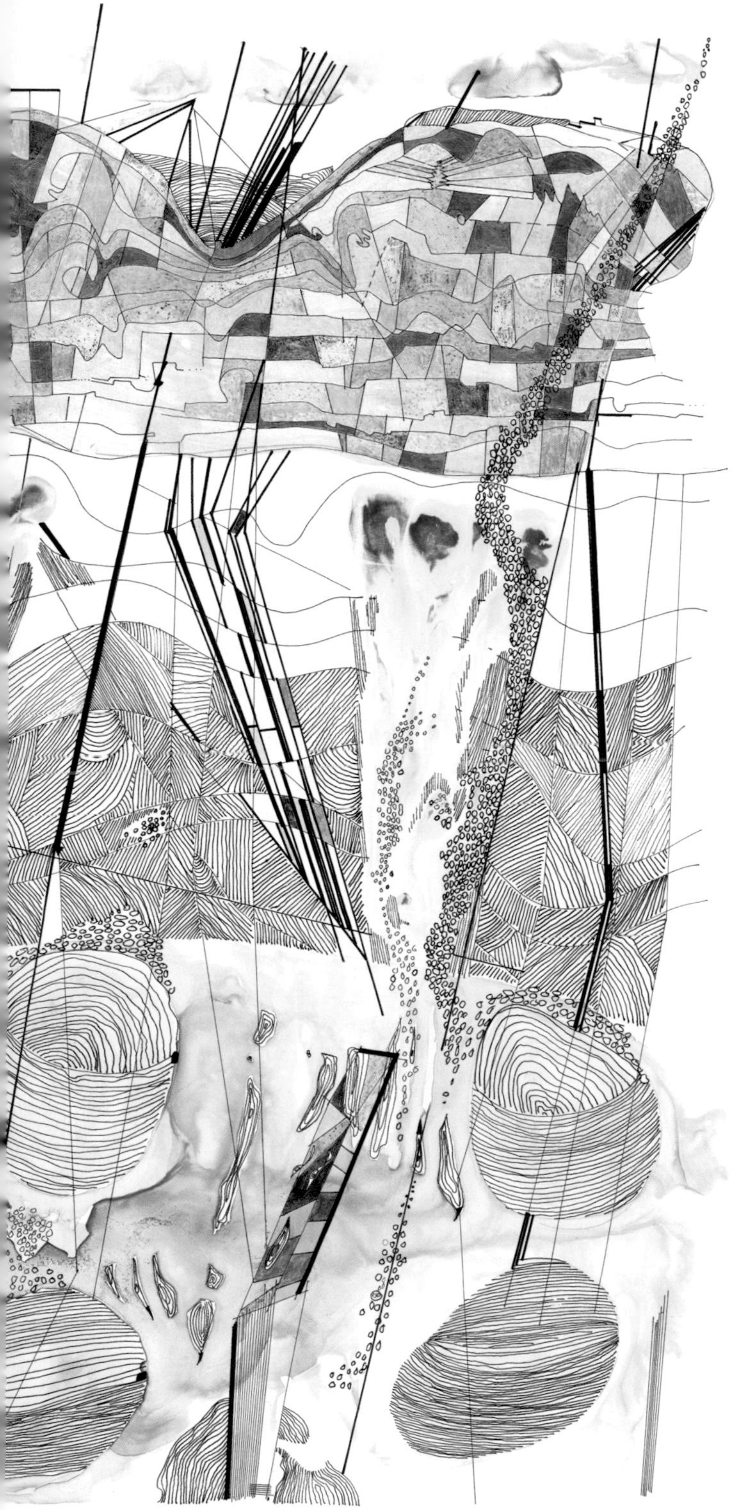

Miller Pollin's material process involves laying down radiant inks on exceptionally smooth Yupo paper. The brilliant color retains the water action and sets up a syncopation of color and pattern. The color refers only to itself and not to any local description of the natural phenomena or their real-world appearance. Each color added to the composition is an intuitive response to the previous one and sets up an internal combustion chamber of action and reaction. She transforms the mechanical pen into a finely-tuned reed instrument. Each mark she makes is irreversible. The process forces an acceptance of each move, however satisfying it may (or may not) be. She has to contend with the consequences of each decision and move the creative process forward, somehow. She does this with a sense of discovery and delight, as is evident in the image.

On top of the vibrant color applied with a brush, Miller Pollin details the image with pen work. While the mechanical pen is a signature instrument of an architect, the manner in which she uses it is anything but traditional. The line work is complex and functions in several significant ways. Overall, the line elements establish a lattice work screen across the surface of the image. Then, looking at detail sections, the line elements disconnect, dissolving the flatness of the screen and opening into an active, volumetric space. Sometimes they are built into a pattern creating a tonal passage. In others they articulate volumetric forms as in Cell Structure 3 derived from a grape cell image. Here yellow circles are formed into little vessels with tops and insides.

Cell Structure 3 | 2017

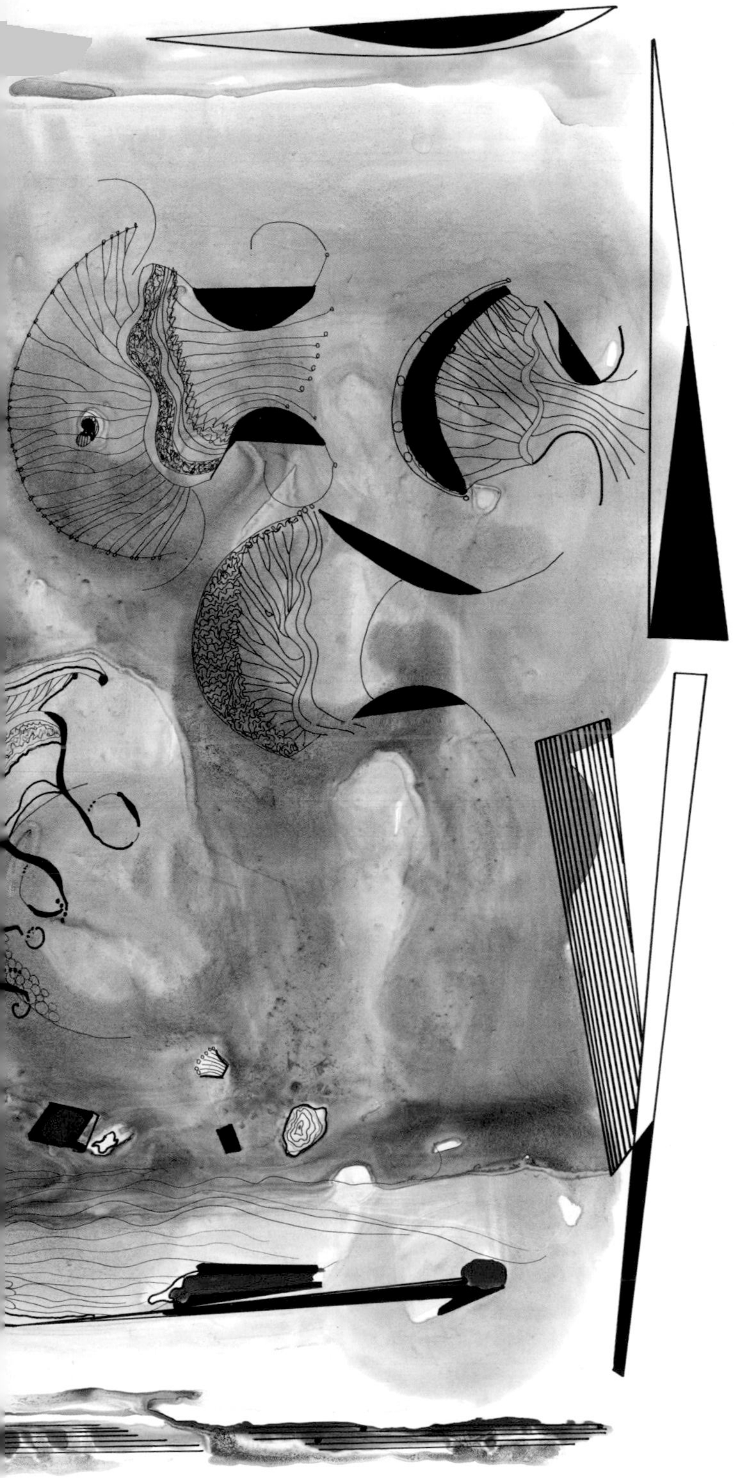

Finally, she inserts long perspectival elements through the space, setting into motion every aspect of the image, as in Cell Structure 3. These diagonals upset what would otherwise be an orderly overlay of spatial screens. Close reading of the image moves us through a carefully calibrated spatial sequence, first of all a flat overall screen, then opening into volumetric space in the smaller forms, and finally re-flattening space at the next level. Each layer is a doorway into seemingly infinite subdivisions.

The landscape format of her imagery is cinematic, with a 1 to 2 ratio. Diving into the microscopic world, we emerge into a vastness that is dazzling and alive. The elements of ink, color and paper all interact as if a festival of sound.

Andreas Weber, in his book Matter and Desire, argues for a poetic materialism. Describing the linden tree he says, 'The sky is folded into the calyx of every petal. This is it, the overwhelming experience of simultaneity, the synchronous presence of all possibilities—of growth, maturation, and decay—the totality of being, the newborn laughing coyly in the face of disintegration with the causal ease of a child's tears, all of this concentrated in the damask of a single petal.' Miller Pollin projects this same infusing of life and promise.

Cell Structure 4 | 2017

On watercolor paper these two images sketch the complexity of individual seeds. Both of these examples examine a type of seed wind dispersal

Nemesia Versicolor | 22"(H) x 30"(W) | 2016
Seed with peripheral wing to assist wind dispersal

Spergularia Media | 22"(H) x 30"(W) | 2016

Greater sea-spurry peripheral wing that assists in wind dispersal

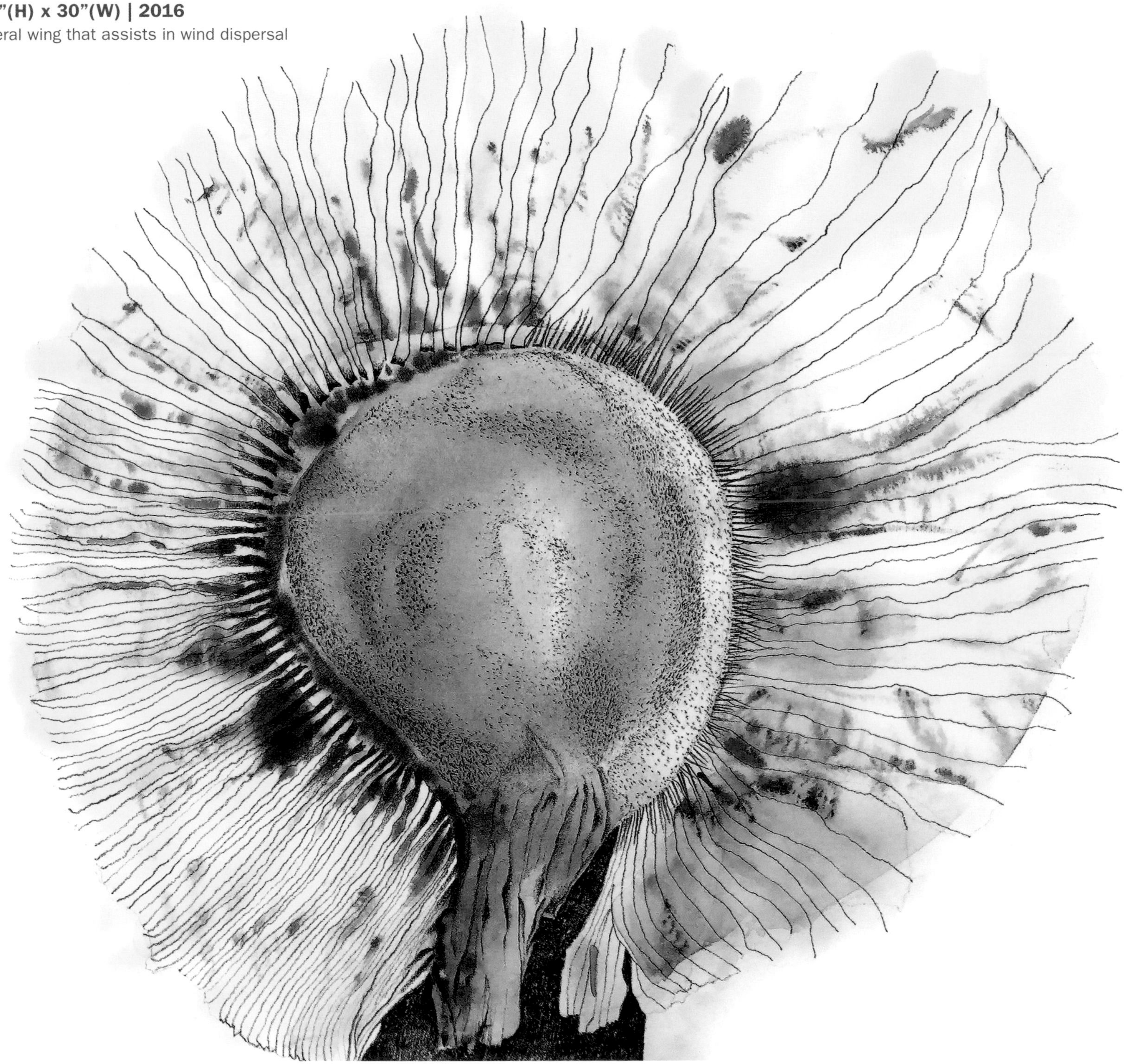

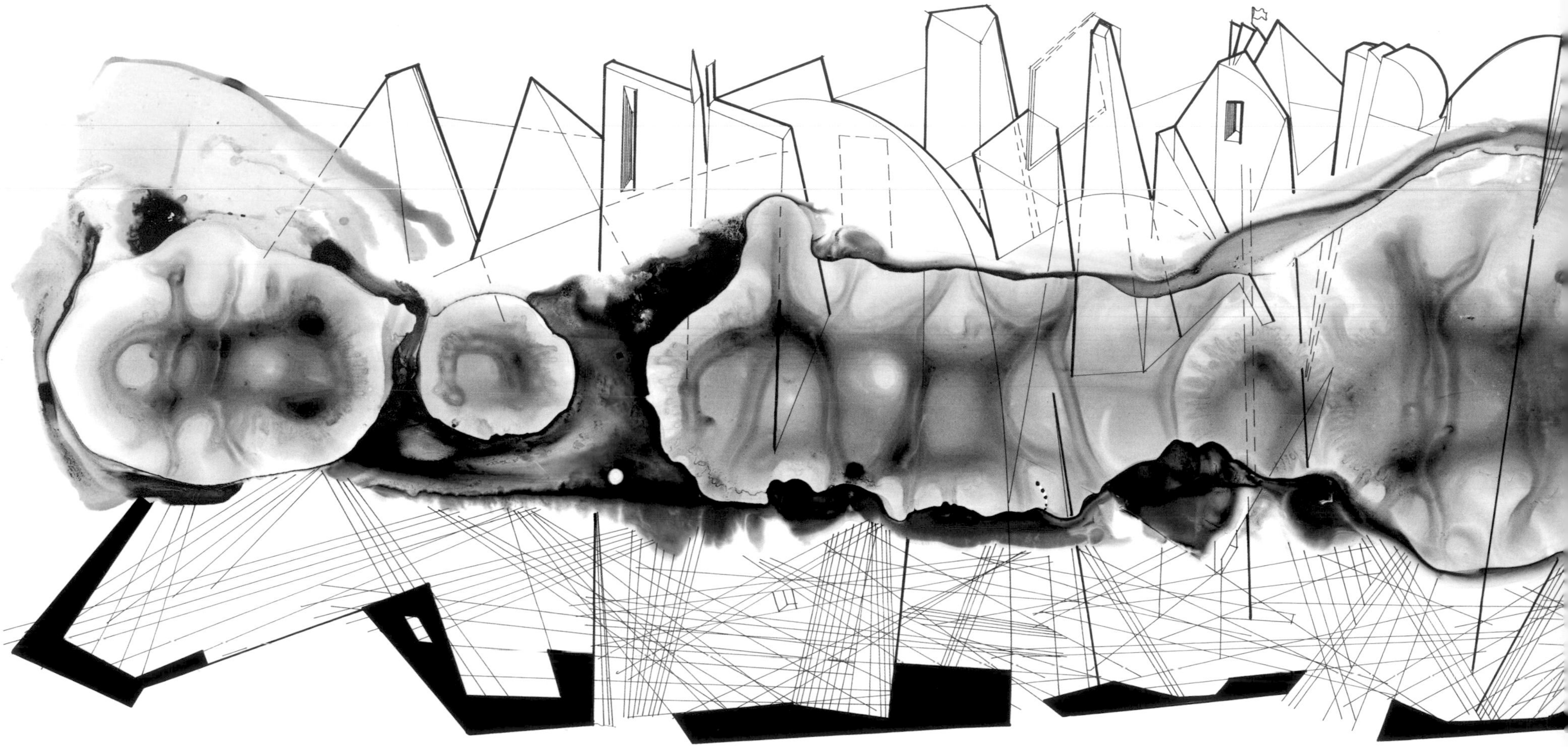

Urban Lake
2017

TOPOGRAPHY DRAWINGS

Water Color and Ink on Yupo Paper | 15"(H) x 60"(W)

The Topography Drawings combine water color and pen and ink on Yupo paper. The aqueous layer becomes the loose aerial-view shape of the lake, while the pen and ink layer is capturing the lines of topography, person-made vessels or architectonic elements.

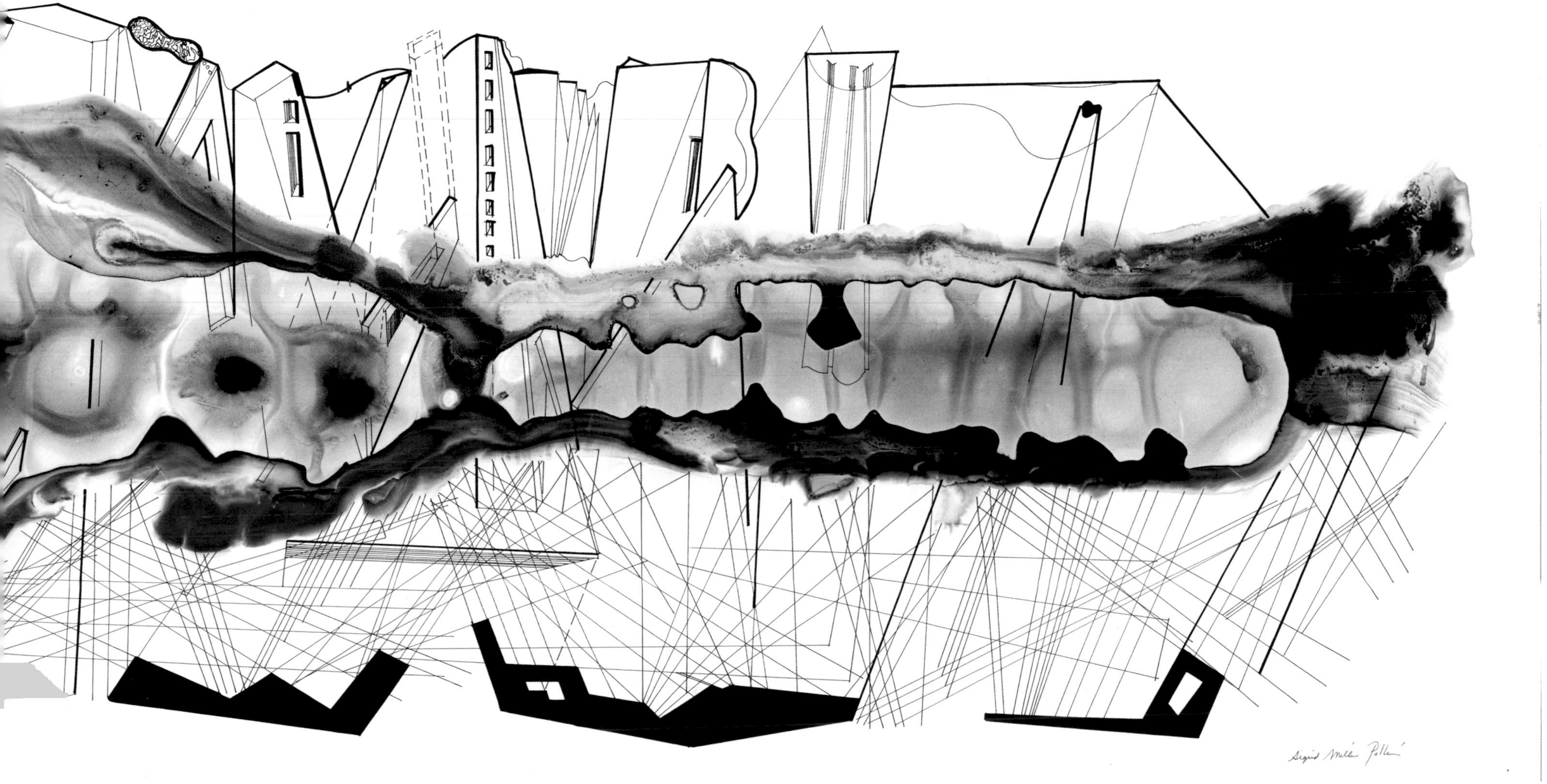

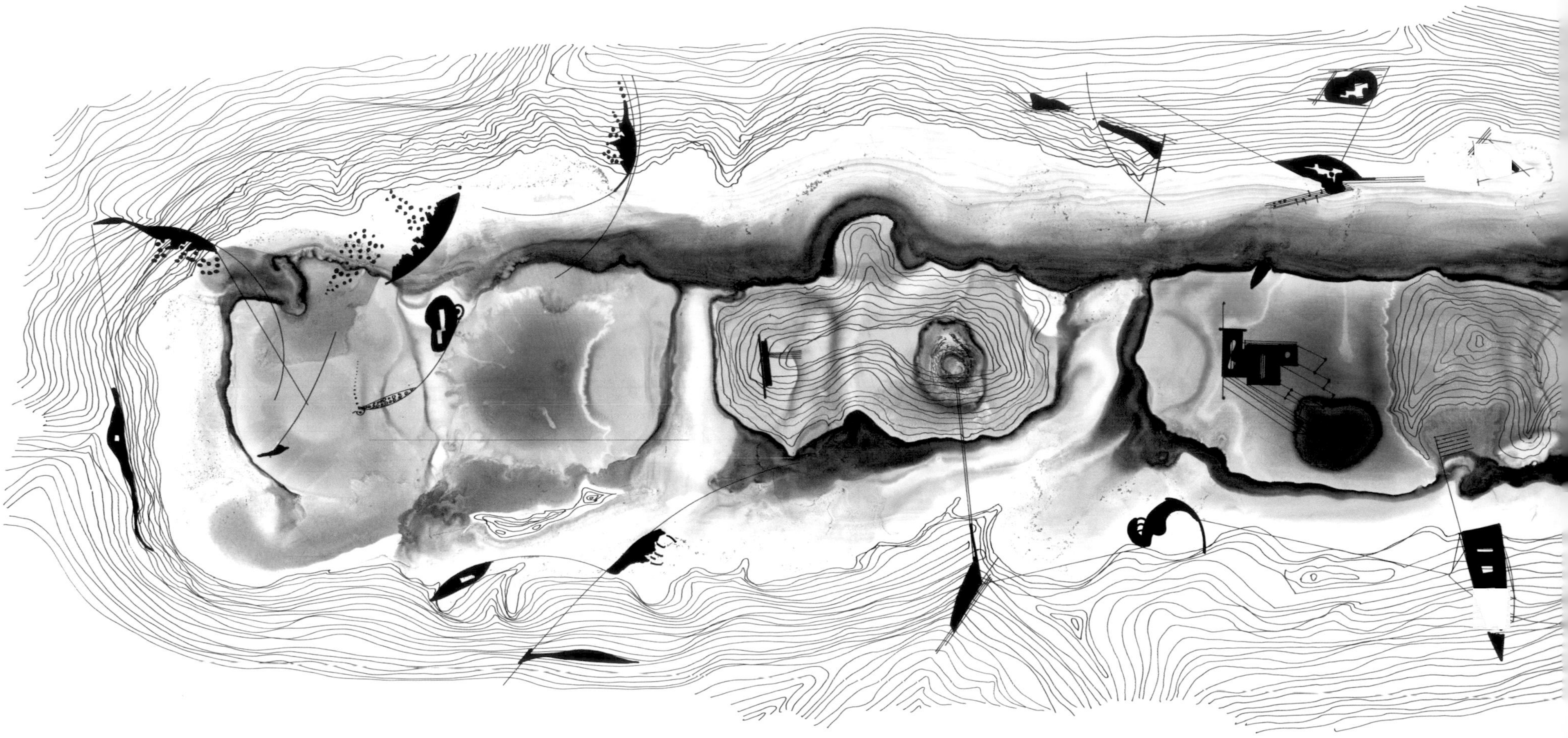

Lake Topography
2017

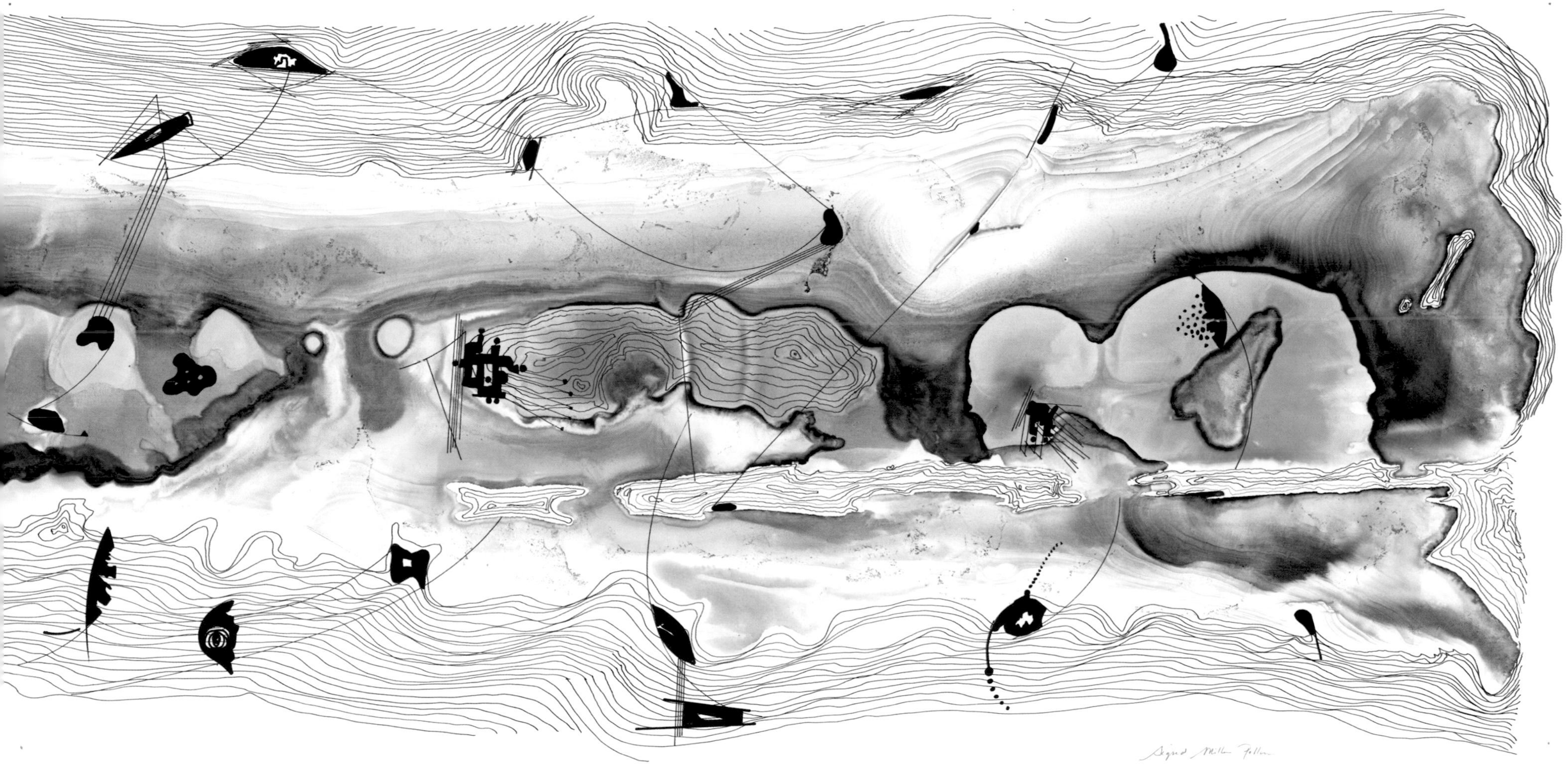

[CREDITS]

Production Team

Moises Acosta
Marcel Alvarez
Andrew Bagge
Noa Barak
Hernan Barufaldi
Jill Browning
Allison Buthray
Victoria Capaldo
Serena Chow
Jean Crossman
Chad DeSisto
Lilly Donahue
Ana Escalante-Lentz
Ray Q. Galano
Rene Glynn
Seth Hoffman
Wendy Ing
Cortland Knopp
Callie Krekorian
Matt Lieb
Ryan Luczkowiak
Christopher Mansfield
Tom McMahon
Sherry Ng
Kevin O'Brien
Eric Olsen
Gustavo Pardo
Shinyoung Park
Eduardo Perez
Ruth Pollin-Galay
Carol Pope
Juan Carlos Ramirez
Laura Sakata
Julie Sarsynski
Eric Sautter
Neetu Singh
Cecelia Valinotto

Photo Credits

Ed Acker
Biography | Pg. XI

Tom Bonner
Jumping Rocks: House I, II, & III | Pg. 42-43, 46-48, 52-54, 56-57, 60-64, 66-67
1290 Studio & Residence: House I, II, & III | Pg. 79-81, 87-89, 93-94, 96-97
Wave House | Pg. 114, 118-120, 122-123
La Sierra Commuter Rail Station | Pg. 128, 130-132
Loring Building | Pg. 200-201, 204-205

Benny Chan Fotoworks
House for a Magician | Pg. 98, 102-103, 106-108, 110-113

Ngoc Doan
Gordon Hall | Pg. 12
Crotty Hall | Pg. 22-23

Adam Dubich
Wave House | Pg. 126

Ray Q. Galano
Jumping Rocks: House I, II, & III | Pg. 40
Riverside Chamber of Commerce | Pg. 134

Ned Grey
Moore House | Pg. 164, 168-169

Marco Guzman
Jumping Rocks: House I, II, & III | Pg. 41, 42, 49, 56
Wave House | Pg. 116
Colton Senior Housing | Pg. 247-248
1290 Studio & Residence | Pg. 71
Cockburn House | Pg. 235

Shelly Harrison
1290 Studio & Residence | Pg. 68, 76-77
Opalinski House | Pg. 216, 218, 220-224, 226-227

TJ LeClair
Wave House | Pg. 117, 120, 124

Peter Mauss ESTO Photographics
Gordon Hall | Pg. 04, 07-09, 12-15
Crotty Hall | Pg. 16, 18, 20-21, 26-31, 34-35
1290 Studio & Residence | Pg. 78, 82-83, 86, 90-92, 95
Straw Avenue | Pg. 140, 144-145, 148-149, 152-153
Pat's House | Pg. A Prefabricated Home | Pg. 154, 158, 162
Ruthie Lane | Pg. 182-183, 186-189, 192-193
Hemmer Corrales House | Pg. 170-171, 174-176, 178-179

Sigrid Miller Pollin
Ransohoff House | Pg. 228, 230-233
Cockburn House | Pg. 234, 237-239

Alexander Vertikoff
University Place | Pg. 206, 208, 212-213
Colton Senior Housing | Pg. 242, 244, 246, 249- 250